Study
And
Learning

Second Edition

The Development of Skill,
Attitude and Style

Wayne R. Herlin
Laura J. Albrecht-Munk
Douglas J. Bell

 KENDALL/HUNT PUBLISHING COMPANY
4050 Westmark Drive   Dubuque, Iowa 52002

This edition has been printed directly from camera-ready copy.

Copyright © 1995 by Kendall/Hunt Publishing Company

ISBN 0-7872-0320-3

Printed in the United States of America
10 9 8 7 6

About The Authors

Wayne R. Herlin is Professor of General Studies and Assistant Dean of Student Life at Brigham Young University. He earned B.A. and Ph.D. degrees at the University of Utah in English and educational psychology, respectively, and an M.A., degree at Stanford University in counseling. Post-doctoral study at Appalachian State University, led to certification as a developmental educator.

Publication experience includes editor of the *Utah Reading Review* and *College Reading and Learning Association Newsletter,* and co-author of *Critical Reading, Improving Reading Speed and Comprehension,* and *Successful Study Skills.* He has also authored several home study courses and dozens of journal articles.

A member of the BYU faculty since 1964, he has taught study skills, reading, English, and educational psychology classes. He served as operations coordinator for general education, was co-founder of the BYU Learning Services Center.

Laura J. Albrecht-Munk is Associate Director of the Counseling Center at Saint Louis University. She received her B.A. degree (1981) in history from the University of Washington, and her M.Ed. degree (1985) in educational psychology from Brigham Young University.

A SLU staff member since 1989, she has taught freshman orientation, counseling, and communication classes. As administrator in the counseling center she has supervised educational outreach and programming. As a clinical counselor she has provided individual and group psychotherapy.

Albrecht-Munk was a member of the Brigham Young University faculty from 1985 to 1989. As instructor of General Studies she taught courses on effective study skills and student development.

Douglas J. Bell is Associate Clinical Professor at Brigham Young University. He received a B.S. degree (1970) from Brigham Young University in Business Management and a Master of Business Administration degree (1971) from the University of Utah. He was awarded a Ph.D. (1984) from Brigham Young University in Higher Education Administration. Post doctoral work at Appalachian State University led to certification as a developmental educator.

As administrator at BYU, he served as Director of Registration and Director of Admissions. He was president of the Utah Association of Collegiate Registrars and Admissions Officers and was member and chair of several national association committees. He has done extensive research on decision making and has published numerous articles on leadership and decision making. He has given more than a dozen presentations at national association meetings.

As a faculty member at BYU, he has designed curriculum for courses in study skills, career choice, leadership, and computer literacy. He has taught courses in student development, business, and educational leadership. As counselor, he has concentrated on helping students achieve academic success and develop sound decisions for college majors and careers.

Contents

Chapter 4

Chapter 5

Part Two

Chapter 6

Chapter 7

Chapter 8

Chapter 9

Chapter 10

Chapter 11

Part Three

Supplemental Readings and Worksheets

Preface

The typical college level *how to study* textbook is a collection of systematic techniques for effective study. Francis Robinson's *Effective Study* (now out of print) and Walter Pauk's *How to Study in College* (1989) are examples of powerful ideas to help students study more effectively. If techniques were the only concern of a good student, textbooks such as these would be excellent guides to the new student entering college who is wondering how to make the transition from a largely guided high school learning atmosphere to a college atmosphere in which the student is left mostly on his or her own. Research findings in the 1980's, however, indicate that being a good student goes far beyond mere application of study skills. Ruth Talbott Keimig, in her 1983 ASHE-ERIC report, *Raising Academic Standards: A Guide to Learning Improvement*, developed the thesis that the least useful process of changing student learning consists of remedial courses of the type that would use the typical "how-to" approach to study. Keimig felt that an educational experience using learning theory principles emphasizing overall student development is the most effective approach to changing a student's intellectual learning processes.

A second critical look at learning in colleges grew out of reports from researchers who have struggled with learning patterns of students in European universities. The results of their research can be summarized by referring to a report by Noel Entwistle and Paul Ramsden in their book, *Understanding Student Learning,* published in England in 1983. They first noted that a wide variety of classroom and individual interventions can be effective in changing a student's learning habits. Second, they noted that no one system or technique works for all, no formula is a panacea for success; rather, improved learning ability resides in coming to grips with those attitudes toward knowledge that lead a student to be what Entwistle and Ramsden termed either a *surface* learner or a *deep* learner.

The authors of this textbook have felt for some time that the typical array of study skills textbooks has left a significant segment of learning development unattended. We have no serious quarrel with most study technique approaches, although we are aware that such technique approaches to college study have only minimally changed students habits and have too often been naive in expecting to make a quick and easy difference. We have therefore chosen to balance in this textbook several phases of college learning.

First, we want students to look at learning as a multi-faceted developmental process: to understand that intellectual development is intertwined with all other human development. Second, students should recognize that deep learning patterns grow out of an ethical attitude towards knowledge as well as out of intellectual exercises. Third, students should see their own styles of learning as a foundation for ever-widening experiences with learning. Fourth, students should examine their personal style of learning to see the effect it has on specific learning requirements placed on her or him in the college setting. Considering learning as a developmental process, the authors want to help students develop and apply a personal attitude of learning, looking at the typical study skills and techniques as a smorgasbord of ideas to be considered as they develop an intellectual identity in the college environment.

Obviously, it is difficult to present a complete smorgasbord of learning skills in one book. The extent of the book, however, is not nearly as important as how it encourages students to make purposeful decisions about learning. In this respect, students need to know what study skills *experts* recommend, and also need to make their own selections within their level of development. *Study and learning is not just the development of skill— but the development of skill, attitude, and style.*

We wish to express our appreciation to many contributors who encouraged us to undertake the mammoth and often frustrating task of writing a textbook. We wish to thank our colleagues at Brigham Young University and Saint Louis University who challenged and supported us in our effort, and who were more than willing to give us constructive criticism. A special thanks to our families for their love, support, patience, and encouragement throughout the many months of writing.

Our final note of gratitude goes to Brigham Young University and Saint Louis University, whose policies encourage and support scholarship in a way that is most generous.

Wayne R. Herlin
Laura J. Albrecht-Munk
Douglas J. Bell

Chapter 1

Introduction To College Learning

---

*"They Can Make Me Go To College
But They Can't Make Me Think"*

At the beginning of fall semester, a student came to college driving an old Buick. Besides being loaded to the brim with sports equipment, clothes, books, plants and other items, the Buick sported a bumper sticker which read, *"They Can Make Me Go to College but They Can't Make Me Think."* Reading the statement conjured up all sorts of mental images: the student kicking and screaming as the parents shoved him into the car saying, *"You may hate us now, but in four years you will thank us!"* or the student demanding, *"Why do I have to go to college?"* and the parents replying, *"Because we said so. Now stop your complaining; it will be good for you!"* or as the student climbs into his car to leave for college, he waves good-bye and drives off chuckling under his breath, *"They can make me go to college but they can't make me think!"*

Whoever wrote that bumper sticker knew a lot about the hard realities of intellectual development. He or she understood that thinking can only be the by-product of personal will, motivation, and attitude. Nobody but yourself can make you think!

Growth and development of any kind does not happen without effort. Consider the accomplishments of some of the great athletes of our time— Kristi Yamaguchi, Carl Lewis or Larry Byrd. Do you suppose that their tremendous physical ability, skill and stamina were due to luck? Not likely. If not luck, then what? What qualities do you think make a "champion"?

Your list might include such qualities as physical strength (the result of hours of body conditioning), determination, positive attitude, motivation, enthusiasm, skill, or a willingness to make sacrifices. Now, make a mental switch from the sports arena and the physical, to the classroom and the intellectual. Doing well in the classroom and being a successful student is not about luck either. Just like physical ability, intellectual growth and skill is the result of commitment, effort, exercise and training.

John E. Anderson, president of the Center for Sports Psychology in Colorado Springs, was a psychologist who worked with the U.S. ski team at the 1994 Winter Olympics in Lillehammer, Norway. In his work with Olympic athletes, Anderson pinpointed six qualities that make a champion on any "field" (Readers Digest, February 1994, pp. 117-120), but, for our purposes here, his principles have been adapted to fit the "champion" on the "academic field."

Dare to dream. Envisioning (imagining in your minds eye) what you want to accomplish or become, is the first step on the road to success. What kind of student do you imagine yourself being? How do you see yourself using your knowledge and education in helping others in the work place, at home, in your community? Can you visualize yourself as an intellectual "champion"?

Get fired up! Be driven to be and do your very best—always. Keep the internal torch for learning burning. Be excited about your opportunities as a college student and curious about what you do not know. Enthusiasm makes the difference.

Aim high. Don't set your sights too low; you are likely to live up to your expectations. Believe you can be and do something great and worthwhile with the talents you have and the knowledge you will receive.

Plan more than one strategy. As a champion, always have a strategy or a game plan to direct your efforts. Sometimes things do not work out the way you thought they would, and you need to be prepared with a back up plan. If you do not do well on your anatomy exam, what are you going to do about it? If you decide engineering is not what you want to do, what next?

Bounce back. Life is made up of both victories and defeats. Be happy about what you do well, and do not let your set backs trip you up or get you down. Let your failures be an inspiration to you to get back at it again. Take a different approach or improve your present one.

Don't give up. There is satisfaction in completing a difficult task against the odds. College will be challenging. It is supposed to be. Hang in there when the going gets tough. Believe in yourself and ask for help when you need it.

In a nutshell, becoming an "intellectual champion" is all about commitment—commitment to oneself and to learning.

Personal Commitment to Learning

An incredible story about personal commitment to learning comes from The Autobiography of Malcolm X (1965). When Malcolm X entered prison in 1947 he had only an eighth-grade education. While in prison, he met a fellow convict who eventually inspired him to educate himself by improving his vocabulary and reading. *Once Malcolm X discovered his appetite for knowledge, he consciously committed himself to learning all he could.* When he was released from prison, he took with him a curiosity and a desire for learning that could not be quenched. Note how the following quote from Malcolm X (1965) describes his intense desire to develop his intellectual capacity:

As my word base broadened, I could for the first time pick up a book and read and now begin to understand what the book was saying. Anyone who has read a great deal can imagine the new world that was opened. . . . I never had been so truly free in my life. . . . When I had progressed to really serious reading,

> every night at about ten p.m. I would be outraged with the ``lights out.'' It always seemed to catch me right in the middle of something engrossing. Fortunately, right outside my door was a corridor light that cast a glow into my room. The glow was enough to read by, once my eyes adjusted to it. So when ``lights out'' came, I would sit on the floor where I could continue reading in that glow . . . My homemade education gave me, with every additional book I read, a little bit more sensitivity to the deafness, dumbness, and blindness that was afflicting the black race in America. (pp. 174- 180)

You are going to college because you want to grow intellectually—you want to become educated. *The responsibility of educators in higher education is to provide you with a solid curriculum and to establish an open learning environment that provides you with opportunities to improve your attitude, skill, and knowledge.* Your responsibility as a student is to decide how you will take advantage of those learning opportunities. Like Malcolm X, your intellectual development will be a product of your willingness to engage in activities that stimulate your thinking toward increasing levels of complexity.

If you do not already have an appetite for knowledge and learning, now is the time to discover it. Be actively involved in the learning process by assuming responsibility for your intellectual development, and by making choices that assure a successful college experience. Strive to improve your thinking, acquire further knowledge, and then apply that knowledge to bettering your own and others' lives. As Malcolm X found out, learning does not have to be experienced as a burden to bind you down or a drudgery to hold you back—it is meant to make you free.

Balanced Development and
Its Influence on Intellectual Wellness

Beyond a personal commitment to becoming an "intellectual champion", maintaining a sense of wellness and balance in life is also important to your intellectual development. Your intellectual self and its wellness are just one dimension of your life. According to Hettler (1980), five additional dimensions of wellness contribute to or distract from total wellness, and hence impact on your intellectual development. The other dimensions are occupational, physical, spiritual, emotional, and social wellness.

4

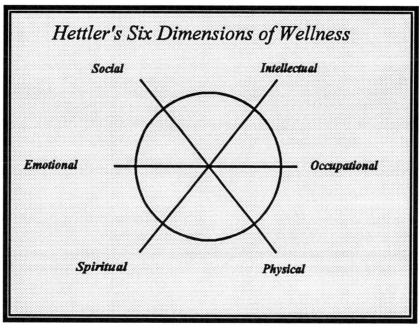

Figure 1.1 Hettler's Dimensions of Wellness.

Hettler (1980) presents his wellness model (Figure 1.1) as a circle with six separate, but connecting parts. The interconnectedness among the six dimensions illustrates that each is important to the total well-being and functioning of a person. If an individual experiences wellness in any one area, that wellness extends to the other dimensions. Conversely, a lack of well-being in any area adversely affects wellness in the other dimensions. For example, feeling physically tired or lethargic due to lack of exercise and sleep, or poor nutrition, could affect your ability to concentrate on your homework, inhibit your desire to socialize with friends, and cause undue feelings of stress and anxiety. How do you think being satisfied and happy in your career might affect the other areas of your life? For a person who is illiterate, how might his or her illiteracy affect each area? *Wellness in all six dimensions will bring a balance, or an integration of the total person.*

Adopting a wellness-oriented lifestyle means avoiding unhealthy behavior patterns by becoming aware of choices within each wellness dimension and making decisions toward a healthy existence. Because comprehensive wellness is important for your intellectual development, you need to know what constitutes development and wellness in each of the dimensions.

Six Dimensions of Wellness

Intellectual development is characterized by the willingness to engage in activities that are intellectually challenging and stimulating. Intellectual wellness encourages creative thought and resourcefulness in using available sources, inside and outside the classroom, to improve and expand existing knowledge and skills. There are myriad opportunities to learn: cultural events, forums, lectures, books, people, T.V., films, and internship experiences, to name just a few. An intellectually well person searches out these types of learning experiences in order to broaden perspective and increase complexity of thinking.

Occupational development and wellness are characterized by choosing a suitable college major and a career. This effort in college is followed by making choices in your work that are likely to ensure greater job and life satisfaction, like taking advantage of opportunities to learn new job skills or leaving a job that is not consistent with your values.

Physical wellness and development are measured by the degree to which you are physically fit and healthy through exercise and good nutrition. Taking necessary steps to prevent disease or illness by visiting your doctor regularly and by providing proper self-care (i.e., drinking adequate amounts of water and protecting your skin from sun damage), also characterizes physical wellness.

Spiritual development is marked by an ongoing involvement in seeking greater levels of purpose, meaning, and significance in your life. Spiritual wellness is characterized by a deep appreciation and respect for all life and believing that your life has a definite purpose.

Emotional development is the increasing ability to become self-aware and express your feelings appropriately. Emotional wellness includes a healthy coping style, recognized by the ability to manage impulses and feelings, accept responsibility for your actions, and to feel good about yourself. It also includes having the skill to develop close personal relationships.

Social development and wellness encourage mature, meaningful family, friend, and work relationships that are positive and respectful. Social wellness also includes contributing to the general welfare of your community by volunteering and serving others, and by treating the environment well.

When you commit yourself to a wellness-oriented lifestyle, you can be sure that your intellectual development will be reinforced.

Staying Intellectually Motivated and In Balance

Undoubtedly, as a student you have experienced times when you lacked interest in your schoolwork and learning. Maybe you understood your lack of motivation as laziness, boredom, or a sign of "not being cut out for school." A breakdown in your intellectual motivation can be triggered by many things. In relation to Hettler's wellness model (Figure 1.1), breakdown in motivation will likely be the result of limited wellness in one or more of the other five wellness dimensions. The following is an explanation of how limited wellness in each of these dimensions could directly affect your intellectual development and motivation to learn and what you might do to prevent it.

Occupational Wellness

Going through college undecided about what you want to do in life constitutes limited wellness. In fact, Robinson (1970) claims a lack of vocational choice to be one reason for poor motivation among students. He cites research (1970, p. 106) which indicates that students who have decided on a major usually study more, get better grades, and complete college more often than those who are undecided about their majors. If you are a freshman and have not decided on a major, do not fret. There is time and opportunity for you to explore your interests, but your search must be an active one. There are actually many juniors and seniors out there, undecided about their majors, who have expected the right major to come to them without any conscious effort on their part. And they are still out there floundering! To prevent lack of occupational choice from affecting your intellectual development and motivation, seek out resources in the career center at your college. There you will find and have access to helpful information on various majors and careers. Trained counselors and staff members will assist you in your decision-making and in your eventual choice of a major and career.

Physical Wellness

Continued physical activity, good nutritional habits, and proper use of the medical system when appropriate are necessary for your overall health and well-being. If you get regular exercise, eat the right amount and kind of food, and avoid substances and practices that are harmful to your health—drugs, caffeine, tobacco, alcohol, and promiscuous unprotected sex—your chances of feeling and staying healthy are much improved over leading a life of self-neglect or abuse to your health. Feeling good and being healthy have a direct influence on your level of motivation and learning in school. You have only to think back to the last time you were ill, to remember how difficult it was for you to concentrate on your studies—even to have the desire to pick up a book. Of course, some illnesses come no matter what you do to prevent them. But many illnesses may be warded off by taking some preventive measures and by living healthily. For instance, it is inevitable that during mid-terms or final exam week, many students will experience illnesses that can be related to stress and anxiety, such as headaches, insomnia or sleeping too much, colds, stomachaches, etc. Stress levels can be reduced by exercising regularly, eating healthful foods, taking vitamins, and getting enough sleep. To facilitate your physical wellness, check out the recreational and athletic opportunities and resources on your campus. When you are not feeling well, visit the health center. Involve yourself in educational opportunities that support physical wellness and emphasize healthful living. By making a conscious effort to stay active and healthy, you increase your capacity to stay motivated and alert in your studies.

Spiritual Wellness

How one develops a greater sense of spiritual wellness is a very private matter, one that differs from person to person; but spiritual wellness can be said to involve a personal attitude of deep appreciation and respect for oneself, for one's fellow human beings, for nature, and for a power beyond oneself. It is often marked by personal involvement in seeking meaning and purpose in human existence. What do your answers to the following questions say about your own spiritual wellness? How do you treat yourself and others? Do you find meaning and significance in your life? Are you tolerant of others who are different from you?

8

Limited spiritual wellness will affect intellectual motivation. Generally, where there is a lack of appreciation for life, there is a lack of appreciation for learning, because most of learning is learning about oneself, other people and the elements of life. Examine how your intellect and personal motivation might be affected by your lack of spiritual well-being. How might you go about improving your spirituality? Are there resources on your campus that could help you?

Emotional Wellness

With any demanding experience, for example, with going to college, one's emotional well-being is bound to be tried. Feelings of stress and anxiety associated with getting projects or papers in on time or studying for a test are common; feelings of loneliness are felt because of moving away from family and friends; feelings of depression, worry, and fear are just beneath the surface of consciousness. At these times, limited emotional wellness will be the result of an unhealthy coping style. Emotional concerns and worries you may have about yourself or others can interfere with your ability to study and concentrate. Robinson (1970) listed distracting personal problems as a major reason for poor motivation among college students. Emotional concerns and worries that result from personal problems ``make us inefficient by distracting our attention, by preventing normal healthy habits of living, and by giving us a dour outlook on life (p. 105)." If you need to make some emotional adjustments in your life or you need help with a relationship, take the necessary steps to find assistance. Your college counseling center promotes growth and development in the emotional wellness dimension through personal counseling, support groups, workshops, and other mental health programs. It will be a good resource for helping you strengthen your emotional well-being. Talking with a trusted friend, faculty or family member, resident assistant or member of the clergy could also prove to be a helpful support.

Social Wellness

Students who have difficulty in their interpersonal relationships, who feel alone and isolated, who feel as though they do not belong to a group or are an insignificant part of a community, will manifest limited social wellness. A primary concern for many college students is worry that they will not make friends and be accepted by their peers. Just how well a student adjusts socially could determine how well he or she adjusts academically. If you feel inadequate or insecure in your social relationships, you are apt to be distracted from studies, and the possibility of academic success is diminished. There are many opportunities, resources, and places, on or nearby your campus, to meet people and help you adjust better socially: living in dorms; joining sororities, fraternities, service and environmental groups and other clubs; and volunteering in your community. Do not forget that family members can be a great support too.

Just as too little social life can interfere with your attention to academics, so can too much social activity affect academic motivation. Do not become so overly involved in social activity that you lose sight of your intellectual pursuits and what is most important at college. Finding a social balance will be important to your overall intellectual and academic performance.

Getting Involved in an Academic World

Speaking of students who develop a wellness life-style, Frederick Leafgren (1989) observed, *"A wellness-oriented life-style results not only in a strong personal commitment to one's well-being but also in a strong commitment to continued involvement in the institution (p. 157)."* Students learn by becoming involved. The more involved you are inside and outside of the classroom, the greater chance you have of leaving your campus a more educated person. A fear might be that getting involved in other learning experiences outside classroom academics would detour your efforts and affect your grades. Consider what one talented former Brigham Young University student, who was awarded the Rhodes Scholarship, said when asked what made his undergraduate experience a success: *"The first principle I followed was that busy people can do more things and do them better than not-so-busy people. I noticed when I played freshman basketball, that*

10

despite the four hours required for daily practice, my grades were higher in-season than during the off-season. During the season I simply knew I had much more to accomplish so I wasted less time. I learned a lesson from this and established the general policy of never turning down a learning opportunity on the excuse I was too busy with coursework" (quote taken from BYU's Daily Universe, November 10, 1975, 29, No. 49, p.44). A controlled and balanced involvement in your college community can enhance your educational experience and intellectual development.

Campus Resources

Part of getting involved in school and on campus is learning what is out there for you. *On your campus there are various organizations, services, and people that can play an important role in your overall development as a college student.* Your campus is equipped with many resources meant to enhance the development of the whole person. Your challenge is to find, seek out, use and learn from these resources. An excellent way to become acquainted with your college campus is to acquire a student handbook. In it you will find a lot of information about your campus policies, resources, clubs and organizations, schedules (athletic events, etc.) and much more. The following list of resources is not comprehensive by any means, but it does list some of the most important resources that could be helpful to you at some point in your college career. Make the effort to locate and visit these resources on your campus.

Occupational/Academic Resources

Career Planning Office—Do not wait until you are a senior to visit this office! Here you will receive help and guidance in major selection, career exploration and development, and job-search related skills.

Academic Advising—Sometimes it is difficult to decide on what classes to take and when to take them. If you need assistance in course selection, an academic advisor can help.

Educational Services (academic skills)—Most colleges provide some type of educational support for students who want to improve their reading, writing, and study skills, like notetaking, test-taking, listening and time management.

Financial Aid and Scholarships—Advice and information on scholarships and loans are available at this office.

Instructional Media Services—This is a great resource if you need to purchase or use basic media material and equipment for class projects.

Physical Resources

Recreation Center—Drop-in recreation and opportunities for informal play are available at the recreation center, as well as exercise equipment and programs. Intramural sports programs are an opportunity for formal athletic participation.

Health Center—This is a convenient resource to have on campus when you are ill and in need of a nurse or doctor. Some health centers offer programming in the area of personal health and wellness, including things like blood pressure and cholesterol screenings; CPR and nutrition classes.

Alcohol Awareness Program—Generally, this type of program is more educational in nature than it is treatment focused. Usually the purpose of a program like this is to make students aware of their negative drinking habits and patterns, and to encourage healthier decision-making around alcohol use.

Disability Related Services—This office helps those students who are physically, emotionally, or learning disabled to get the most out of their education by providing the necessary accommodations for participation in the classroom.

Dining Services—Everyone has to eat! Find out where the various dining locations are on your campus.

Spiritual Resources

Campus Ministry Office—This office usually concerns itself with the spiritual life of the college community. Programs, worship services, and counseling may be provided to nurture faith development.

Chapel or campus church—There might be a chapel, church, or synagogue on campus or close to campus which you could visit for worship and quiet reflection.

Emotional Resources

Counseling Center—Most college counseling centers are staffed with licensed counselors and psychologists who are trained to help students with personal or relational concerns like roommate conflicts, stress, and depression.

Residence Life—If you just need a listening ear, try talking with your Resident Assistant. He or she may be able to help you or direct you to an appropriate resource.

Social Resources

Student Government—Student Government provides ample leadership opportunities. If you are interested in improving the quality of education on your campus, then you should get involved in student government.

Student Clubs and Organizations—An array of academic, professional and social clubs, as well as a variety of honor societies, probably exists on your campus. Getting involved in clubs and organizations is a great way to learn and to meet people.

Volunteer Program—You can make a difference in your community and enhance your educational experience by volunteering your time and talents toward helping others.

Residence Life—If you choose to live on campus, your hall will essentially become your home away from home and be a good source for making friends and social contacts.

Law Enforcement and Public Safety—The purpose of this office is to create a campus environment that is safe and comfortable. Security, crime prevention, and parking are just some of the responsibilities of this office. For your safety, check to see if the Public Safety office on your campus provides an escort service.

Intellectual Resources

Library—The library is an important learning and study resource on campus. Frequent it often!

Computer Services—Most campuses make computers available for student use to complete classroom assignments.

Faculty—Seek help from and ask questions of your professors when you want to understand more clearly. Most faculty members welcome student inquiries inside, as well as outside the classroom.

A Word on This Textbook

This textbook is a book of involvement. You will become a better student and a more effective learner as you become involved by commitment, as suggested in chapter 2; as you approach learning deeply, as defined in chapter 3; as you develop and enhance your learning style, as explained in chapters 4 and 5; and as you select and adapt learning techniques, as reviewed in sequence in the six chapters of part II of the text. You are encouraged to contemplate also the supplemental readings, and apply their wisdom to your study and learning choices. Do not be bound by *a single* technique. That is *not* what this book is teaching. It is better that you follow Gibbs' (1985) approach to your developing skill, attitude, and style of learning.

> The students themselves are in the best position to judge the appropriateness and value of new techniques. Whether a technique suits an individual, whether it meets the demands of the learning tasks, and whether it can be used appropriately, given the present level of intellectual development of the individual can only be decided by the individual himself. Our [we teachers'] job is to help the individual make the decision. (p. 154)

Now read on—learn and enjoy!

References

Anderson, John E. "What Makes A Champion." Reader's Digest, Pleasantville, New York: The Reader's Digest Association, Inc., February, 1994, 144, No. 862, pp. 117-120.

Astin, A.W. ``Student Involvement: A Developmental Theory for Higher Education." Journal of College Student Personnel, 1984, 25, pp. 297-308.

Gibbs, G. "Teaching Study Skills." In Entwistle, N.J., New Directions in Educational Psychology: 1. Learning and Teaching, London: The Falmer Press 1985.

Hettler, W. "Wellness, Promotion on a University Campus." Family and Community Health. The Journal of Health Promotion and Maintenance, 1980, 3(1), pp. 77-92.

Leafgren, F.A. "Health and Wellness Programs." In M.L. Upcraft, J.N. Gardner, and Associates, The Freshman Year Experience. San Francisco: 1989.

Malcolm X and Haley, A. The Autobiography of Malcolm X, New York: Random House, Inc., 1965.

Robinson, F. P. Effective Study. New York: Harper and Row, 1970.

Part One

Learning As Development

Chapter 2

How College Students Develop and Learn

What is the learning process you experience as a college student? How does the college experience restructure your thinking? Have you made up your minds on critical issues? Are there thinking methods that make new college students stubborn or confused when looking at critical issues?

This chapter is about how you view your own learning, depending on what stage of development you have achieved as you enter college, what stages you progress through during your college experiences, and what stage you arrive at as you prepare to leave college for your life's career. You will be introduced to a theory of intellectual and ethical development. The possible cognitive (intellectual) and ethical (moral) development during the college years will be examined in detail. As you look at this theory, look also at yourself. How do you fit into this theoretical picture? What is your personal reality within the stages of college student maturity?

William G. Perry, Jr. (1952) and a colleague, Charles P. Whitlock, working in Harvard University's Bureau of Study Counsel, encountered what they interpreted as personality differences in students' thinking and learning patterns. They described the hypothetical students in this way.

> Sammy was intelligent. As he went on in school he perceived another principle. He saw . . . that more moral value was put on whether reading was 'done' than upon its outcome. . . . Reading was clearly not a means to an end but a problem of conscience.

A student was quoted having said:

> *I see what you're doing. You're trying to get us to think while we read. But suppose we think something the author doesn't think, or something the teacher doesn't think. What will happen to us then?*

From this early observation of (mostly freshmen) Harvard students, Perry began to observe personality differences in students that might account for their unique attitudes toward learning. In 1954, under Perry's guidance, the Harvard Bureau of Study Counsel began a "descriptive" study (Perry 1968b) of student differences in meeting the "diversity and relativism of thought and values" that were apparent among liberally educated students in a highly diversified university.

Perry and his colleagues became aware that what they thought were unique and relatively stable personality differences actually were evolving developmental patterns, patterns that changed in a student from fall to spring of the academic year and probably would change further from year to year. The patterns changed as students met the challenges of a demanding faculty who expected more than mere memorization and recitation; they expected thinking, learning, and intellectual creation.

Three book-sized reports followed Perry's studies (Perry 1968a, 1968b, 1970). These three publications form the basic source material for the following simplified explanation of Perry's theory of cognitive and ethical growth among college students. The authors of this chapter take responsibility for any distortion caused by their simplification; the original ideas are credited fully to Perry.

Elements of the Perry Developmental Scheme

To understand Perry's developmental scheme, you will need to locate nine positions along a stair-like progression that implies growth in intellectual power and in ethical commitment. The growth pattern may be represented as in Figure 2.1 by a diagram of nine steps, each showing distinct developmental characteristics manifest by college-age adults as they experience the challenges of college life, whether in the classroom or in the myriad other living-learning centers—dormitories, cafeterias, apartments, church gatherings, rap session—wherever students interact.

Perry's nine levels of characteristics, called "positions," often are difficult to understand and observe because the steps are small and their characteristics are many. To help yourself understand the levels, simplify the nine developmental positions to just three broad stages. Perry did this, labeling each stage in succession as (1) dualism, (2) relativism, and (3) commitments in relativism. Figure 2.1 shows these three stages (labeled) along with the nine positions (as yet unlabeled) which they include. Students may enter the university operating intellectually and ethically at any level, but Perry (1968b) found that most Harvard students, by the *end* of the freshman year, displayed behavior typical of positions 3, 4, or 5 (early relativism), while most seniors operated from positions 6,7, or 8 (late relativism).

Position 1 is so naively dualistic that Perry doubted any Harvard students could have started there and survived the year, while position 9 is of such ethically committed and intellectually grounded maturity that seldom did any student consistently display that level of serene intellectual self-assurance. The positions 1 and 9, then, are the extremes of the three stages. In between are the three broad stages, with small increments of growth taking the student from dualism to eventually making commitments in relativism.

The Three Perry Stages Described

In order to grasp the developmental picture that Perry discovered as he and his colleagues interviewed Harvard university students over their four-year college experiences, look first at a description of the three stages. After you get a feeling for the stages of development through the college years, you can look further at some problems in sequential development and at Perry's subdivision of the stages into his nine positions.

Dualism

A student in the stage of dualism assumes all information to be classifiable as either right or wrong, good or bad, all one thing or all the other. People, knowledge, and values are seen as absolutes, all concretely placed at one pole or another. Uncertainty is unnatural and must be explained in terms of certain knowledge. The external environment controls: the student

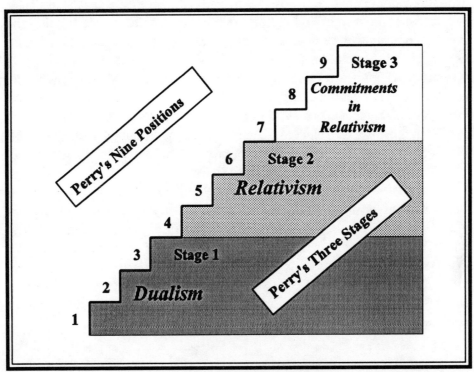

Figure 2.1 Perry's Nine Positions and Three Stages.

turns outside him- or herself to accept authority figures, such as parents, teachers, textbooks, or similar "sure" sources of "right." "Correct" decisions are based on such authorities. Learning is a matter of memorizing the "right" answer, which is the province of established authorities. Dualistic thinkers are unable to analyze or synthesize ideas because multiple points of view are unacceptable.

22

As the student moves from lower dualistic positions toward higher positions, the concept of **multiplicity enters the dualistic stage**. Multiplicity appears on the surface to be a second stage, wherein greater tolerance of people's differences is allowed. But, the attitude that everyone has a right to his or her own opinion because the facts are not yet in, really is a cynical adaptation of the belief that when all the facts are in, there will still be right and wrong; but no one knows the facts, hence no one has a right to be the authority. Multiplicity as a subphase of dualism prepares the student for the eventual jump into Perry's second stage, known as relativism.

Relativism

When the student becomes more capable of evaluating knowledge, he or she moves out of dualism into relativism. Relativism becomes evident when the student grows out of dualism by way of multiplicity and **sees facts in relation** to their context and no longer views them as paired polar opposites. In relativism, knowledge is always evaluated relative to the context in which it lies and the circumstance under which it is applied. In relativism, absolutes disappear as the guiding force of thinking. Evaluation of information at the relativistic stage is a process wherein the student shifts from external control to the **student's internal reference points**. The problem at the relativistic stage, however, is that the student has given up the comfort of outside authorities but has not yet met the challenge of making firm decisions on the basis of a consistent internal interpretation of context. At the relativistic level there is a **lack of acceptance of responsibility for making choices.**

Commitments in Relativism

At some point in the relativistic stage students find it necessary to make some kind of commitment. It is as though the student has discovered that she or he must make a commitment to something: a career, a marriage partner, even an idea. The

committed student thus begins to see her or his role in terms of personal values that form the basis of commitment. The three positions within the commitment stage that will be described later basically represent advancing levels of personal consistency and the development of value systems that guide commitments.

Transitions and Deflections

You now have a picture of Perry's three developmental stages, but before attempting to understand the labels and descriptions of each of the nine discrete Perry positions, you need to realize that development through the positions, and from stage to stage, is neither routine nor automatic. Growth takes place in response to resolution of conflicts between the comfort of a particular position and challenges from other people's ideas (teachers', classmates', etc.) to that position. Movement from position to position leads to the more broadly conceived stage development.

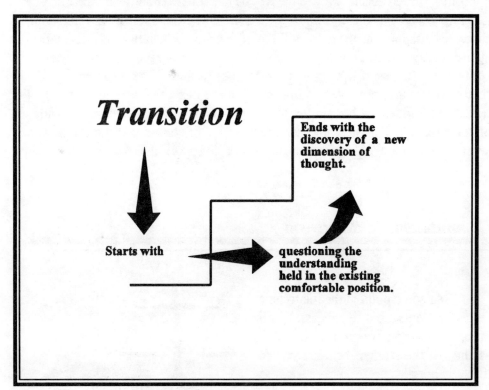

Transition

Ends with the discovery of a new dimension of thought.

Starts with

questioning the understanding held in the existing comfortable position.

Figure 2.2 Transition Between Perry's Steps.

24

Transitions

Colleges and universities are centers of intellectual learning and discovery. No student can attend a liberal arts college without having her or his "comfortable" beliefs challenged by new "discoveries." In the Perry scheme, the concept of transition from one position or stage to another becomes critical. Transitions are represented by the vertical risers in the diagrammatic stairs of Figure 2.1. The transition from one position to another is illustrated in Figure 2.2, wherein the transition is always the result of new idea encounters that trigger a questioning challenge to an existing position (Perry, 1981). Thus by questioning position on the Perry scale, the student provides the dynamic of change that leads to his or her own development. Colleges and universities deliberately foster these challenges.

Not every challenge to the comfort of a student's existing position will set in motion a transitional experience, but continued daily challenges eventually cause sufficient disequilibrium to give way to alternative interpretations of the world and a transition to new developmental positions. Movement from position to position causes sufficient change that a student will eventually evolve to a whole new stage of intellectual and ethical development.

Deflections

Out of the transitional struggle the expected development would be movement upward to the next developmental stage. While Perry (1968a) expected this growth pattern, he also noted three detours in the pattern, so-called *deflections, which* he labeled *temporizing, retreat,* and *escape.* If the challenges at a student's current developmental stage are too strong, too devastating, or too far beyond what the student can ethically or intellectually cope with, the student may react with a kind of defiance, a personal resentfulness or alienation. In Perry's terms, one may then be *deflected* from ethical and intellectual growth--by *temporizing* (simply avoiding any change for a prolonged period, as much as a year or more), *retreating* (from the positions in the dualistic stage, denying the possibility of even the existence of other developmental stages), or *escaping* (settling in at relativistic stage while rejecting any implications for further growth).

With an understanding of the developmental pattern of Perry's three stages with their nine positions, and of the possibility of periodic detours or deflections from the pattern, you are ready to consider a description of the scheme of Perry's mainline intellectual and ethical development through the college years (1968b, 1981,).

As noted in Figure 2.1, positions 1, 2, and 3 are positions of *dualism* leading to *multiplicity*. *Dualism*, remember, represents the view that there are only two sides to any issue, good and bad, right and wrong, or we and they. *Multiplicity* admits to a diversity of opinions and values, but only because the "right" answers "out there" have not yet been discovered. Because the "right" answers are unknown, everyone has equal claim to his or her own opinions. Nobody is wrong because nobody is right. Positions 1, 2, and 3 start as dualism and are so labeled; but they give way to multiplicity as repeated attacks on the concept of dualism tear away at its comfortable naivete.

Position 1 is extreme dualism, encompassing we-right-good on the one hand against they-wrong-bad on the other hand. Authorities (including teachers) are absolute; their word is unquestioned. Obedience, hard work, and determination are the sole criteria for success.

Position 2 is the beginning of multiplistic substitutions for dualism. Intellectual uncertainties occur because authorities purposely withhold answers while students struggle to learn them, or because "good" and "bad" authorities differ. "Bad" authorities are viewed as frauds, and "good" authorities as helpful.

Position 3 is an acceptance of an intellectual world in which even the "good" authorities don't know everything. By study, research, and diligence they will begin to understand, but for now some truths must await discovery. Thus at position 3, diversity is legitimate temporarily, but until more is known, standards remain puzzling and multiple opinions are acceptable.

By the time position 3 takes hold, the student faces the dilemma of losing the comfortable moral anchor of clinging to the "right." By now the "right" has been repeatedly challenged, and some "rights" have toppled before an onslaught of uncertainty. The student, both intellectually and ethically, must reconstruct her or his world of values and assumptions. In position 3 the student has accepted multiplicity as legitimate in some areas.

The particular line of thinking now arises, "In how many areas of human knowledge must the absolute answer be challenged?" In politics and

26

literature a challenge is acceptable. But in science, mathematics, or even religion, should the dualistic anchor be challenged?

The challenges of transition from position 3 to position 4 are those that move one from dualism to relativism. They are so basic to the requirements for intellectual success in a university setting that two manifestations of position 4 emerge. *Position 4a is a position of neatly ordering some ideas as being multiplistic while others are dualistic: the unknown is multiplistic and the known is dualistic.* In some things anyone's opinion is acceptable, while in other things the "authorities" know and have spoken, and "right" must prevail. Those who develop to position 4a typically are students who exhibit more trust in authority, who are more willing to adhere to rules and expectations. For them, duality is preserved where it is important ethically, while they are free intellectually to explore uncertainty with the authorities, who also are perceived as "not knowing" yet. Students do wonder, though, how authorities can grade them in areas of uncertainty, a dilemma that has potential to spark a transition to a higher position. Position 4a is at the height of multiplicity, a parallel clinging to duality in some areas while assuming that "everyone has a personal right to his or her own opinion."

In position 4b relativism is in full view. Students adjust to multiplicity by concluding directly that authorities are not really asking for right answers, but are demanding certain patterns of thought. The teacher does not merely ask what the student thinks about an issue, but how she or he supports the opinion with data and logic. This adjustment in ethical reaction to right and wrong is relativistic. "Right" is replaced by a process and grading is also seen as a process, not a result. Both positions 4a and 4b still cling to the "proper" relationship to authority while beginning to cope with the dualistic orderings of the world.

Positions 4a and 4b, possess an awareness of the pending collapse of dualism and begin to genuinely meet the dilemmas of a relativistic world; a world in which solutions must consider many variables that work well in some contexts, while not at all in others. The transition from positions 4a and 4b to position 5 is a major resolution of intellectual and ethical conflict.

Such a transitional dilemma leads to full relativism in Perry's sense — a type of thinking that requires two intellectual necessities: *(1) observing that all "truth" must have a context or setting in which it acts within the universe; and (2) understanding that "truth" requires each individual to think about his or her own way of thinking about the world.* This requirement causes one to look at himself or herself in relation to the world's "truth" and begin to think about thinking, as well as merely think.

Position 5 accepts a relativistic world in which not only students but authorities differ in their interpretations of "truth," because they base their thinking on different theoretical arrangements of "truth." Position 5 is at the center of Perry's stage of relativism; it is also the pivotal point in his developmental scale (1968b). *At position 5, a student comes fully to accept a generally relativistic world, one in which knowledge really is not divided into two opposing camps but depends on context.* The student has finally rejected dualistic interpretations of "truth." For better or for worse (itself a dualistic cliché), the student deals with "truth" in ways that demand open investigation and a complete willingness to acquire knowledge. As mentioned earlier, however, a conviction is missing, along with an acceptance of any commitment. Even the inclination to apply knowledge is an intellectual exercise in an unguided world.

The lack of moral or ethical commitment at position 5 leads one to the realization that some decisions have to be made if only to get along in life; and these decisions require some kind of value system, some ordering of priorities, or at least some recognition of a value hierarchy. *Position 6 is a realization that decisions have to be made and that decisions require value judgments.* This is the final position in the relativism stage, and its realization that decisions require some criterion of choice becomes the transition to the three positions of the commitments-in-relativism stage.

Position 7 is a position of acknowledging one's first significant commitment. In spite of a relativistic world, the student discovers that the value hierarchy "out there" has personal meaning and needs priorities. A feeling arises, "This is my best choice, given my interpretation of the context as I understand it." The choice is value-laden and is also based on a consideration of the "facts" of the universe.

In position 8, a system of values has formed. Several commitments are made that have a pattern similar to that of earlier pledges. The commitments are balanced against the context of the world and the newly developed value system. Some of the commitments are very deep, some highly tentative.

Perry never actually found any students at Harvard who fully reached the position 9 level, which he described as one of serene maturity. (1981) He described the ninth position in a statement: "This is how life will be. I must be wholehearted while tentative, fight for my values yet respect others', believe my deepest values right yet be ready to learn." *At position 9 the student (perhaps poststudent, mature adult) has experienced many commitments that have led to a firmly entrenched system of commitments that are powerfully based, but maintain a respect for others and a humility that welcomes recurring challenge, scrutiny, and evaluation.*

28

Evaluating Yourself in the Perry Stages and Positions

As you read the above Perry stage and position descriptions you may have found yourself described by one of them. Read them again while asking yourself if you accept a truly relativistic world. Do you challenge the "truths" in your biology text, your physics text, or your math text? Have you been willing to read beyond your assigned course materials to see if the material is universally accepted? Have you noticed genuine differences in ideas taught in different classes? Have you thought about the differences? Are you engaging your professors in conversations in their offices? Do you tell them of your uncertainty and seek more than just clarifications or brief tutorings? Do you ask true questions of substance? Have your conversations with other students centered on ethical issues growing out of intellectual discoveries? Have you endured a period of doubt while you searched  for a particular "truth"? Have you attended extra-curricular forums, lectures, seminars, or workshops just so that you could learn for yourself?

These are all marks of transition towards more complex stages of development. If the experiences in the previous paragraph are foreign to you, consider yourself in a position below 5. Remember that you are not even to position 5 yet unless you have engaged in regular self-analysis of your learning in a context that is not given by an authority. In a relativistic world, the "truth" can be seen from many points of view. The higher levels are marked by a distinct system of values that have met the challenge of time, thought, and experience.

Do not mistake strong religious commitment for positions 8 and 9. Positions 1 and 2 actually show more overt "commitment" to religious beliefs than do positions 8 and 9. At position 2 one might argue vehemently for his or her beliefs. At position 8 one might choose not to argue at all because one understands that the religious principles themselves have met the test of time and will argue eloquently for themselves. A mature thinker may choose wholeheartedly and calmly to discuss scriptures and conversion with a deep conviction while respecting the less fixed positions of others.

One of the authors grew up as a Perry position 1 or 2 Republican. He knew "right" and "wrong" in politics because he had heard and reheard his father and uncle for hours at a time try to top each other in damning the Franklin Roosevelt administration and the New Deal. There came a time, finally, when the author voted Democrat in a state election. Never have such unsettled feelings attended any other action that he had done in his lifetime! Yet the author boasts a Ph.D. in educational psychology. The point to all this? Your actual Perry position in intellectual and ethical growth may be less developed than you think.

Don't despair as you try to evaluate yourself; just be realistic and honest. It is important to know yourself and to give yourself a pattern for growth. At the end of four years of college you should be educated, not merely trained. And an education inevitably means intellectual development in the midst of change. Experience and change allow the student's values to be strongly grounded in serious self-scrutiny. Healthy commitments are based on values that are reviewed, tested, and found worthwhile in the contexts of life's purposes. To do less leaves a student naive and either uncommitted to anything, or convinced without foundation to something one doesn't really understand. The uncommitted position leads to cynical non-action. A position of unfounded conviction leads to overreaction and then to despair, when a dualistic position collapses.

Learning Applications

1.   Obtain a copy of Perry's 1968 Harvard College report, <u>Intellectual and Ethical Development in the College Years</u>, from your library or resource center and study the end-fold diagram of the Perry scheme. As you study the diagram, answer the following questions:

   a.   Why are the terms *embeddedness* and *actualization* placed where they are on the diagram?

   b.   If a person in your class absolutely insists that another college is "better" than the one you are attending and will neither define "better" nor discuss why, but gets angry when you do not accept his statement, what Perry position is he manifesting and to what extent is he displaying any form of deflection?

   c.   What is the relationship of values to commitment?

   d.   What are two additional questions that can be raised to understand Perry's diagram? (You may have more than two.)

2.   Draw a diagram of your own that shows Perry's scheme. Label all stages, positions, and deflections. Show how transitions relate to your education and experience.

3.   Obtain three scenarios of individuals' lives, beliefs, writings, etc. For each scenario postulate a stage and position, and defend your choice on the basis of the critical characteristics and evidence given in the scenario.

4.   Estimate your own Perry stage and position on the basis of anecdotal evidence and your own writing samples. Explain why the evidence supports the designations.

5.   Read the autobiography of Malcolm X (see the readings in the end of the text) and discuss the stages of Perry's model that Malcolm passed through in his struggle to understand himself.

References

Chickering, A.W. (ed.). The Modern American College, San Francisco: Jossey-Bass, 1981.

Dewey, J. Art As Experience, New York: G.P. Putnam, Capricorn Books, 1934.

Kolb, D. A. "Learning Styles and Disciplinary Differences." In Chickering, A.W. (ed.), The Modern American College, San Francisco: Jossey-Bass, 1981.

Kolb, D. A. Experiential Learning: Experience as the Source of Learning and Development, Englewood Cliffs, NJ: Prentice-Hall, 1984.

Perry, W. G. Jr. Patterns of Development in Thought and Values of Students in a Liberal Arts College. United States Department of Health, Education, and Welfare, Office of Education, Bureau of Research, Final Report, April 1968a.

Perry, W. G. Jr. Forms of Intellectual and Ethical Development in the College Years. Cambridge, MA: Harvard University Press, 1968b.

Perry, W. G. Jr. "Cognitive and Ethical Growth: The Making of Meaning," in Chickering, A.W. (ed.). The Modern American College, San Francisco: Jossey-Bass, 1981.

Perry, W. G. Jr. and Whitlock, C.P. "The Right to Read Rapidly," Atlantic Monthly, November 1952, pp. 88-96.

Chapter 3

Deep
vs.
Surface
Learning

What is the difference between a surface and a deep approach to learning? Which approach do you take in your college learning opportunities? Are you intrinsically or extrinsically motivated?

In the 1970s and 1980s, a body of research in learning and study came out of Europe, mostly from Sweden and England. The research persuades serious students to at least consider the alternatives to learning and study schemes that have been based mostly on American educational psychology. Essentially, American research has relied on quantitative examination of process and outcome, while the Swedish-English model has been based on the qualitative reports by researchers who have interviewed students and reported their own reaction.

The European direction can be exemplified by the learning style contrast that Marton (1975) and Saljo (1984, 1975) have labeled *"deep"* learning and *"surface"* learning. Throughout this chapter you will be looking at definitions, relationships, and applications of deep and surface learning in an attempt to help you understand how you study, and how you might more effectively learn.

33

In the verses below, Alexander Pope ("Essay on Criticism," Part II, lines 215-232) expressed an attitude toward learning that is helpful for you to understand and apply.

> *A **little learning** is a dangerous thing;*
> *Drink deep, or taste not the Pierian spring.*
> *There shallow draughts intoxicate the brain,*
> *And drinking largely sobers us again.*
> *Fired at first sight with what the Muse imparts,*
> *In fearless youth we tempt the heights of Arts,*
> *While from the bounded level of our mind*
> *Short views we take, nor see the lengths behind;*
> *But more advanced, behold with strange surprise*
> *New distant scenes of endless science rise!*
> *So pleased at first the towering Alps we try,*
> *Mount o'er the vales, and seem to tread the sky,*
> *The eternal snows appear already past,*
> *And the first clouds and mountains seem the last;*
> *But, those attained, we tremble to survey*
> *The growing labours of the lengthened way,*
> *The increasing prospects tire our wandering eyes,*
> *Hills peep o'er hills, and Alps on Alps arise!*

In Perry's developmental scheme, Pope might have been saying,

> *A dualism is a dangerous thing;*
> *But relativism's not the Pierian spring.*
> *Not yet committed? Intoxicated brain?*
> *Commit thyself—be sober again.*

Pope decried "a little learning" (surface learning, dualism), anticipated "distant scenes of endless science" (relativism), and warned of "the growing labors of the lengthened way" (deep learning, commitments in relativism), while he was yet a very young man, and 200 years before the psychologists took learning seriously as a phenomenon for investigation.

34

Deep and Surface Learning

"Deep" and "surface" relate to differences in how students carry out (or "approach") their studies. *Marton and Saljo (1984) argue that students learn differently, not merely because of prior knowledge or because some students are "brighter" than others, but because the very process of learning is different for different students.* Deep and surface learning does not mean there are deep learners or surface learners, rather there are deep approaches and surface approaches that learners take to their learning opportunities.

Marton and Saljo (1984) asked their students how they handled specific learning tasks assigned to them for their study. The students were asked such questions as "Can you describe how you went about reading the text?" "Was there anything you found difficult?" "While reading, was there anything that struck you as particularly important?" etc.

From these interviews, it was noted that some readers failed to get the point simply because they did not look for it; others sporadically tried to memorize the text; and some saw themselves as "empty" vessels to be filled with learning. At times the students who memorized became so tense in trying to memorize text that their overanxiety to perform well led to what Marton and Saljo called *hyperintention*—resulting in missing the meaning of the information.

Other readers were successful in understanding the point of their learning tasks because they looked for relationships within the text, or between the text and the outside world; and the last group attempted to make critical judgments, logical conclusions, or new arrangements of ideas.

As Marton and Saljo analyzed each interview response, they were able to categorize them along a continuum of depth of understanding, whose two polar opposites were "surface" at the one extreme and "deep" at the other. As you come to view your own learning approach, try to view it within a continuous gradation with points along a continuum, and not as one of two extremes, either totally surface or totally deep.

The European educational psychologists who have used Marton and Saljo's surface and deep approach terminology have adapted the original catagories to purposes of their own research. *Surface learning* has been characterized by Entwistle and Ramsden (1983) in the following way:

Surface Learning

Surface learning deals essentially with unrelated sets of information. Unrelatedness would include defining learning tasks as separate and isolated from each other. For example, a surface approach would view organic chemistry and biology as two discrete subjects, each with department-tight bodies of knowledge; or history and economics as unrelated explanations of how people have interacted in society.

Surface learning defines learning as highly memorization-centered. Memorization as learning is central to the surface approach. Learning is simply defined as "How much do I have to memorize to pass this course?" Or "I could have passed that test if only I had memorized the part the professor included in her test."

Surface learning involves little or no reflection of ideas. Unreflectiveness interprets learning in an external way. The learning task is seen as passive—the teacher's problem, not the student's—a matter that is external to the student's interest, a process of accumulating material for a test, not of extracting meaning for oneself.

These three aspects of the surface approach to learning will be contrasted next with a deep approach, but first compare each with Perry's scale. Would you support the assertion that a surface approach grows naturally out of a dualistic view of life? Did it occur to you to think of a surface approach and Perry dualism as being worthy of your comparative analysis? At what Perry level, and at what learning approach level, were you operating as you read this chapter?

Entwistle and Ramsden (1983) conceptualized the deep approach to learning with the following concepts.

Deep Learning

Deep learning includes personalizing experience. Personalized experience includes relating the learning task to one's own life and knowledge. For example, a student who has taken some chemistry classes could easily view the biology of organisms as an example of applied organic chemistry. History would be seen as encompassing economic as well as political views of human interactions. Any new topic would have a personal tie to whatever the student already knows.

Deep learning observes whole-part relationships. A learning task is seen as parts of an integratable whole. The student tries to put the parts together into meaningful relationships, learning from meaning more than from memory. In fact, memory is created from meaningful relationships, not from rote effort. Evidence to conclusion, generalization to detail, multiple sources compared, present task to previous tasks related—all these relationships and more are actively sought as part of a deep approach to learning.

Deep learning senses meaning as an integration of the whole with its purpose. In the deep approach, the purpose of the task is clearly seen in order to understand relevant meaning as well as internal relationships. The structure, intent, and perspective impose a discernable pattern on the task.

To help you understand the contrast between surface and deep approaches to learning, look at Figure 3.1. Remember that while the definitions and comparisons have emphasized the polar extremes, individual learning approaches would approach one pole or the other in varying degrees. (Entwistle and Ramsden 1983, p. 137)

Surface Approach vs. Deep Approach	
Unrelatedness:	**Personal Relatedness:**
☞Task separate ☞Treat as its own ideas ☞Elements of task are separate	☞Task integral to self ☞Treat as part of one's whole development ☞Elements of task may be related to already learned knowledge
Memorization:	**Meaning Relationships:**
☞Task is a memory task ☞Intend to memorize what is needed to pass the course	☞Task is a relationship task ☞Intend to integrate, relate, see connections, understand
Unreflectiveness:	**Reflection of Meaning:**
☞Task defined externally ☞Material accepted without critique ☞Passive approach: soaking in ideas as they pass by	☞Task defined by its purpose ☞Reflect on material from a broad perspective ☞Impose meaning: impose a pattern on ideas

Figure 3.1 Comparison of Deep and Surface Approaches

Surface/Deep Approaches and Related Views of Learning

To enrich your understanding of surface and deep learning strategies, two additional concepts of learning style (European definition) that show the relationship of each to the general concepts of surface and deep learning are detailed below. If you will look at the two related views, your understanding of surface and deep learning should be greatly enhanced.

Svensson (1976) analyzed student reports of learning experiences based on two considerations: (1) what students do *while* they are trying to learn, and (2) what the learning *product itself* is. Adding outcome to process, Svensson shifted the emphasis on learning from Marton and Saljo's view of process alone to include the *organizational* aspects of learning. What Svensson noticed was that learning outcomes vary in their organizational pattern and consistency.

Atomistic learning lacks consistency. It is characterized by memorization of very specific details without putting the details together. Usually the atomistic learner also lacks some of the details that otherwise would fit together into integrated meaning.

Holistic learning shows consistent organizational pattern. The holistic learner tends to see fit, organization, and pattern, with analysis and interpretation based on the observed patterns. Specifics of the organization vary with content and discipline, of course, but organization of meaning is always present in the holistic learner.

The differences between surface/deep learning on the one hand, and atomistic/holistic learning on the other, are important and can serve to enrich your understanding as a learner. **For most purposes, atomistic outcomes may be equated with surface approaches and holistic outcomes equated with deep approaches.** What understanding the atomistic/holistic dichotomy does, compared with the surface/deep dichotomy, is highlight a learning skill that emphasizes handling learning material by careful construction of integrated unity, bringing to bear insight and closure to large bodies of information. The deep approach moves the learner in that direction. The holistic learner demonstrates that kind of learning outcome.

Marton and Saljo (1983, p. 52) claim the following:

> [There is] ...a paradoxical circular relation between approach to learning and motivation to learn. . . . Intrinsic motivation (interest) serves to lead to a deep approach and extrinsic motivation (concern with demands) to a surface approach. On the other hand, adopting a surface approach means that the learner focuses on the *text* or tasks themselves and not on what they are about. But it is hardly possible to be interested in a *text* unless one is paying attention to what it is about. Not being motivated by an interest in the *text* tends thus to lead to the adoption of a surface approach, and the adoption of a surface approach tends to block any interest in the *text*.

The argument on the circularity of motivational source and learning approach suggests that if your interest in learning is determined by course demands only, you will be more concerned with how many pages to read, what details you *must* remember, or what the outside expectations are. Your interest in the requirement triggers a surface approach, and your surface approach blocks the development of intrinsic interest. You are caught in a self-perpetuating cycle of surface learning.

Saljo (1979) analyzed the responses of adult learners to the question, "What does learning mean to you?" His findings isolated five distinguishable conceptions of learning that bear a close resemblance to developmentally based learning applications.

Learning is:

1. Increased knowledge
2. Memorization
3. Acquisition and utilization of facts
4. Abstraction of meaning
5. Interpreting and understanding reality

How do these five developmental learning levels relate to surface and deep approaches to learning? Van Rossum and Schenk (1984) studied Saljo's levels and quantified the results. Figure 3.2 illustrates how the individuals' expressed conceptions of learning compared with their preferred choice of learning approach.

Conceptions Held	Surface Approach Used	Deep Approach Used
Increased knowledge	6	0
Memorization	19	4
Acquisition/utilization of facts	8	4
Abstraction of meaning	1	11
Understanding reality	1	12

Figure 3.2 Conceptions and Deep and Surface Approaches

The meaning of Saljo's developmental conceptions of learning, as related to Marton and Saljo's surface/deep learning approach, can be understood by noticing that levels one and two are expressed by learners who prefer surface approaches.

*Knowledge (level one) is the **what** of learning.*

*Memorization (level two) is the **how** of learning.*

Surface learning can be clearly seen an effort to increase one's knowledge by memorization processes. Viewed this way, Saljo's developmental conceptions define surface learning in terms of **what** and **how,** and place surface learning at a naive level of development. (Remember that memorization and knowledge intake tend to be dualistic in the Perry scheme.)

At the other end of Saljo's developmental conceptions, levels four and five are expressed by learners who prefer deep approaches.

*Abstraction (level four) is **how one learns**.*

*Understanding reality (level five) is **what one learns**.*

Abstraction is an organizing process, and understanding requires that reality be placed in meaningful relationships. These conceptions were held by learners who approached learning deeply, as can be seen from Figure 3.2. Again, as with surface approaches, the meaning of deep approaches is enhanced by seeing both the *how* and *what* of deep learning. (The consideration of many variables to abstract understanding from reality moves the deep learner at least to the Perry relativism stage.)

Saljo's third conception appears to be a middle ground between surface and deep learning.

*Acquisition is an unspecified **how** that begins to put facts into a context that allows their use.*

Obviously, the third conception has aspects of both surface and deep approaches. That explains its middle position and its even split of learners who preferred surface and deep approaches to learning. Not much can be applied to an understanding of surface and deep learning from level three except to notice the transitional fit in what can be viewed as a developmental ordering of how learning is conceived.

If Saljo's conceptions are truly developmental, two application questions deserve an answer: (1) Where do you fit on the developmental levels? and (2) What can you do if you are not satisfied with your own development?

Strategies for Deep Learning

Part II of this textbook concentrates on skills of study and learning. In that section you will deal with how to read, how to attend to lectures, how to handle evaluations and assessments, how to think, and how to remember. Then why should you look at strategies here? In this chapter your attitude and overall approach to learning are given preference over what specific skills you might use. Here you should think strategy, while in Part II you should think tactics. Here you think about learning broadly; there you must think specifically.

An important strategy hint you should consider will grow out of chapters 4 and 5. In those chapters you will learn about styles of learning. The hint is to learn what your style is and take advantage of its strengths. At the same time, overcome the weaknesses of your style by broadening your ability to adopt alternative styles of learning when they will serve you better. As you become more flexible as a learner, you will also find yourself developing your cognitive and ethical levels, thus freeing yourself to be a true student intellectually.

Learning Applications

1. Relate the five developmental learning conceptions represented in Figure 3.2 to Perry's developmental stages.

2. Choose a content course you are now enrolled in, which you will call your target content course (TCC). Answer the questions here relative to deep and surface approaches and your chosen TCC.

    a. What learning requirements in your TCC appear to be unrelated to other parts of the course? How could they be changed to make them related?

    b. What memorization chores are a part of your TCC? Devise a memorization strategy for each that uses meaning relatedness to assist.

    c. What in your TCC appears to you to be there purely as an arbitrary whim of your instructor? Find two or more logical reasons why your instructor included it as an important part of the course.

References

Entwistle, N.J. "Contrasting Perspectives on Learning," in Marton, F., Hounsel, D., and Entwistle, N.J. (eds.), The Experience of Learning, 1984.

Entwistle, N.J. and Ramsden, P. Understanding Student Learning. London: Croom-Helm; New York: Nichols Publishing Co., 1983.

Marton, F. "On Non-verbatim Learning I: Level of Processing and Level of Outcome." Scandinavian Journal of Psychology, 1975, 16, pp. 273-279.

Marton, F. and Saljo, R. "On Qualitative Differences in Learning I: Outcome and Processes," British Journal of Educational Psychology, 1976a, 46, pp. 4-11.

Marton, F. and Saljo, R. "On Qualitative Differences in Learning II: Outcome as a Function of the Learner's Conception of the Task," British Journal of Educational Psychology, 1976b, 46, pp.115-127.

Marton, F. and Saljo, R., "Approaches to Learning." In Marton, F., Hounsell, D., and Entwistle, N.J. (eds.),The Experience of Learning, 1984.

Saljo, R. Qualitative Differences in Learning as a Function of the Learner's Conception of the Task. Gothenburg: Acta Universitatis Gothoburgensis, 1975.

Saljo, R. "Learning in the Learner's Perspective I: Some Common-Sense Conceptions." In Reports from theDepartment of Education, University of Goteborg, 1979, 76.

Svensson, L. Study Skill and Learning. Gothenburg: Acts Universitatis Gothoburgensis, 1976.

Svensson, L. "On Qualitative Differences in Learning III: Study Skill and Learning" British Journal of Educational Psychology, 1977, 47, pp. 233-243.

Van Rossum, E.J. and Schenck, S.M. "The Relationship Between Learning Conception, Study Strategy, and Learning Outcome. "British Journal of Educational Psychology, 1984, 54, pp. 73-83.

44

Chapter 4

Styles of Learning

How do you learn best? What are your weaknesses in learning? How does your learning style match with surface and deep learning approaches? Does your learning style match with your instructors? Does it matter?

Learning is a developmental process. Cognitive abilities develop as one moves from more simplistic thinking levels to abstract, more complex thinking levels. Even though learning is a process, it is a very personalized process. Not everyone learns the same way, and not all aspects of learning differences are related to intelligence or ability. Individual differences in learning reflect personal learning preferences and play an important role in the development of learning styles.

In this chapter you will have opportunity to look at David A. Kolb's theory of learning style and Carl G. Jung's theory of psychological types, and then consider your own learning in light of each theory. You will look at variety of styles rather than at depth of learning approach, but as you review variety, relate it to depth, for both variety and depth affect your own style of learning.

What is Learning Style?

Learning style, the way a person prefers to learn, is defined similarly by several different writers. Clayton and Ralston (1978) refer to learning style as the student's consistent and preferred way of responding to stimuli in the context of learning. Kolb (1984) defined learning style as the way a student perceives (takes information in) and processes (makes experience a part of self) information. Herrmann (1988) expressed learning style in relation to brain dominance, relating hemispheres of the brain to how a person prefers to learn, understands and expresses something, solves a problem, or selects a learning experience. Gregory (1979) says, "Learning Style consists of distinctive behaviors which serve as indicators of how a person learns from and adapts to his environment (input/output)." However it is defined, *learning style seems to involve the most comfortable and natural way a person goes about learning information.*

In their book <u>Introduction to Type in College</u>, John DiTiberio and Allen Hammer (1993) illustrate the idea of preference in learning style with a simple writing exercise which follows:

On the line below, write your name as you would normally do.

_____

On this line, write your name again but use your other hand.

_____

Naturally, signing your name with your preferred or dominant hand was easy. But what was it like to sign your name with your less-preferred hand? Undoubtedly, it felt awkward or unnatural, took longer, and required greater concentration (it probably looked funny too!) Even though you prefer using your dominant hand when you write, that does not mean you could not use your other hand if necessary—it just would not be as natural and comfortable for you. Like writing, you have a preferred way of learning. This is called **learning style**.

46

The Kolb Model for Experiential Learning

Chapter two presented Perry's theory of intellectual development as only one picture of how college students develop as young adults in their lifetime. This section of the chapter is presented for you to consider how you interact with your intellectual growth to shape your own particular style of learning.

The theory of learning style developed by David A. Kolb (1981, 1984) views learning as experiential in nature. Kolb borrowed the concept of experiential learning from the educational philosopher John Dewey (1934). Dewey viewed learning as a cyclic series of experiences, the outgrowth of which is learning. Therefore, as you think of learning as Kolb views it, think of having experiences from which learning is acquired. Learning, then, affects your development, thus making Kolb's theory also developmental in character. In summary, Kolb's sequence follows first, **experience**; second, **learning**; and third, **development**. Following Dewey's cyclic model, the sequence then repeats itself with a slightly altered set of circumstances. In this cyclic process, through selective experiences, learning takes on preferred modes, and development leads to preferred learning styles.

Kolb's Experiential Learning Cycle

Kolb viewed learning as resulting from four kinds of experience that ideally should occur with optimum regularity and should be a part of any learning. These experiences he labeled as (1) **concrete experience** (hands-on action, including direct emotional participation in the experience); (2) **reflective observation** (pausing to view and think about the experience); (3) **abstract conceptualization** (relating the experience to other, similar experience, thereby giving the experience broader meaning); and (4) **active experimentation** (doing something on a trial basis with the ingredients of the experience). According to Kolb, these four experiences are recurring, cyclic, and cumulative (see Figure 4.1). The cumulative nature of the experiences leads to learning, which in turn leads to development.

Development does not occur evenly in the four areas of experience, even though it theoretically should if one could assume regular developmental cycles. What happens is that the learner gets uneven doses of experience, depending on environment and interest. Schools, for example, may emphasize

47

lecture over hands-on action, or abstract thinking over trying out an idea in actual practice. An early interest in mechanical devices may lead a youngster to take his or her toys apart without thinking about why the parts function as they do. As these experiences accumulate, the direction of development is such that individuals begin to prefer some experiences over others because they have become more successful or more comfortable in some than in others. Since experience leads to learning and learning leads to development, students come to differentiate their experiences into preferred learning styles. One student prefers hands-on experience, while another prefers quiet reflection about experience. A third prefers attaching abstract meaning to experience, while a fourth is impatient to try out new ideas.

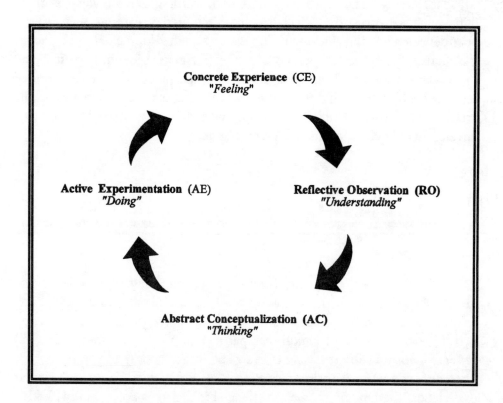

Figure 4.1   Kolb's Experiential Learning Cycle.

48

Skyler MacDonald

(40) If you had a little more space, it might be easier to read

Beginning of 1st Nephi

Destruction of Jerusalum

Leave possessions

Lehi is commanded to take his family into the wilderness and leave Jerusalum

Lehi sees a vision and prophesies in Jerusalem

Laman went to Laban and asked for the plates
[Almost killed]

Nephi, Sam, Laman, + Lemuel return to Jerusalem to obtain the brass plates

They gather up their possessions and try to trade for the plates
[Almost killed] [Angel]

The Spirit

Nephi slays Laban and takes the plates. Zoram goes with them back into the wilderness

Family / Rod of Iron / Tree

Lehi sees a vision of the Tree of Life

Lehi's sons return to Jerusalum to have Ismael and his household to go into the wilderness with them

Guides / Directs

The tribe recieves the Liahona

interpretations

Nephi is shown in vision the tree of life, the land of promise and the destruction of his people

revelations

Lehi's sons marry the daughters of Ismael

[Murmuring] [Anger]

Nephi breaks his bow

Construction

Nephi is commanded to build a ship

[Brothers oppose]

The ship is finished

They start sailing to the promised land.

Nephi is bound

Great Storm

Calming of the Sea

They land in the promised land and inhabit it, tilling the earth and planting seed

End of 1st Nephi

This is a summary of First Nephi and the main events that take place. First Nephi is one of my favorite books in the Book of Mormon because it shows the growth of a great leader and prophet, guided by the Lord to the promised land.

    I used a timeline diagram.

To illustrate the learning cycle, consider Sir Isaac Newton's experience watching an apple fall from a tree, which eventually led to his theory on gravity. As the story goes, in 1666 Newton observed an apple falling off a tree in his garden. This experience influenced further observation and reflection, conceptualization of ideas and formulas, and experimentation on the effects and pulls of gravity, particularly in relation to planetary motion, until nearly twenty years later his concept of universal gravitation sprang forth. Newton had succeeded in calculating a planet's orbit around the sun as slightly elliptic. The idea that learning is a cyclic process, continual and ongoing, cumulative in nature, wherein experience gradually lends itself to new experience and a higher level of complexity of learning, is comparable to Newton's eventual arrival at his theory.

Kolb's Development of Learning Styles

Kolb's learning cycle emphasizes the equal interrelationship among the four learning experiences or modes in their value in the learning process—abstract thinking is not valued over concrete thinking, and neither is understanding valued over doing. Ideally, effective learning requires the flexible use of all four learning modes. Realistically, however, few people are equally effective and flexible in each of the learning processes. The tension created by the dialectic interplay between the opposite learning abilities (feeling opposed to thinking and doing opposed to understanding) forces the learner to reduce the tension by suppressing a particular mode in favor of the other, making one or the other more dominant. Facing new experiences, the learner must decide which set of learning abilities to use in the learning situation. *How one consistently and characteristically resolves the tension between the concrete and abstract dimension on the one hand, and the active and reflective dimension on the other, determines which learning modes will be either specialized in or ignored.* This gives rise to one's unique learning style.

Kolb (1984, pp. 76-77) explained the development of learning style in this way:

As a result of our hereditary equipment, our particular past life experience, and the demands of our present environment, most people develop learning styles that emphasize some learning ability over others. Through socialization experiences in family, school, work, we come to resolve the conflicts between being active and reflective and between being immediate and analytical in characteristic ways, thus leading to reliance on one of the four basic forms of knowing: divergence, assimilation, convergence, and accommodation. Some people develop minds that excel at assimilating disparate facts into coherent theories, yet these same people are incapable of or uninterested in deducing hypotheses from the theory. Others are logical geniuses but find it impossible to involve and surrender themselves to an experience. And so on. A mathematician may come to place great emphasis on abstract concepts, whereas a poet may value concrete experience more highly. A manager may be primarily concerned with the active application of ideas, whereas a naturalist may develop his observational skills highly. Each of us in a unique way develops a learning style that has some weak and some strong points.

Generally, the more heavily you rely on a particular learning style, the less balanced you are considered to be in learning. The more adaptive forms of learning emerge when you use all four learning modes in combination. Kolb (1984) refers to individuals who have developed learning styles that emphasize balance in all four learning modes through integrative learning experiences as "mixed types."

Kolb's Four Learning Styles

Diverger, **assimilator**, **converger**, and **accommodator** are the names of Kolb's four Learning Styles. Each learning style combines different learning modes: the diverger combines the learning preferences of concrete experience and reflective observation, the assimilator has an orientation toward reflective observation and abstract conceptualization, the converger emphasizes abstract conceptualization and active experimentation, and the accommodator relies primarily on the learning preferences for active experimentation and concrete experience (see figure 4.2). Even though most people will rely more heavily on a particular learning style, that does not mean the other learning modes are not used. Learning styles are not fixed but are flexible orientations. Each learning style is not devoid of the influences of the other learning modes, even though one may be preferred.

50

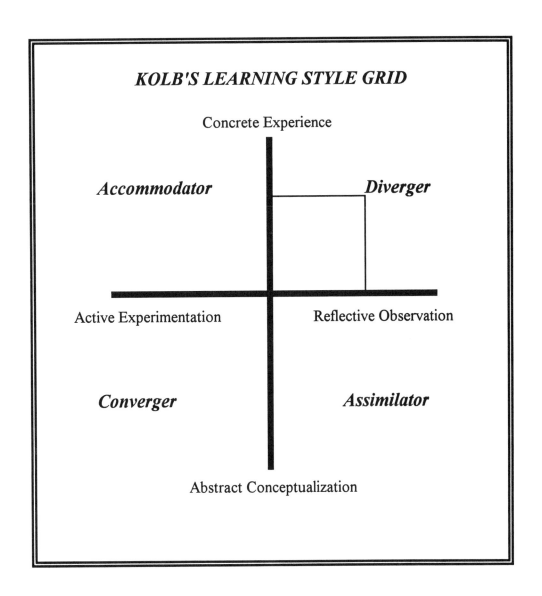

Figure 4.2 Kolb's Learning Style Grid

What follows is a general description of the characteristics of the four learning styles. The descriptions may seem to simplify the individual thinking processes, but keep in mind that an individual's thought process tends to be highly complex. The information below will prove useful in helping you identify and assess your learning strengths and weaknesses, but be careful not to stereotype your learning by concluding that the description conclusively explains how you learn.

The Diverger (Explorer)

The word *diverge* means to branch off or to go in different directions. Persons with divergent learning styles may be viewed as types of "explorers" in their thinking process. They tend to be imaginative and enjoy learning situations that call for the generation of ideas like brainstorming. They are also good at gathering information, evaluating it, and arranging it into meaningful wholes. Divergers are best at viewing concrete situations from many different points of view. Their multiple perspectives in opinion are appreciated and valued by others. These are people who enjoy being around others because they enjoy involving themselves in personal ways. Overreliance on the reflective mode could cause the diverger to become paralyzed by too many alternatives, however, resulting in indecisiveness. Too much emphasis on perceiving information concretely may influence scattered thinking, making organization of information difficult.

The Converger (Builder)

To *converge* means to come together. Convergers are deductive reasoners who tend to be efficient at defining problems, drawing conclusions, solving problems, and making decisions. As practical learners, they find value in the pragmatic application of knowledge. They work best when there is a single solution to a problem. At times controlled in their expression of emotion, convergers would rather deal with technical tasks than with interpersonal issues. Hasty decision-making could result if convergers are too action-oriented. If overly abstract in the way they perceive information, important problems and opportunities may go unrecognized and unnoticed, causing the wrong problem to be solved.

The Assimilator (Planner)

To *assimilate* means to absorb or incorporate. Being less focused on people, the assimilators prefer dealing with abstract concepts and ideas. As inductive reasoners, they are efficient at reasoning from particular facts or observations and drawing general conclusions by examining how separate ideas and concepts fit together. Because assimilators tend to be good at

52

understanding the meaning of ideas, they have the ability to create theoretical models. Ideas are judged and valued on whether they are logically sound and precise more than by their practical value. Conceptualizing too abstractly may lead to impractical thinking, making ideas and theories nonapplicable. If overly reflective in the way they process information, assimilators may have difficulties directing their work to a practical end.

The Accommodator (Facilitator)

To *accommodate* means to adapt. Accommodators adapt well to changing environments and enjoy getting involved in new experiences. They like seeking opportunities and taking risks. Their major strength lies in doing things and carrying out plans and tasks. Sometimes accommodators are viewed as "pushy" because of their active and task-oriented style. Their decision-making and problem-solving process tends to be intuitive rather than logical. They rely on other people's analytical skills more than on their own. Accommodators who rely too heavily on active experimentation may become overly action-oriented, the result being premature decision-making and problem-solving without a sound basis for their choices. Getting overly involved in "doing" could also result in "spinning their wheels," or getting caught up in meaningless activity.

Kolb's Learning Style Inventory

Kolb has devised a self-report inventory that measures your preference for activities that are representative of Kolb's four lines of experience: concrete experience, reflective observation, abstract conceptualization, and active experimentation. If you take the Learning Style Inventory (LSI), the results will indicate your strengths and weaknesses in relation to the learning cycle by showing what four learning modes are developed and underdeveloped. Your dominant learning style is also identified by placement in one of four quadrants (diverger, assimilator, converger, accommodator) according to which combination of learning modes you prefer.

Your profile will reflect only your perception of how you think you learn. Because it is a self-selected, subjective assessment, it cannot measure your learning style with more accuracy than your own self-knowledge allows. The benefit of being introduced to learning style assessments in this chapter is to help you draw a picture of your learning strengths and weaknesses.

Kolb's Developmental Model and Stages of Development

According to Kolb, learning is viewed as an experiential outcome leading from an *acquisition* stage in early years to *specialization* of learning style in the college years, and finally to *integration* of style in middle adulthood.

Kolb's developmental model (1984, p.141), seen in figure 4.3, is slightly reformulated to represent another view of Kolb's acquisition stage. (Kolb originally showed the upper cone only, from the center circle up; the authors have added the lower cone to imply the acquisition stage is a period in one's life when experiences are expanding as well as differentiating to the second stage of specialization.)

Acquisition Stage

In Kolb's developmental theory, even very young children begin to acquire learning style preferences that affect heavily their willingness or unwillingness to learn in specific learning environments. This is Kolb's acquisition stage of development. It covers roughly ages birth to adolescence (0 to 15). *In this stage the youngster gains a sense of herself or himself, including the acquisition of strong learning style preferences.* She or he differentiates from the accumulation of experiences those that have personal meaning, in order to shape a unique personality. This differentiated human being is one who goes off to college, ready to learn in her or his own preferred way.

54

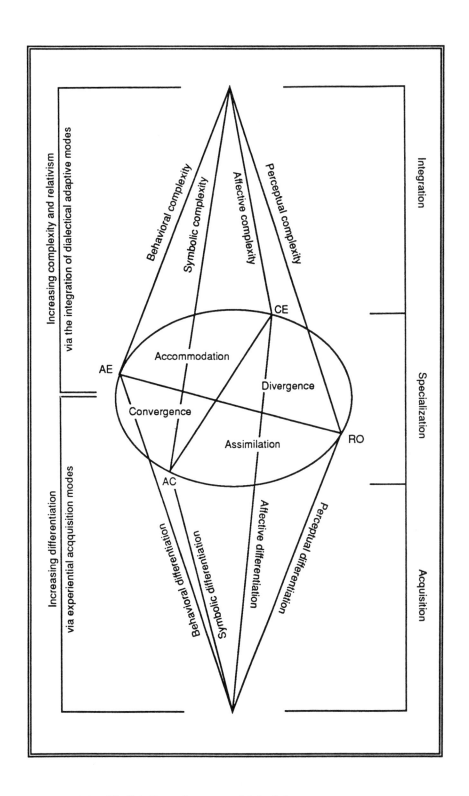

Figure 4.3 Kolb's Developmental Model.

55

Specialization Stage

At the specialization stage, learning style preferences are the strongest. Individual preferences have developed because of differentiation along the four lines of experience (concrete experience, reflective observation, abstract conceptualization, and active experimentation), some lines developing further than others, due to personal choices and socialization factors. As the differentiation intensifies, the distance along developmental paths in the four experience lines increases. Out of this specialization stage comes your strong sense of individuality.

The specialization stage extends throughout the college years into the early career-building years, and on until counterbalancing life forces (environmental impacts such as the promotion to foreman, supervisor, or manager; community involvement that demands a new set of experiences; or lay church volunteer work) *create a learning demand that is not met by the ready learning style.*

The prior acquisition of a preferred learning style is supported in the specialization stage of young adulthood as long as college and career choices are compatible with the preferred learning style. Not surprisingly, though, some learning styles conflict with some career and educational choices. Kolb (1981) reviewed such cases of occasional bright engineering freshmen who, having been admitted to one of the top technical universities in the country, now experienced loss of drive in their studies and increase of confusion in their choices. Kolb concluded that this confusion had to stem from conflicts between their chosen majors and their preferred learning styles. They found they could not learn in the way they preferred, while their professors (themselves brilliant engineers who in their teaching assumed that all engineers learned the way the professors preferred) insisted on specific learning modes.

Integration Stage

Take a look at your college experience and your general education requirements. Which courses did you dread? Why did you dread them? Not all your answers are a matter of ability; some are a matter of choice. *You have specialized your learning style preference and may be afraid to try learning experiences that have become uncomfortable. But one of the wonderful things about a college education is that you will have to try them anyway, or leave the university.* The university is a force toward integration as well as

56

toward specialization. Like it or not, you will gradually integrate your now-specialized learning style.

Your specialized learning style will guide you to a college major and will get you your first career employment. It also will help you achieve a sense of individuality. Because it serves a critical developmental function in your life, you will cling to it. But a counterforce will gradually emerge that will strengthen with increasing specialization. The further apart or more pronounced the dependency on particular experience lines, the greater the need to integrate experience along all the lines. Much of the counterforce is simply the fact that nobody ever lives in an environment that is purely the product of a single experience or of mere repetition of the same kinds of experiences.

Your particular learning style may not fulfill everything you want in life. There may be more to life than your learning style can give you. Consider these intrusions, for example: You, a future mathematician, spent two years of your life as a volunteer missionary for your church, or as a Peace Corps worker for your country. People, not figures, were your concern. Or a stimulating lecture by the scientist-director of the Royal Institution of Great Britain opened your mind to the poetic insight of scientists and the artistic symmetry of scientific phenomena. Or you graduate and take a job as a reporter on a major newspaper staff. You are successful until you become city editor and direct others' efforts, not just do your own. All these scenarios and thousands more refuse to let you continue to hold only one specialized learning style. At some point, usually well into middle adulthood, the restrictions of society's institutions—even your own drive to personal need fulfillment—demand that you integrate your experiences into a balanced learning style. The integration may not be total or perfect, but the pull creates a mature sense of selective application of learning styles that Kolb has labeled integration. Kolb (1984, p. 145) described this integration as follows:

> With this new awareness, the person experiences a shift in the frame of reference used to experience life, evaluate activities, and make choices...For the reflective person, the awakening of the active mode brings a new sense of risk to life. Rather than being influenced, one now sees opportunities to influence. For the person who has specialized in the active mode, the emergence of the reflective side broadens the range of choice and deepens the ability to sense implications of actions. For the specialist in the concrete mode, the abstract perspective gives new continuity and direction to experience. The abstract specialist with a new sense of immediate experience finds new life and meaning in abstract constructions of reality. The net effect of these shifts in perspective is an increasing experience of self as process. A learning process that has previously been blocked by the repression of the nonspecialized adaptive modes is now experienced deeply to be the essence of self.

Learning Implications of Kolb's Learning Theory

Understanding the learning process and its implications toward the development of your learning style is an important beginning in helping you improve your learning skills. For instance, if you are having trouble learning new material, it may be because you are trying to learn in a way that is not consistent with your natural style. Kolb's ideas are presented here to help you identify your learning strengths and to start you thinking how you might go about developing a greater learning capacity in those learning processes that are less developed. Even though a strongly preferred style of learning may serve you well enough in beginning a chosen major or career, to limit yourself to one style only, no matter which style, will prevent your becoming a deep learner. The diverger will be a surface learner in the atomistic sense; the assimilator will be limited to the *how* of deep learning without the *what*; the converger will fail to treat abstract concepts as true abstractions, but will act only on "memorized" abstract words; and the accommodator will act naively, without conceptual depth. The deep approach to learning will ultimately require the full cycle of experience in reasonable balance and in repeated experiential episodes.

Psychological Types and the Myers-Briggs Type Indicator

Two things should be evident at this point: people are unique in their adaptiveness to their learning environment, and that uniqueness is reflected in personal learning styles.

This section of the chapter will approach learning style from a psychological perspective, drawing on Carl G. Jung's theory of psychological types. The Myers-Briggs Type Indicator, an assessment device based on Jung's theory, will be discussed and applied to learning style. From the discussion you should consider your own learning style in light of Jung's theory and compare your "type" with earlier discussions of learning styles.

58

Psychological Types

Differing from the popular Freudian view of his day that man was determined and shaped solely by factors outside of himself, Carl G. Jung believed that individuals' subjective, inner realities and experiences were important factors in explaining differences in psychological processes. Jung's theory of psychological types explains the differences in people's mental functioning or processing. His term "psychological types" refers to individual preferences or habitual attitudes in mental or psychological functioning which characterize or "type" in specific ways. Kolb describes the development of learning style as the result of preference or choice among mental activities. *Similarly, development of psychological types occurs as specific mental functions become preferred or differentiated from other mental functions.* Whether discussing learning styles or psychological types, development consists of favoring naturally preferred functions and ignoring less preferred mental processes. Jung believed that individuals were predisposed due to hereditary elements to prefer certain mental functions over others, but he also recognized the influence of environmental factors as either positively or negatively reinforcing dominant or less dominant mental functions.

Myers-Briggs Type Indicator

The Myers-Briggs Type Indicator (MBTI) is based on Jung's theory of psychological types. It is a measurement of personality. Developed by Katherine Briggs and Isabel Briggs Myers, the MBTI is designed to assess your preferences on four scales: extroversion/introversion, sensing/intuition, thinking/feeling, and judgment/perception. Notice that each scale has two opposites. Just as you have a preferred way of learning, you have a preferred way of being in the world. Even though a person may display a particular predominance or preference on each of the four scales, he or she is likely to possess to some degree the opposite attitude or function.

Myers-Briggs Scales

Extroversion (E) and Introversion (I) define a person's attitude and orientation toward the world. A person who prefers Extroversion is inclined to direct his or her attention outside of self and focus attention on people and events. A person who prefers Introversion is inclined to direct his or her attention inward to inner realities and experiences by paying attention to feelings and thoughts. Common adjectives often used to describe an extrovert are sociable, action-oriented, assertive and spontaneous (Myers and McCaulley, 1985). Introverts are often described as contemplative, cautious and private.

Sensing (S) and Intuition (N) describe how a person acquires or gathers information. Individuals who prefer Sensing perceive the present moment through their senses (how things look, feel, taste, sound or smell) and tend to focus on the practical rather than on the abstract. An individual who prefers Intuition goes beyond the information by inferring possibility and meaning by way of insight or "hunches."

Thinking (T) and Feeling (F) describe ways a person makes judgments or decisions. People who prefer Thinking like to decide things objectively and logically by weighing information in a detached way. Those who prefer Feeling like to decide things subjectively according to what is important to them and to others.

Judging (J) and Perceiving (P) describe how a person relates to the outside world. A person who prefers Judging likes to organize and structure the outer world by concluding and settling things. A person who prefers Perceiving likes to adapt to the world by being open and flexible with new options.

Your MBTI results yield a four-letter code or type that indicates preferences on the four scales. For instance, a person whose type is INFP has preferences for Introversion, Intuition, Feeling, and Perceiving. There are sixteen possible types (ISFJ, ENTJ, INTP, etc.) Can you guess what your type might be? You may know that you prefer to pay attention to your feelings and thoughts over your external environment. Perhaps you prefer acquiring information by focusing on the big picture rather than on details. Maybe you prefer to make decisions by what is important to you and not by what seems logical. You may prefer to relate to the world by keeping your options open to new experiences rather than deciding on things immediately.

Of course, to accurately know what your type is, you will have to take the MBTI. Like the Learning Style Inventory, the MBTI may be available through your college's assessment center.

Learning "Styles" and Type Preference

According to Jung's type theory, personality preferences or the function of type influences the way a person learns. Each type has a style of learning that comes naturally. Your type can help you identify how you are likely to learn and what you will tend to respond to as a learner. The outlines which follow summarize some of the learning "styles" associated with each scale. They are adapted from the works of DiTiberio and Hammer, 1993; Keirsey and Bates, 1984; and Myers and McCaulley, 1985.

Extroversion (E)

♦ Derives energy from being around others
♦ Likes to study in interactive groups
♦ Acts quickly on projects or assignments
♦ Learns best by involvement and action
♦ Prefers group discussion

Introversion (I)

♦ Recovers energy by being alone
♦ Prefers private study with quiet concentration
♦ Focuses on projects that require a long attention span
♦ Learns best by pausing to ponder and think

Sensing (S)

- Prefers practical approaches to learning
- Learns facts and details easily
- Depends on skills already learned
- Trusts past experience
- Likes personal, hands-on involvement
- Prefers multiple choice tests

Intuition (N)

- Prefers innovative approaches to learning
- Seeks to go beyond factual information
- Takes risk in new learning situations
- Values "hunches"
- Likes learning that is explorative
- Prefers essay tests

Thinking (T)

- Uses logic to guide learning and decision-making
- Likes to relate to learning material objectively
- Learns by being challenged
- Prefers learning subjects that require critical ability

Feeling (F)

- Uses values and feelings to guide learning and decision-making
- Likes to relate to material personally
- Learns by being supported and encouraged
- Prefers learning people-oriented subjects that require subjective ability

Judging (J)

- Task and outcome oriented
- Works steadily toward closure
- Prefers "work before play"
- Likes to plan work and study time
- Prefers to concentrate on a few tasks at a time

Perceiving (P)

- Process oriented
- Works in bursts of energy
- Prefers "play before work"
- Likes to be spontaneous in work and study
- Likes to work on more than one project at a time and remain open to new information

Type Development

Societal forces, individual choices, and natural preferences are the factors involved in differentiation among mental functions and development of psychological types. Jung (1933, p. 564) described this process below:

> It is hardly possible—owing to the inclemency of general conditions—for anyone to bring all his psychological functions to simultaneous development. The very conditions of society enforce a man to apply himself first and foremost to the differentiation of that function with which he is either most gifted by Nature, or which provides his most effective means for social success. Very frequently, indeed as a general rule, a man identifies himself more or less completely with the most favored, hence the most developed, function. It is this circumstance which gives rise to psychological types.

For Jung (1933, p. 561), the process of differentiation is individuation, or the process of "forming and specializing the individual nature"; this process gives rise to personal types. A sense of individuality is achieved through the acquisition and development of preferences among mental functions.

Specialization, in the way ascribed to Kolb, can be compared to Jung's description of differentiation in type development. As you recall, a person in the specialization stage of development has dominant modes of learning which are more specialized. Specialization is needed to establish a sense of individuality and to function in a world that demands specialized skill. *Myers and McCaulley's (1985) theory of type development assumes that youth is the time for specialization, when competence and skill are achieved and preferred or dominant functions are emphasized.* The course of personal development in youth and young adulthood is significantly shaped by choices made and by the application of those choices to life tasks.

Type development does not end with the specialization around dominant mental functions. Myers and McCaulley (1985, pp. 15 and 65) explained development the following way.

> Development comes from striving for excellence in those functions that hold the greatest interest and from becoming at least passable in the other less interesting, but essential functions. . . It [type development] is a process of getting greater command of preferred functions, adequate command of less-preferred functions, and comfort in both the extroverted and introverted attitudes.

63

In type development, a more complete, mature development involves adequate use of the less preferred functions and attitudes. In Kolb's integrative stage of development, integration between the less preferred and preferred learning modes is considered the ultimate level of growth and development. Kolb and Myers and McCaulley all assert that it is generally during midlife and beyond that individuals begin to use and depend on their less dominant modes or functions in learning. Whether many individuals reach this stage at which each function can easily be used when a particular learning situation requires it is questionable. This advanced stage of adult development may be only a theoretical extrapolation of observed data, much as Perry's ninth position of commitment was only theorized, not actually observed.

Choosing a College Major and Occupation

How far should you take your LSI or MBTI results? Should you use them to guide your choice in a college major or future career? Kolb (1981, p. 239) researched correlations between learning-style orientations and choices in undergraduate majors. In a study done with managers who reported their undergraduate majors, Kolb found that those with divergent learning styles tended to have majors like psychology, history, English and political science; those with assimilative learning styles were economics, mathematics and chemistry majors; convergers tended to have engineering backgrounds; and those with accommodative styles tended to graduate in business. A conclusion drawn from the study was that one's undergraduate education was an important factor in the development of learning style, either by the process of choosing a certain discipline, or by the process of socialization in the course of learning, or both. *The implication is that people tend to choose majors that are consistent with their learning styles.* Kolb also suggests that a match between your learning style and the demands of your major may result in greater personal commitment and motivation to learning, as well as a feeling that the workload is lighter.

Your MBTI results can give some helpful insight into how you go about choosing a major. DiTiberio and Hammer (1993) indicate that the first and last letters of your MBTI type can indicate your preferred style of exploring majors and careers. For instance, EJ Types tend to have a clear sense of direction, so they will tend to decide a major by selecting quickly. IJ Types want to be sure they make the right choice, so they might spend a lot of time "doing their homework" before making a final decision. EP Types often make decisions by trial and error, so it is important to them to experience as many majors as possible before making a selection. IP Types often wonder "what they want to be when they grow up," and they might want to delay a decision about a major until they can consider many options.

Students normally gravitate toward subjects and majors that interest them and that provide opportunities to use their preferences. *However, if you find yourself in a major that does not correlate with your learning style, do not automatically assume that you are in the wrong major. Remember, each learning style combines other preferences, and your choice in major may reflect a viable but less favored learning mode, one that can be relied on to support quality work and intense interest.* Although there is some support for the suggestion to select a major that is compatible with your learning style, do not base your choice of major solely on your LSI or MBTI results. There are other inventories, like the Strong Interest Blank and the Jackson Vocational Interest Survey, designed to help you in your personal career assessment. There are also helpful value-oriented computer programs, like Sigi, that help you look at related aspects of your personality. Choosing a major is an important task and should be done with as much information as possible.

Summary

Two different theories on the development of learning style have been presented in this chapter. Kolb's theory on experiential learning describes learning style as the way a person perceives information concretely or abstractly and processes information reflectively or actively. Jung's theory of psychological types suggests how personality orientation or the function of "type" affects one's learning.

Knowing more about your learning style should contribute to your learning effectiveness. Take time to become a better learner by integrating the information presented in this chapter. Capitalize on your learning strengths and evaluate how your weaknesses interfere with your learning. Finally, consider how your weaknesses might clash with learning style expectations of faculty in various departments and colleges.

Suggestions on how you might go about improving your own learning style are the subject of the next chapter, Understanding Your Own Learning Style. Upcoming chapters will focus on how to use your learning style effectively in the application of study skills.

1. Make arrangements with your instructor or with your counseling center to take the LSI or MBTI. For results most representative of your true style of learning, you should take these tests before you read the chapter so that the discussion of the inventories' theoretical bases will not influence your responses. Remember that these inventories are not tests in the sense of right and wrong answers. Rather, they are inventories of preferences, with no reference to better or worse choices. Answer all the questions and respond to all the situations according to how you feel personally. When you have completed the inventories, have your instructor or a counselor discuss with you how the results fit your learning profile.

2. If you took the Kolb Learning Style Inventory, look at the skewed kite-shaped profile of preferences that shows relative preference along each dimension and at the rectangular figure that shows a resultant preference for a particular learning style. Compare the quadrant descriptors with your own self-view. Note also whether the resultant rectangle is large, small, skinny-vertical, or skinny-horizontal. Lines of the rectangle close to the grid line means very little strength of preference of one polar opposite over the other. Based on the shape and size of the rectangle, consider whether your growth in the Kolb developmental scheme is not yet fully specialized or has gone beyond specialization to integration. (Hint: Large rectangles show strong preference and strong specialization. Small rectangles show little preference and little specialization, but say nothing about why.) What do your Kolb diagrams say about your use of Kolb's complete experiential learning cycle?

3. If you took the Myers-Briggs Type Indicator, compare your MBTI type preferences with your own self-assessment and against Kolb's LSI. Are the types and the styles coherent? Do they fit each other and your view of yourself? What do they tell you about your personality strengths and weaknesses as they affect your desire to be a student? What kind of student do they suggest you are? How well do you accept their indication? How should you or the inventory results change for you to become a deep learner? How should they change for you to become the kind of learner you want to be? What do they suggest about your Perry developmental stage and position?

References

DiTiberio, J. K., and Hammer, A. L. Booklet: Introduction to Type in College. Palo Alto: Consulting Psychologists Press, 1993.

Clayton, C. S., and Ralston, Y. Learning: Their Impact on Teaching and Administration, AAHE-ERIC/Higher Education Research Report, No. 10. Washington, D.C.: American Association for Higher Education, 1978.

Gregory, A. "Learning/Teaching Styles: Potent Forces Behind Them." Educational Leadership, Jan 1979, 36, 234-236.

Jung, C. G. Psychological Types. New York: Harcourt, Brace and Company, 1933.Keirsey, D., and Bates, M. Please Understand Me. Del Mar, CA: Prometheus Nemesis Books, 1984.

Kolb, D. A. Experiential Learning: Experience as the Source of Learning and Development. Englewood Cliffs, NJ: Prentice-Hall, 1984.

Kolb, D. A. ``Learning Styles and Disciplinary Differences," in Chickering, A. W., and Associates, The Modern American College. San Francisco: Jossey-Bass Publishers, 1981.

Kolb, D. A. Learning Style Inventory: Technical Manual. Boston: McBer and Company, 1976.

Margerison, C. J., and Lewis, R. G. How Work Preferences Relate to Learning Styles. Bedfordshire, England: Management and Organization Development Research Centre, Cranfield School of Management, 1979.

McCarthy, B. The 4-Mat System. Barrington, IL: Excel Inc., 1980.

Myers, I. B., and McCaulley, M. H. Manual: A Guide to the Development and Use of the Myers-Briggs Type Indicator. Palo Alto: Consulting Psychologists Press, 1985.

Smith, R. M. Learning How to Learn. Chicago: Follett Publishing Company, 1982.

Chapter 5

Understanding Your Own Learning Style

How can understanding your learning style help you to become a better student? What learning path will you chart to increase your learning power? What learning strategies will help you excel?

Thinking about how you learn and then using that knowledge in developing a personal approach to learning will help you face your educational challenges competently. You will be empowered by understanding your learning strengths and limitations and by knowing where you need improvement. Capitalizing on what you do best will help you find alternative ways to supplement your learning in areas that are difficult for you, or are inconsistent with your particular learning style.

This chapter will further your understanding of learning style by helping you interpret your individual test scores and plan a learning strategy to enhance your strengths and overcome your limitations.

Enhancing the Process of Learning How to Learn

Understanding learning style enhances the process of learning how to learn, first, *by developing an awareness of how you learn*; second, *by strategizing personalized learning plans*; and third, *by taking the necessary steps to carry out your plans of action.*

Brundage and MacKeracher (1980, p. 30) support this three-step sequence this way:

Learning how to learn involves a set of processes in which the individual learner acts at least partially as his own manager of change, and his focus of change is his own self-concept and learning processes. This requires that the learner be able to conceptualize his own learning process and be able to pay some attention to how he goes about learning . . . [and] trust himself to manage this process.

Develop an Awareness of Yourself as a Learner

The first step to improving your learning approach is to become *aware* of yourself as a learner. A simple way to learn about how you learn is to think of a rewarding or meaningful learning experience that you have had recently or at some other time in the past. This can be a helpful mental exercise in discovering how you prefer to learn. A lot can be understood by answering the following questions:

What was your most rewarding learning experience? Why?

What does your experience tell you about how you like to learn?

The following scenario depicts a meaningful learning experience. From the short description below, what can you guess about Cindy's learning style by her choice and interest in the topic, chosen learning activities, and personal reaction to the overall learning experience? What learning limitations might you guess she has, in light of what she did not say she enjoyed?

70

One of Cindy's most memorable learning experiences happened while taking a history class in high school. Every student was assigned to work with two other students in the class, and together they were to select a topic of their choice. The entire group was responsible for planning, organizing, and presenting a whole week of activities to the class. Cindy's group chose to present the topic of juvenile delinquency. After much brainstorming, discussion, and planning, the group decided on the following class activities: films on juvenile delinquency; a skit on teenage abuse of alcohol; a class discussion on pertinent issues affecting teenagers, such as drugs, alcohol, and crime; and a field trip to a local juvenile reform facility. What Cindy particularly liked about this learning experience was the opportunity to learn more about a subject she was interested in, to work and interact with other students in a group, to be responsible for planning and developing the week's activities and carrying them out, to have the opportunity to be creative and imaginative in the planning, and to hear what other students thought and felt about the topic.

Not only can your meaningful learning experiences paint a clearer picture of your learning style, but your everyday experiences can also say something about how you learn. To illustrate, consider the following:

Describe how you learned to ride a bicycle.

When you browse in a bookstore, what section do you spend the most time in?

If you had the task of putting together an unassembled desk, how would you go about it?

How did you learn your multiplication tables?

How did you decide which college to attend?

Answering questions like the ones stated above will help you develop a more comprehensive picture of yourself as a learner. The more aware you are of experiences and the more you understand them in light of your learning style, the better equipped you will be to learn. Below are some additional questions, adapted from an AAHE Bulletin (1982), to further stimulate your thinking about how you learn.

71

What learning experiences have you had that you did not like or that you found affected you negatively?

How did the negative learning experience affect your performance?

What subjects do you find are easiest or most difficult? Why?

What learning activities do you have difficulty with? What kinds of learning activity do you succeed at?

How do your learning strengths and weaknesses support or clash with the learning style expectations of your professors?

Testing is another way to greater self-understanding. The previous chapter went into depth on the development of learning styles. An explanation of the Kolb Learning Style Inventory and the Myers-Briggs Type Indicator was given to familiarize you with definitions of learning style, to get you thinking about how you learn, and to help you understand that how you learn affects your entire learning experience. The information derived from taking these self-assessment instruments will help you evaluate your strengths and weaknesses in relation to how you learn from everyday experiences.

When interpreting your test results, you want to know the conditions under which you learn best and learn least well. You will want to identify what learning approaches fit your learning style and what classes will pose learning challenges or difficulties. You will want to fully diagnose your strengths and limitations in order to understand how your style affects your ability to approach learning deeply. After interpreting your scores, you should have a fairly good working knowledge of your learning style. (How to determine learning preferences and general learning style for each of the above mentioned tests is discussed in chapter 4.)

Develop a Strategy for Improving Your Learning Style

After you have examined your preferred ways of processing information, it is time to chart a learning path that will increase your learning effectiveness. The second step to improving your learning approach is to develop a learning *strategy* by capitalizing on your learning strengths and supplementing your learning needs. Start by developing a *learning plan* that includes *learning strengths you want to reinforce, learning hurdles you need to overcome,* and *specific learning strategies for improving your learning skills.* By combining your test results with your awareness of self, you are ready to personalize your learning plan.

Personal Learning Plan

Describe the preferences of your learning style.

- What are my strengths?
- What kind of learning situations do I work well in?
- What classroom approaches do I favor?
- What classes do I prefer to take?
- How do my strengths show up in my writing and in the way I study?
- What majors am I interested in?

List the specific limitations associated with your learning style.

- What learning situations are difficult for me?
- What subjects do I tend to avoid?
- What learning processes could I improve on?
- What kinds of learning activities cause me stress?
- How do my limitations affect my writing and the way I study?
- What classroom approaches do I have difficulty learning from?

Explain how you will improve your overall learning approach and style.

- What classes can I take to improve my thinking ability?
- How will I change the way I take classroom notes to make them more comprehensive and useful?
- How can I use my learning strengths to help others?
- Where should I study to better concentrate on my work?
- Who could I study with that can help me in math?
- Is this the right major for me, given my strengths and weaknesses?

Developing learning skills in areas of weakness is the most challenging way to improve your learning style because it requires a lot of hard work. *Kolb (1981) suggests two other ways to improve your ability to learn: (1) by developing work and learning relationships with people whose learning strengths and weaknesses are different from yours, and (2) by improving the fit between your learning strengths and the kinds of learning and problem-solving experiences you face.*

You can learn a lot from people who value learning differently than you do. Learn to appreciate different learning styles. Develop relationships with those who have different skills than you. If you prefer to study in a group setting, you could learn more if the group consisted of individuals who have varying learning styles. Different perspectives and approaches to learning can add a depth to your learning that studying with a group of individuals of your same learning style could not.

Sometimes students choose a major that does not reflect their aptitudes or their learning style. You may improve the match between your learning style and learning situation by changing your focus of study to an area that requires certain abilities and skills you feel more comfortable with. Level of difficulty alone should not suggest that a particular major might be wrong for you. You should expect college to be difficult. Therefore you must consider factors other than level of difficulty when making the decision to change your major—for instance, your level of interest, motivation, and depth of understanding. Improving the match between your learning style and learning situation may also mean concentrating on those learning activities that lie in your area of learning strength and then relying on other people in your areas of learning weakness through tutoring or studying with someone who has strength where you have weakness.

Figure 5.1 describes ways you can develop your learning skills in relation to Kolb's four learning styles. These suggestions only point you in the direction of ways to improve your skills. You must implement the suggestions by coming up with specific activities to guide your learning.

Act on Your Planned Strategy

The final step to improving your learning approach is to carry out or *act on* the activities in your learning plan. Your selected activities should be organized to increase your learning competence. It is up to you to initiate your plan and bring about this greater learning competence.

ACCOMMODATOR

Ways to develop accommodative learning skills:

☞ Carry out tasks and plans quickly

☞ Involve yourself in challenging experiences

☞ Adapt to changing circumstances

☞ Deal with people

☞ Get involved in leading

DIVERGER

Ways to develop divergent learning skills:

☞ Get personally involved with people

☞ Be responsive and sensitive to feelings and values

☞ Listen with an open and responsive mind

☞ Exercise imagination and brainstorming

☞ View information from many perspectives

CONVERGER

Ways to develop convergent learning skills:

☞ Find practical uses for ideas

☞ Define problems clearly

☞ Choose the best solution to problems

☞ Make decisions based on finding solutions

☞ Consciously set goals

ASSIMILATOR

Ways to develop assimilative learning skills:

☞ Look for the meaning in information

☞ Absorb observations into an integrated explanation

☞ Organize information

☞ Create conceptual models

☞ Test ideas and theories

Figure 5.1 Developing Your Learning Skills.

Occasionally you will need to evaluate your learning plan to determine whether your chosen activities are helping you to improve your learning effectiveness. Approach your learning plan flexibly. Do not hesitate to alter your plan if your learning needs have changed. The objective is to provide yourself with continued opportunities to improve your learning style.

Developing an awareness of your learning strengths and weaknesses, planning how to best utilize your strengths and improve your weaknesses, and charting a deliberate course for change are not easy learning tasks. However, if done seriously, they will be the most beneficial things you could do for yourself as a learner.

Case Examples of Learning Style

The three case examples described below will serve as good illustrations of how you might go through the process of interpreting your own test scores and any other information you have about your learning style. A good self-interpretation will help you assess your learning preferences, limitations, and plans for improving your learning skills.

The Case of Jim.

Jim is a 23-year-old senior majoring in mathematics.

> **LSI**. Jim's learning style is a **Converger**. His preferred learning abilities are doing and thinking. The Converger learning style is primarily characteristic of deductive reasoning and practical application of information.
>
> **MBTI**. Jim's type is **ISTJ** (introversion, sensing, thinking, judgment). The ISTJ type is characterized by a quiet and private orientation, preferring to deal with the reality of the present, and emphasizing a reliance on facts, logic, and analysis.

Preferences. Jim will tend most of the time to be controlled in his expression of emotion. This does not mean that he does not feel. On the contrary, Jim may feel very intensely about some things, but he will tend not to show his emotions because he prefers to deal with his environment

76

practically and sensibly. Even in times of crisis or great emotion, Jim may look very composed. While watching an emotional movie, for instance, Jim may try to analyze or second guess what will happen next, not be surprised by feeling an uncontrolled reaction.

As an introvert, Jim tends to be a quiet, private, and rather serious. He will have a difficult time interacting with people on an interpersonal level where social skills are expected and required. Jim will rely heavily on logic instead of on his perceptive capabilities to understand others. He will feel more comfortable interacting with people on technical issues rather than interpersonal issues. Although Jim likes his privacy and may prefer dealing with people on an individual basis, he may occasionally enjoy interacting interpersonally with a small group of people around whom he feels comfortable. He tends to be a very dependable, reliable, and loyal person to those whom he does befriend.

An abstract and practical approach to thinking comes very naturally to Jim. He tends to be good at deductive reasoning and efficient at breaking down complex thought into parts, then systematically reaching conclusions from factual material. Jim prefers dealing with separate facts and details rather than concentrating on understanding relationships between them. He has the ability to absorb, memorize, and recall factual information accurately and quickly.

Jim most often prefers a structured learning environment. He feels most comfortable in a classroom situation where he knows the exact procedures and rules for operating efficiently in the class. For example, he might become anxious and frustrated if a professor does not provide a syllabus which directs the students' reading and preparation well in advance. A professor who is not systematic or orderly in her or his lecture presentation may be disrupting to Jim.

Jim is very good at time management. He will tend to be task-specific and outcome-oriented. He is a planner and a goal-setter and will work very efficiently when there is a course of action to follow. Jim could be an asset to any study group or project because he is hardworking and persevering in his attempt to get things done. Once a plan is set, he will tend not to deviate from it. He will act decisively and logically in making decisions, but can at times be too hasty in deciding quickly.

Limitations. Jim's most pronounced limitation seems to be his inability to synthesize and integrate material. Predominantly processing information logically, rationally, and systematically, Jim lacks the skill to relate material conceptually and holistically. Certain classes that require this kind of deep analysis of material will be difficult for Jim. He will tend to feel like a "fish out of water" in classes where creative, divergent, and imaginative thinking are expected or required. He will tend to be inhibited in learning situations where he is asked to risk with new skills.

Jim's special attention to memorizing facts and detail emphasizes short-term memory learning. He may have a greater tendency to forget information more quickly because he does not visualize, synthesize, or conceptualize information, which tend to be long-term memory processes. Jim needs to learn how to rehearse information by combining and relating separate facts and details into patterns, concepts, and theories.

Preferred Classroom Approaches. Jim will probably vary between preferring obtaining information through more passive means, such as textbook reading and actual hands-on experience. Jim will most likely prefer testing situations that require the recall of memorized material, for example, multiple choice tests or tests in which the answer is found through following a set procedure. Essay questions or comprehensive exams that require synthesized understanding of information will tend to challenge Jim.

Learning in Relation to a Surface or Deep Approach. Jim's approach to learning may lack the quality and depth associated with a deep learning approach because of his emphasis on the memorization of information, as opposed to the understanding of information. His approach to learning tends to be more task-oriented than process-oriented. To increase his conceptualizing and synthesizing abilities, Jim must begin to trust his intuition and imagination. Relaxing during the learning experience and trusting and believing in his capacity to think will create a positive self-esteem that would seem necessary for him to take learning risks and to be creative.

Learning Strategies. Jim might benefit socially by developing his interpersonal skills. He might do this by learning how to respond more personally and sensitively to others by placing greater value on feelings and subjective experience. Because Jim learns more by doing than by listening, he may need to improve his listening abilities by being more open to others. Participation in interpersonal workshops or seminars would be extremely helpful in increasing Jim's interpersonal confidence. He may also want to make a concerted effort to involve himself in more social activities with friends whom he trusts and feels comfortable around.

To increase his ability to think in more divergent ways, Jim will need to direct his mind purposely to work in unsystematic ways by participating in such activities as brainstorming groups, imagining creative ways of problem-solving, reading books that will get his mind thinking in divergent ways, or taking specific classes that encourage him to think creatively.

78

When reading or listening to lectures, Jim will need to force himself to summarize and integrate concepts and ideas at the end of a chapter or lecture to reinforce his holistic understanding. Strengthening this skill is important for increasing Jim's ability to think more deeply.

While reading or taking notes, Jim may be too perfectionistic about details, easily getting caught up in memorizing every fact that he thinks is important. He would benefit from taking less copious notes and by skimming reading material when necessary. By use of techniques like the SQ3R (see chapter 8), the conceptualizing and synthesizing of main ideas will be encouraged.

Jim has great skill in analytical thinking. He could be a help to many people who lack this skill. Through tutoring or teaching others, Jim would continue to strengthen his own analytical ability.

While studying for an essay exam, it would be helpful for Jim to formulate essay questions and answers to those questions as preparation and practice for taking an actual essay exam.

To maintain a sense of balance in his life, Jim would do well to plan time for fun activities and relaxation.

The Case of Jenny.

Jenny is 21 years old. She is majoring in psychology and has plans to continue in a master's program in social work.

> **LSI**. Jenny's learning style is a **Diverger**. Her preferred learning abilities are feeling and understanding. The Diverger learning style is characteristic of imaginative and explorative thinking, gathering information, and relying on feeling-based judgment.
>
> **MBTI**. Jenny's type is **ISFJ** (introversion, sensing, feeling, judgment). The ISFJ type is characterized by perceptiveness, perseverance, practicality, conscientiousness, and a sensitivity to others' feelings.

Preferences. Jenny basically likes being around and interacting with people. She tends to be very perceptive to interpersonal dynamics and communications. She likes dealing with people on an emotional level and tends to respond sensitively to people's feelings. Jenny will often find great satisfaction in supporting persons in need. Her career choice to be a social worker seems to support this. Jenny tends to relate with empathy and reflectively, but when she is under stress or has a deadline to meet, her contact with people may become more practical and structured.

Jenny prefers to socialize with smaller, more intimate groups of people. She may feel shy or somewhat self-conscious interacting with larger groups of people whom she does not know well.

Making decisions and solving problems will come easily for Jenny if she has a "feeling" for what the right choice or solution is. If she has mixed feelings about something, her feelings become confused; or if she has too many choices to choose from, she may tend to be indecisive.

Jenny prefers a more practical, feeling-based approach to learning. Classes like psychology, sociology, or history—which teach about people's experiences, ways of life, and attitudes—will be enjoyed over classes that deal with abstract concepts and ideas like mathematics, economics, or certain sciences. Jenny will tend to be highly motivated to read articles, books, novels, etc., about collective human problems or personal life experiences. She will have little difficulty internalizing and understanding information that deals with people.

In general, but mostly in classes that require more abstract thinking, memorization will be the main process by which Jenny will learn. The idea that practice makes perfect influences the way Jenny approaches her learning and studying. She will likely have a systematic approach of going over material again and again until she learns it.

Jenny is naturally persevering. When she has a task or project deadline, she will prefer to work methodically and systematically at accomplishing it. She will tend not to procrastinate her obligations, starting early and consistently hammering away at them.

Depending on the required subject or task, Jenny will prefer to study alone in quiet concentration, but she could feel comfortable working in a small group with others who are serious about the learning task.

Limitations. Jenny is oriented more toward people than toward working with things or symbols. Dealing with abstract concepts will generally be very difficult for Jenny. Her performance in classes that require the logical analysis of information will be strained. She may even try to avoid subjects that require this type of thinking.

Because Jenny tends to rely heavily on memorizing information, she emphasizes short-term memory learning. Her focus on memorizing detail makes looking at information conceptually and holistically more difficult. She lacks certain skill in the integration and synthesis of material. Jenny will tend to do well in classes that require the regurgitation of information, but she will struggle with those classes that insist on a deeper level of understanding. Jenny's creative abilities will likely lie dormant because she approaches learning in a structured, safe, controlled manner. She may struggle with feeling confident in her academic abilities.

At times, Jenny may tend to perceive her environment too subjectively, and thus her feelings will be easily stirred.

Preferred Classroom Approaches. Jenny tends to enjoy learning in a personal way through discussion with others, teaching others, or having "hands-on" experience. She will also learn well from lecture-type classes and may tend to be a copious notetaker. Jenny may prefer teaching approaches that are orderly and structured rather than open and flexible. She will like things clearly stated by professors. Jenny will tend to do well on essay exams as long as they require the parroting of information.

Learning in Relation to a Surface or Deep Approach. Jenny's approach to learning may tend to be more surface in the atomistic sense. She knows how to learn facts and details but has difficulty relating separate ideas into wholes. To strengthen her learning, Jenny needs to exercise her capacity to "see the whole picture."

Learning Strategies. Jenny can memorize abstract concepts well, but she has difficulty understanding what they mean. In order for Jenny to grasp abstract meaning, she must learn in very concrete ways. That means she will have to rely on visual models, drawings, illustrations, or other more tangible manipulations to draw meaning from abstract concepts. Practice in thinking abstractly will improve reasoning ability, so involving herself in learning opportunities is important and necessary.

If Jenny is rereading chapters two and three times, she is wasting precious study time that could be used more effectively. Adopting a good reading skill technique that encourages the integration of material as she reads, for example, recitation and rehearsal of ideas, would improve her comprehension and cut down her study time. Jenny would also benefit from taking time to summarize and integrate ideas and concepts after reading or listening to a lecture.

If Jenny wants to improve her ability to think creatively, she must take learning risks. She can build her trust and confidence in her thinking by relying on what she already has—her perceptiveness and intuitiveness. She has and uses these abilities in dealing with other people, but she needs to channel them to other learning experiences. Jenny needs to trust herself to think on her own. In approaching a task like writing a paper, she could enhance her creativity by not approaching the writing in a controlled way, wherein each sentence of the first draft has to be perfect. Going with the flow of ideas, uninhibited that first time through, is important for her creative thought. Afterwards she can go back and tidy the paper up by identifying general themes discovered among the facts and eliminating unnecessary information. The challenge for Jenny will be letting go of the control.

Jenny should take every opportunity to continue strengthening her interpersonal and intrapersonal skills. Her strong empathic, perceptive, and intuitive ability will aid her effectiveness as a social worker.

The Case of Kathy.

Kathy is a college sophomore interested in the sciences, particularly biology. She has tentative plans to pursue a medical profession.

> **LSI**. Kathy's learning style is an **Assimilator**; however, her scores do not indicate she is strongly an Assimilator. Kathy views herself as processing information by reflecting and doing. There is a stronger indication that Kathy prefers thinking over feeling when it comes to perceiving information. The Assimilator learning style is characteristic of inductive reasoning. Kathy can reflect on a wide range of information, putting it into concise, logical form.
>
> **MBTI**. Kathy's type is **ESTP** (extroversion, sensing, thinking, perception). It should be noted that Kathy's judgment/perception attitude score (fourth code number) showed only a very slight preference for perception, which suggests that her style of dealing with the world includes a more balanced position between being decisive and organized, as well as being spontaneous and adaptable. The ESTP type is characterized by being in touch with the external environment, being realistic and practical in dealing with present realities, and getting all they can out of life.

Preferences. Kathy tends to interact with people she works with objectively and practically. Although her working interpersonal style may at times lack a "personal touch" because she tends to relate to others routinely and matter-of-factly, at other times she will come across as very friendly, adaptable, and good natured. On a more intimate, casual level, Kathy may be more consistent in being responsive to other people's feelings and points of view than she is in the work place. However, because she tends to put more emphasis on conducting herself logically, feeling values may sometimes be overlooked, not only in regard to other people but also in regard to herself.

Kathy will generally be more outcome than process oriented in her approach to work. If she is involved in a project, she will make a conscientious, systematic effort to reach her goals and objectives on schedule and see that they are done correctly. However, her orientation toward work

82

will not always be structured and outcome oriented. Kathy can also be flexible and spontaneous to changing situations. Although deadlines will be recognized and worked toward, Kathy will not necessarily feel bound by a need to follow a particular course of action if a project or situation requires further consideration.

Kathy can be direct in making decisions, but at times she may lack a clear sense of direction. There will be times when Kathy may feel the need to follow standard procedures to solve a problem. At other times she may see a need to be more process oriented and adaptable in making a decision. During these times, looking for a satisfying solution to a problem becomes more important than following a set procedure. How Kathy decides to solve a problem or make a decision will tend to be situational or by trial and error. She will be good at seeing the present realities of a situation and meeting the needs of the moment. However Kathy decides to solve a problem, she will usually make her decisions or judgments on logic rather than rely on personal feelings.

Kathy tends to favor an abstract and practical approach to thinking, preferring to work with facts and getting involved in firsthand experiences. However, she also enjoys learning experiences that allow for some creative thinking. Being good at reasoning from facts, Kathy has skill to understand the meaning of ideas by examining how concepts and ideas relate to each other as long as the abstractions and theories are not irrelevant. She will have very good memorization skills, but she can also rely on her ability to conceptualize and synthesize material if the learning situation requires it. As with decision-making, Kathy will tend to judge the value of any idea by logic rather than by personal values or feelings.

Limitations. Compared to Jim (case #1) and Jenny (case #2), Kathy seems to be a more "balanced" learner in that she has a greater adaptive ability to different learning experiences than either Jim or Jenny. Nonetheless, she has her particular learning challenges. Because Kathy tends to be more situational in the way she approaches learning and the problems she faces daily, there may be some pressure to be the "right person at the right time." This could become a limitation if she finds the challenge too difficult to deal with and if she acts too quickly without weighing the pros and cons of a situation.

Because Kathy generally relies on her logical approach, she will at times overlook feeling values. Undoubtedly, she will face learning experiences that require more reliance on feeling-based judgment. She would benefit from developing a greater appreciation for how feeling values enhance certain learning experiences. Not only may she overlook feeling values in learning, but she may at times overlook what other people care about.

Preferred Classroom Approaches. Kathy will probably prefer several approaches to learning, depending on what subject she is studying. There may be learning situations in which she will prefer firsthand experiences. Other times she will prefer learning by reading or listening to a lecture. It is difficult to say what testing situations Kathy will most prefer and do the best in. She may tend to do best on tests that require the recall of memorized material, but because of her conceptual abilities, she may also perform well on essay exams. With multiple choice tests, Kathy will need to trust her hunches more often.

Learning in Relation to a Surface or Deep Approach. Kathy's style of learning seems more oriented toward a deeper learning level. Her strong cerebral approach will usually get her thinking about the *whats* and the *hows* of understanding information—grasping the facts but also seeing how the facts relate to one another.

Learning Strategies. Kathy seems to have a nice balance between committing and sticking to her goals or tasks at hand, but she is also able to adapt and be spontaneous if the situation requires it. She should continue to nurture this attitude because it brings a more balanced perspective to her living.

To develop a greater appreciation for feeling-value, Kathy could make a more conscious effort to consider others' feelings and points of view by appreciating their ideas and merits and taking time to understand how they feel and think. She could seek out some new opportunities to deal with people in less logical ways.

Much of Kathy's learning strength comes from focusing on immediate experience—her memory for detail, acute observation skills, and practicality. However, she would benefit from strengthening her ability to perceive her environment more intuitively by responding to her hunches or going with her gut feelings more frequently. Kathy will probably benefit from engaging in physical activities to reduce stress.

Learning Application

Complete the **Learning Styles Worksheet** located at the end of this chapter. It is designed to help you develop a greater awareness of your learning strengths and weaknesses and to guide you in planning your course for change. Use the information from your test results and self-observations to answer the questions. Think deeply and thoroughly about each question before you answer it.

84

Learning Style Worksheet

1. If you have taken the LSI or MBTI, record your results below.

   LSI _____   MBTI _____

2. Combine your test results with your own understanding of how you learn; describe the preferences of your learning style.

3. What specific limitations are associated with your learning style that will affect your choices and performance in learning activities, decision-making, and problem-solving?

4.   Which courses do you anticipate having difficulty in? How might you compensate?

5.   What classroom learning approaches (lectures, discussion, etc.) best suit your learning style? How will you adapt to or supplement those approaches that do not fit your learning style?

6.   How do your learning strengths and limitations match surface and deep learning approaches? What would enhance your ability to approach learning deeply?

7. If you have not already decided on a major or career, what possible areas might you explore, in light of your learning style information (in conjunction with your interests)?

8. What specific learning strategies might you develop to improve your overall learning skills? (Learning strategies can include enhancement of strengths as well as improvement of learning limitations.)

9. What do your learning style and your willingness or resistance to change in style tell you about your Perry position in cognitive and ethical development?

References

Brundage, D. H., and MacKeracher, D. Adult Learning Principles and Their Application to Program Planning. Toronto: Ministry of Education, Ontario, 1980.

Claxton, C., Adams, D., and Williams, D. "Using Student Learning Styles in Teaching." American Association for Higher Education Bulletin, May 1982, 34(9), 1, 7-10

Keirsey, D., and Bates, M. Please Understand Me. Del Mar, CA: Prometheus nemesis Books, 1984.

Kolb, D. A. Experiential Learning: Experience as the Source of Learning and Development. Englewood Cliffs, NJ: Prentice-Hall, 1984.

Kolb, D. A. Learning Style Inventory Self-Scoring Inventory and Interpretation Booklet. Boston: McBer and Company, 1981.

Myers, I. B., and McCaulley, M. H. Manual: A Guide to the Development and Use of the Myers-Briggs Type Indicator. Palo Alto: Consulting Psychologists Press, 1985.

Perry, W. G. Jr. Forms of Ethical Development in the College Years. Cambridge, MA: Harvard University Press, 1968.

Part Two

Developing And Applying Learning Skills

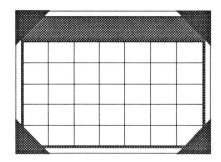

Chapter 6
Taking Charge of Your Time

How important is time management to a college student? Can you create a lifestyle that will improve your success in college? What is it that you value the most in life? Do your values have an impact on your goals? Once you have defined a goal, how can you make sure it is accomplished?

Former radio station chief executive and Salt Lake City Mayor Earl J. Glade (1959) calculated that under proper time management, a seventy-year span could be stepped up to the equivalent productive span of over one hundred years in terms of accomplishment, simply by paying attention to how one uses his or her time.

Looking at time another way, a salaried worker at $30,000 annual salary, plus 25 percent fringe benefits, earns $771.15 per week, $18.03 per hour, or 30 cents per minute. A student probably could not immediately earn that high a salary, but a high school student could easily be investing half that much in temporarily lost earnings, $9.01 an hour or 15 cents a minute. Based on a 40-hour work week, a student is forgoing over $360 while attending college. The significant question is *"How do you invest your time as a student who has ostensibly postponed entry into the work force so that you can be more productive and more valuable after a period of learning?"*

Shirley Dever (1971) said of time,

> *Time is our most priceless possession. It's easy to squander time in meaningless ways. Sometimes it's even easier to let someone else talk us into spending this precious time in ways which aren't right for us. Many people are miserly with their money; but few think about being careful about the way they spend their time. Yet, along with love, time is probably the most valuable possession we have.*

Alan Lakein (1973) considered time this way:

> *Time is life. It is irreversible and irreplaceable. To waste time is to waste your life, but to control time is to master your life and make the most of it.*

Using time effectively and successfully is probably one of the most vital habits that you can learn while you are in college. Learning to get the most out of your time in college will not only influence how well you succeed in college, but at the same time will prepare you for a lifetime of success. *Taking charge of your time is a habit; habits must be learned by disciplined practice.* The way you take charge of your time now is more habit than plan, and the way you change your time-use patterns will depend on your deliberate attempts to develop new habits.

In this chapter you will look at the occupation of being a student, living a life when, more than at any other time, you are in complete charge of your own time. After previewing your time options as a student, you will be asked to look at goal setting before you look at time planning; time planning is, after all, meaningless unless it is done in the context of reaching goals.

Once you understand your goals and how to achieve those goals by the disciplined use of time, you will be ready to: *Make a commitment to become an efficient student who is moving in a self-determined, meaningful direction.*

College Student: A Self-Starting Occupation

From the day you were born people have been deciding your schedule for you. Your mother probably fed you on schedule. Your school started and ended on schedule. If you worked, your boss told you when to start and when to stop. If you were to fit into what other people did, you had to comply with their time-tables. In fact, at times in your life, the time constraints placed on you were so rigid that you undoubtedly resented being so severely regimented.

So now you are in college. Your day belongs to you and you can do as you please! Class attendance is not required. Right? Before you go too far as a student, look around at the wealth of literature that goes into guiding time management schemes for people. Browse the local bookstore and discover the attention being paid to time management. Numerous books are available. Several shelves will be lined with time planners, life organizers, and schedule-keeping devices. People

from all lifestyles are anxious to improve the use of their time, including business managers, professionals, chief executive officers, and homemakers, to mention a few.

Alan Lakein (1973), a well known time management consultant has praised I.B.M., A.T. & T., Bank of America, Standard Oil, Neil Diamond, Gloria Steinem, and many other clients, both corporate and individual, for profiting from taking charge of their time. In business, time management has become indispensable. The more flexible the demands on one's time, the more tightly one must take charge of time in order to earn a living.

What would happen if a student looked at his or her college career as big business? Olney (1988), comparing a college career to big business, reported the financial value of a college degree over a high school diploma to be $600,000 during a lifetime. That's $1,000 per day in college if one stays to graduation!

A college student may live as flexibly as desired — but only for one semester! The truth about occupations is that success requires taking charge of one's time. Taking charge does not mean slavish use of every minute while working or studying. It does mean, however, that self-discipline and sensible devotion to planning helps to accomplish the goals of the planner. *The principle of personal management is immutable: the more demanding the schedule, the more compelling the requirements, the greater the need for planning and discipline.*

College Life: An Investment in Time

As a student, you will succeed as you find time to invest in your success. Consider, for example, Rex, a freshman who has chosen to major in music and minor in math.

Chemistry 105	(College Chemistry)	3 units
Computers 142	(Introduction)	2 units
English 115	(Freshman English)	3 units
Math 112	(Calculus)	4 units
Music 147R	(Symphony Orchestra)	3 units
Music 149	(Concert Attendance)	0 units
Music 193L	(Music Lab)	0 units
P.E. 201	(Beginning Ballet)	0.5 units
P.E. 191	(Weight Lifting)	0.5 units

Rex's task is to schedule an average number of semester credits and manage his time well enough to ensure success. Closer examination illustrates that the courses he has chosen will make incredible time demands.

You may wonder why a beginning freshman would pile work on as Rex has done. You may even think he has an easy load because he is taking "easy" music and physical education classes. Neither question has any merit for you until you know the basis for his class planning—VALUES. Before making judgement, one needs answers to basic questions. What are his values, and what are his goals? To plan time use—to take charge of one's time—one must first understand the values that set personal direction.

The Random House Webster's College Dictionary defines values as *"the abstract concept of what is right, worthwhile or desirable; principles or standards."* *Simply stated, a personal value is what people consider important to them.* What are the five or six most important things in your life? Do you value security, opportunity, money, achievement, comfort or individuality? How do your values interrelate? Is there a hierarchy? What do you do that reflects your values?

To understand Rex's class planning, one must look closely at his personal values. He values five things in his life very highly:

(1)   Personal achievement (3.98 GPA in high school)
(2)   Constant involvement (he played soccer in high school; he co-edited the yearbook)
(3)   Religious service (he regularly attends church and serves on youth committees)
(4)   Musical creation and performance (he participated in one vocal and two instrumental music groups in high school)
(5)   Intellectual companionship (he loves to learn and has been tremendously moved by his teachers)

Consider Rex's values as you look at his schedule. How is he trying to meet his perceived needs? Has he been realistic in his planning? Does he understand his new competitive college environment? Why does he join the university symphony orchestra and also spend every Saturday morning rehearsing with a church based orchestra? If you knew also that his goals in life include playing in a nationally recognized symphony orchestra and becoming an accomplished composer of music, could you understand why he takes physical education classes ranging from weight training to ballet? From an improved perspective, you can see that one must understand his or her values and understand the college environment before setting goals. With these prior considerations in place, you can begin to take charge of your time. With a clear image of values and goals, how you spend your time begins to take shape and direction.

The first phase in achieving success is setting goals, but goals must relate to values, or they are nothing more than hollow words. Can you imagine Rex setting a goal to earn a million dollars by age 30? More likely, while "Rome burned," he would fiddle. How does one earn a million dollars while practicing three hours a day and using "spare" time to write music? Was Mozart a success? He died a pauper, though he filled the courts of Europe with brilliant music!

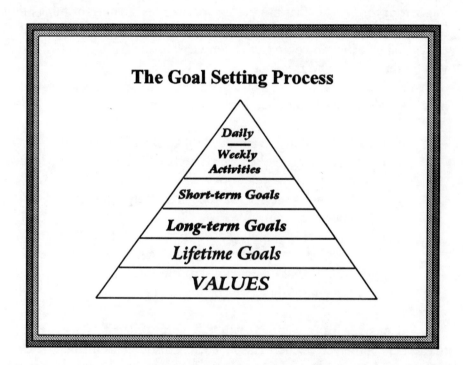

The Goal Setting Process

Daily
—
Weekly
Activities

Short-term Goals

Long-term Goals

Lifetime Goals

VALUES

Figure 6.1 The Goal Setting Pyramid.

Above is a pyramid (see Figure 6.1) which describes a hierachy of the goal setting process. While learning this process, you must begin to see how the final activites you carry out stem from what you consider important—values.

Setting Goals and Determining Activities

Earl Nightingale, a syndicated radio commentator, was extremely successful in a meteoric career in business that quickly netted him a financial fortune. With a million dollars in hand, he began to ask himself what he really wanted to do in life, because he had already achieved his first goal much more quickly than he had ever dreamed possible. As he thought about goals and success, he decided to use his experiences in various ways to inspire others to reach for their own success. In a taped lecture, Nightingale (1972) shared some of his experience with his listeners. Three of his key statements of philosophy are quoted here to guide your efforts toward success:

> *1.   What the mind of man [and woman] can conceive—and believe—it can achieve.*
> *2.   Success is the progressive realization of a worthy goal.*
> *3.   We become what we think about.*

As you evaluate your own life and set your own goals, keep in mind that Nightingale was not necessarily talking about wealth, though one may achieve wealth in the process. Nightingale pointed out that wealth per se had nothing to do with success— achieving worthy goals did.

The reason that people do not reach their potential is that they do not set goals around which to orient their lives and then concentrate their energies and talents on reaching those goals. *We often think we have goals, but after honest examination, we find that what we thought was a goal was simply a wish, or desire, or hope. The difference between hopes and goals is that the latter are actualized into practical plans.* If properly described and implemented, goals become the basis for choices, priorities, and decisions. Hopes, on the other hand, remain vaguely pleasant fantasies that provide the stuff for daydreams and other needed escapes from reality. There is nothing wrong with hopes and dreams, but when we confuse hopes and dreams with actual goals we deceive ourselves into believing that we are being true to ourselves through our fantasies, rather than through our goals, objectives, plans, and achievements.

A goal is an endpoint or a desired state of affairs. Goals arise out of values. They energize you into action and mobilize your resources. Goals have characteristics which make them readily identifiable. The following list of characteristics may help you form goals which are clearly goals and not just wishes.

Characteristics of Personal Goals

1. They are specific.
2. They are measurable.
3. They are realistic.
4. They are compatible with each other.
5. They have due dates for accomplishment.
6. They are written.

The first step in the goal-setting process is to identify specific lifetime goals that fit your values. It is best to write these down and keep them where they can influence your intermediate goals and daily routines. That is their purpose, and that is why you write them down. Remember, you can always change them if you change your mind, but for now they might as well be influencing what you do if you are serious about them at all. A lifetime goal for a student might be "I will continually seek ways to improve my mind through learning and review my progress annually."

The second step is to write down the intermediate (long-term and short-term) goals to achieve in the next few years. Intermediate goals guide your activities within shorter segments of your life. For the college student a long-term goal would be to graduate or complete a program. A short-term goal would include what you want to accomplish by the end of the current quarter or semester. Most time management experts suggest setting both long-term goals (three to ten years) and short-term goals (six months to three years).

Intermediate goals are written down as logical steps to your lifetime goals. And since your lifetime goals reflect your values, your long-term and short-term (intermediate) goals will also reflect your values. A long-term college student goal might include the following written statement: "I will complete my degree program in geography within four years and invite my parents to the graduation ceremony in the spring." A short-term goal would follow this pattern: "I will complete 16 hours of credit during fall semester and receive a minimum accumulative GPA of 3.0."

The third step is to write down the activities for the week or the day which will lead to accomplishing the stated short term goal. Like goals, activities have identifiable characteristics that you should look for as you struggle to write them down.

Characteristics of Effective Activities

1. Activities should relate directly to the stated goal.

2. Activities are very specific. Remember you cannot do a goal, you can only do activities.

3. Every planned activity should have a date, time and place to be carried out.

4. Activities should be repetitive and be carried out daily or weekly. If the activity is not repeatedly done, it will not lead to a change of attitude or goal attainment.

The goal-setting process is straightforward and powerful. The result brings a set of very specific guidelines to your day-by-day choices of activities. To be true to each level of goals is to be true to yourself, your values, and your life. Every level should be included in a comprehensive goal-setting program. Remember, it is not necessary to go through all the steps every week, but, it is healthy to look over what you have previously written down as you do your weekly planning. When you begin to write down your goals, consider the example which follows:

Value: *I prize the personal development and understanding of life I get from reading excellent literature.*

Long Term Goal: *I will read at least 12 books every year to improve my mind and my depth of understanding (6 popular novels and 6 classical novels every year).*

Short Term Goal: *I will read the book My Name Is Asher Lev between October 1st and November 1st.*

Weekly Activity: *To accomplish my goal I will read at least 90 pages per week.*

Daily Activity: *I will read 15 to 30 pages every evening in my room between 10:00 and 11:00 p.m.*

You can see that setting a goal follows a pattern. The foundation might be a commitment to the value of learning, followed by lifetime (descriptive) goals, refined by long-term (measurable) and short-term (specific) goals.

Your goals should be written, looked at often, and altered when you see the need to change them. You should review your values often (monthly). If your written values cease to be your real values, the entire goal structure probably will change. There is nothing wrong with change as long as the change reflects your values. However, you should be concerned when you are involved in activities that do not lead to your goals or reflect basic values. Either the activity is wrong, or the goals and values are wrong. That is why you look at goal and value statements often. Daily, weekly or monthly reviews will be necessary if you want to steer your life in a specific direction.

It is important to be very specific, especially when writing short term goals and activities. In setting up a plan to accomplish goals, specific activities need to be developed. For example, if you wanted to save $7,000 in five years, it would probably not happen if you did not set up an activity. The activity would be to deposit $100 on the first day of each month in an account that paid six percent compound interest.

There are some final reviews that you should work through in your goal-setting process. The questions which follow will act like a checklist to ensure that your goals fit a pattern that will lead to successful achievement.

Questions to Ask About Goals

☐   Is this goal consistent with my personal values?

☐   Am I willing to commit myself to a specific timetable for completion?

☐   Can I measure my progress in increments while working toward accomplishing this goal?

☐   Have I really thought through the commitment necessary and the consequences of setting this goal? Or am I willing to sacrifice and pay the price?

☐   Can I visualize this goal clearly and see myself at the endpoint that it represents? Or is it reasonable to start and complete the project?

☐   Have I thought through the short-term objectives or the specific activities necessary to accomplish this goal?

Daily and Weekly Time Planning

Daily and weekly planning is an important and essential part of college life. Planning in the light of your values and goals brings a greater assurance of success.   As illustrated earlier, the goal-setting process eventually needs specific activities to ensure success.

Planning for daily and weekly activities has become a highly focused activity in our culture.   One would likely see as many day planners as managers at a conference of executives. The final purpose in this chapter is to help you organize and plan your daily schedule.

Setting Priorities: The "To-do" List

After you have reviewed your short-term goals and activities, it is time to set weekly and daily priorities. Priorities are simply activities with time and sequence values attached to them. For instance, you may have decided to stop at the supermarket and then stop at the service station on your way home from school. When you check the fuel gauge of your car, however, you notice that you overestimated your fuel supply, and it is nearly gone. Naturally, stopping at the service station takes on a higher priority than the supermarket, since you may not even make it to the supermarket if you don't stop first to buy gasoline.

In everyone's life there are many similar decisions to be made every day. Some of these will be more important than others. Priorities (time and sequence decisions) will always exist whether one is aware of them or not. The person who feels he or she makes no decisions at all is actually making decisions all the time, even if only deciding not to decide, and thereby decides by default. Thus priority judgments occur, whether done consciously or not. *It is much better to make priority decisions in favor of the things you want out of life (your values and goals) than to let these decisions be made by others, or to let the circumstances dictate the decision.*

102

One student, who was not getting the grades he wanted to reach his goals, was asked by his counselor to make a record of how he spent his time throughout the day. The student wrote down everything he did for the

seventeen waking hours of one day. When he totalled the time, he was surprised to see that he had spent less than an hour-and-a-half in actual study time. *He was more surprised when he realized that even though he had actually spent over three hours in the library, he had studied only about fifty minutes.* Checking over his record, he found that he had entered the library at 10:10 a.m., but by the time he had stopped to talk to a friend, looked around for a good place to study, sharpened his pencil, and stopped to read a few things on the bulletin board on the way back from the pencil sharpener, it was 10:45. He lost the rest of the time in much the same way. A friend had stopped to talk, a trip to get a drink of water ended up taking twenty minutes when he picked up the newspaper, and so on.

This brief anecdote should tell you something very important about priorities. What you should do or think you want to do is often very different from what you actually do. Thus a well-known expression cautions, ***Don't let the things which matter most be at the mercy of the things which matter least.*** Many a person has run out of gas on the way to the supermarket merely because he or she neither planned ahead nor set priorities. If you think seriously about what you want to get accomplished and how long it will likely take, it is easy to plan to give priority to one decision over another.

In any list of things to be done, some will be more urgent or more important than others. Such is the basis of setting priorities. Lakein's system (1973) for handling such a list is both simple and effective. Lakein advised everyone to have a "to-do" list for tasks needing to be done each day. This list contains all the projects, assignments, jobs, etc., that the person wants to accomplish during the day. This system, which Lakein calls his "ABC Method," consists of assigning a value of A, B, or C to each item on the "to-do" list: an A to the side of each high-priority item, a B to each item of medium importance, and a C to each item of low importance.

To illustrate this in terms of a student's life, perhaps your own, look at an example. Suppose you have made the following list of things to do on a particular day:

> *Buy a notebook for class the next day*
>
> *Write a letter home*
>
> *Finish typing an English paper, due next week*
>
> *Do some reading for a report in biology, due tomorrow*
>
> *Watch a special documentary on television*
>
> *Read a favorite book*
>
> *Go window shopping with a friend*
>
> *Spend some time helping to clean the apartment*
>
> *Play some tennis*
>
> *Study for a Spanish exam scheduled at 8:00 tomorrow*
>
> *See a movie that my roommate recommended*

This list may seem a little long, but you will notice that it contains not only items that you *have to do* (writing a letter home, since you are out of money and your checks will bounce if your parents don't put something in your checking account), but it also contains items that you *should do* (outside reading, typing your paper) and that you *want to do* (watching a certain T.V. show, playing tennis). To lead a balanced life, you must ultimately include activities of each type: must, should, and want; but remember, your day is not long enough to do everything, and some of these items are no doubt more important to you than others. Realizing that your time is limited, you look over your list to see which items are the most important to you. That exam in your Spanish class is difficult to ignore. It is a major exam, and you need to bring your grade up. So you write an A to the left of the Spanish exam. You must write home, or at least call (but that would be expensive and things are not that urgent yet); if you write now you will most likely save an expensive call later. You place an A to the left of "write home." You really want to play a few sets of tennis, and you know that if you put it off it will be a long time before you get another chance. Since you feel like work and study have taken up most of your time and you deserve the break, you put an A beside "tennis." The paper you need to type is important, but it is due next

104

week, so you assign a B to this item. You continue this until all the items on your list are assigned a priority. Then you rank all your A priority items by numbering them: A1 for most important, A2 for next most important, and so on. You do this only for the A's since B's and C's should not occupy your attention until all the A's are out of your way. (This brings up an important aside: never work on C's or even B's when there are A's to do. It will be a temptation to do C or B items simply because they are easier and give you a feeling of accomplishment, but resist the temptation and stick to the A's.)

You may find that you tend to give almost everything an A priority ranking (for example, the tennis game when you have an exam and a biology report facing you). If you do, it's possible that you are not keeping your goals in mind. To have a clear idea of what is most important, you should assign priorities that are consistent with the long-term and short-term goals you have set. This will help you gain perspective on the activities of your daily "to-do" list. For example, while cleaning the apartment may seem important to you at the time, it is getting in the way of your more important goals if you let it keep you from studying for your Spanish exam. Keeping your goals of good grades and graduation in mind will help you see that at this particular time studying is an A and cleaning the apartment is probably only a C.

Budgeting Time

If time is life, as Alan Lakein claims, to waste an hour of time is to waste an hour of life. *Budgeting time, then, is the process of deciding how much of your life you are willing to spend to accomplish your goals.* Most college students think they are sacrificing long hours of their life every day just to pay for their educational goals. It may surprise you to know that repeated studies of college students (Kirby, 1977) show that the average weekly investment for education, including study time, during any semester or term is only forty hours! That is no more than a working person's week, and it leaves seventy-two hours every week for other activities after allowing a generous fifty-six hours for sleep. Where is this long-hour sacrifice anyway? The answer is simple: just reread the anecdote of the student who was not getting good grades. That is why a nonworking student can do all his or her school work in a period from 8:00 a.m. to 6:00 p.m. and have evenings free. A working student can work up to twenty hours per week, with planning, and not adversely affect his or her grades. The secret is budgeting and scheduling. *Budgeting is deciding how much time to spend; scheduling is deciding when to spend it. The budget should grow out of your priority or "to-do" list. You look over the items you have listed, estimate how much time will be needed to complete each item, and from that estimate determine how many priorities can be completed in the day or week.* That is all! But to help you budget, here are some suggestions:

1. Budget around your fixed commitments. Class time is already fixed each day. If you work, working hours are usually fixed. Sleeping and eating hours normally are fixed for the most part. Any standing appointment or prescheduled study commitment is also fixed. Time for these fixed commitments is already budgeted (and already scheduled). Be sure you take them into account in your overall budget.

2. Consider your short-term goals. Be sure to budget time for the activities designed to accomplish your goals. If you budget for one item and set goals for another, who are you kidding? Change your budget to fit your goals and priorities, or change your goals and priorities to fit your budget.

3. Budget enough time to study effectively for each subject. On the average, students study from one to three hours outside of class for each hour in class. Your budget should stay flexible to meet your own study needs. Start with two hours study for each class hour, but monitor yourself closely and be ready to adjust.

4. Borrow time when necessary, but never on the no-return plan. Set time aside, preferably evenings and weekends for trade time in case of emergencies. But once you budget two hours for a class see that those two hours are scheduled for another time when emergencies take their place.

Scheduling

One of the freedoms of college life is the extensive personal control the student has over her or his own time. ***Every minute from the waking hour to sleeping is under the student's control.*** Few other phases of life are so freely structured. Perhaps only in retirement is such freedom regained. What a time to advance one's goals! But what a temptation to squander life. Remember, the more flexible the work, the more demanding the schedule.

The fact that college life is under personal control allows a schedule to work for the student. For the college student, life strangely fits and happily complements the schedule. It is the perfect way to get things done. There are dozens of time planners and work organizers on the market, but to schedule your day, all you need is a printed or self-made document that divides the day into hours. It should run from about 7:00 a.m. to midnight to accommodate most students. With such a document you are ready to schedule your week and day. Again, a few basic guidelines will help.

1. *Schedule your fixed activities first.* Fixed activities recur regularly at prescheduled times: class, work, sleep, some study hours. Fixed activities are automatic A priorities when their time comes, and are scheduled routinely once a week.

2. *Make your "To do" list of the tasks to be accomplished during the week.* Flexible activities should be listed on your priority or "To-do" list, and are scheduled daily. List the tasks in order of importance on the day they should take place. Consider how much time you have budgeted for tasks or activities and place them in a time slot. Be sure to include exams, projects or assignments that are due. As the week goes by cross off completed activities and rerank incomplete items on following days.

3. *Schedule specific study time.* For example, list "study psychology" at 10:00 a.m. Monday, Wednesday, and Friday, rather than just listing "study" on the schedule. It is also helpful to state specifically what will be studied, for example, "study Chapter 10." Study time is most efficient when done at the same time and same place everyday. Consistency breeds expectation; expectation breeds results.

4. *Arrange to use nonclass hours during the day to maximum advantage for study.* Study is more effective in the daytime when we are more alert. *Studying as soon after class as possible allows review of notes while the subject is still in mind; waiting longer than 24 hours often causes us to relearn the material.* Careful use of daytime hours also leaves the evening free for projects and other activities.

5. *Schedule some time each week for a separate review.* Review of class should occur at least weekly. Learning occurs when the reviews are separate from original study, and class notes are recapitulated and revised.

6. *Block large segments of time for research, term papers, and projects.* This type of study requires long start-up time, intense concentration, and attention to massive detail. Too much time is lost spinning wheels in one-hour segments. Four-hour blocks are most practical for large projects.

7. *Learn your own "alert" and "dead" hours and schedule accordingly.* If you are a "night" person, forget morning study—but don't forget evening study also. Be yourself, but don't use that as an excuse not to study. (You are too important for that!)

8. *Allow yourself to live a balanced life.* Schedule different types of activities to ensure a greater balance to your life, including such things as church, recreation, and social activities. Sure, you're in school for education — and you should get it — but there are other worthy goals too.

9. *Follow your schedule.* By the time you have reviewed your values, set three levels of goals, made a priority list, budgeted time, and scheduled activities, you might as well follow your schedule. It will actually free you to do many things with a clear conscience. Students often create guilt by doing social activities while not knowing when or if the proper amount of study will be done.

10. *Make your schedule work for you — not you work for your schedule.* Don't fill in all hours. Trade time when needed. If you fail one week, try again next week. Trying and failing is certainly better than not trying at all.

Weekly Planner

As an aid to help you in planning your college week, a two page weekly planner is illustrated on the following pages. Figure 6.2 is an organizing page , which gives space to write out your short-term goals and the associated activities. Next is a block of instructions on how to organize your time and budget the hours for the week. Finally, at the bottom of the page, is a set of instructions on how to organize the weekly schedule which follows on the next page. Figure 6.3 is a schedule which includes space on each day of the week where you can prioritize your tasks. It also gives a schedule of hours between 7:00 a.m. and 11:00 p.m. where you can write down the fixed and flexible time committments which you plan to carry out for the week. Copies of the weekly schedule are available in the suppliments in the back of the book.

Working with your instructor, you will find it helpful to plan your current college activities and to plan for the upcoming week. Remember, after considering your values, set your short-term goals and budget the time you will allocate to accomplish the goals. Prioritize the tasks for the week and begin to schedule time for the activities which are at the top of your priority task list. Remember that some activities are fixed (class time) and others are flexible (movies). The successful college student creates a balance that will allow for time to complete scholarly studies and social activities.

SETTING SHORT-TERM GOALS

Identify your short-term goals and list the activities that will lead to accomplishing your goals. Indicate the time and place you will carry out each activity and then transfer it to your weekly schedule.

Goal #1: _____

Activities: _____

Goal #2: _____

Activities: _____

Goal #3: _____

Activities: _____

Goal #4: _____

Activities: _____

ORGANIZING YOUR TIME

❶ *Build your schedule around your fixed time commitments.* FIXED: organizations, classes, church, and employment. FLEXIBLE: eating, sleeping, study, personal grooming, and recreation.

❷ *Consider your short-term goals.* Budget the time needed for activities that will accomplish each goal, and then schedule the activity.

❸ *Budget enough time to study for each subject.* Most college classes require about two hours of outside work for every hour spent in class. By multiplying your credit load by two, you can get a good idea of the time you should provide for studying each week.

❹ *Study just before or just after class.* Study of class notes should take place the same day as the class. Studying class notes more than 24 hours after the class usually means you must relearn rather than review the material. Previewing just before class facilitates class participation and permanent learning.

❺ *Borrow time--don't steal it.* A few hours each week should be set aside to trade for time borrowed to handle unexpected emergencies.

BUDGETING TIME

Sample Activities	Hours per week	Total
Class Time		
Class/Study	___	
Class/Study	___	
Class/Study	___	
Class/Study	___	
Class/Study	___	
Class/Study	___	
Work		
Time	___	
Travel	___	
Church		
Service Projects	___	
Meetings	___	
Relationships		
Clubs and Projects	___	
Family Visits	___	
Diversion		
Recreation	___	
Exercise	___	
Miscellaneous		
Eating	___	
Traveling	___	
Sleeping	___	
Other	___	
Total Hours Per Week		<u>168</u>

USING THE WEEKLY SCHEDULE

Take 10-15 minutes before the week begins to review your goals, budget your available time and make a list of priorities. Spend 5 minutes each night to review your day and reschedule your priorities and plan the next day. Make any changes you need. Remember: The schedule is designed to serve you. Keep it flexible.

① *Schedule your fixed time commitments first.* This should be done at the beginning of each week.

② *Make a "To-Do" list of the tasks for the week.*
- List your tasks in order of importance on the day they take place. Include any exams, projects or assignments that are due.
- Review your tasks at the end of each day, cross off completed activities and reschedule incomplete items on a future day.

③ *Schedule your flexible time commitments.* These include: studying, eating, grooming, recreation and hobbies, sleeping, etc.
- Allow enough study time for each class. A good rule of thumb is to begin by planning two hours of study for every one hour of class; later adjust up and down according to your experience with each class.
- Set a regular time for study for each class. Your study hours should be as regular as possible and in the same place to avoid distraction.
- Find time for other essential activities.

Figure 6.2 Weekly Planning Worksheet.

WEEKLY SCHEDULE   Name _____   Beginning Date _____   Ending Date _____

Time	MONDAY Prioritized Tasks	TUESDAY Prioritized Tasks	WEDNESDAY Prioritized Tasks	THURSDAY Prioritized Tasks	FRIDAY Prioritized Tasks	SATURDAY Prioritized Tasks	SUNDAY Prioritized Tasks
Schedule							
7 AM							
8							
9							
10							
11							
12 PM							
1							
2							
3							
4							
5							
6							
7							
8							
9							
10							
11							

Figure 6.3   Weekly Schedule.

111

The Planning, Action, and Evaluation Cycle

Writing out your values and setting your goals is periodically done at the start of months, terms, semesters, or years. Budgeting and scheduling are weekly and daily activities. Budgeting and scheduling follow a planning, action, and evaluation cycle, as illustrated in Figure 6.4.

Planning has already been described in the preceding section. Planning, once you learn how, merges with evaluation in the cycle to make the action efficient and effective. Follow the action and evaluation suggestions that follow to see how the cycle leads to taking charge of your time.

Action

Once you have put your schedule on paper you are ready to take action. Do it for one day or one week and then ask yourself, "How did I do?" Beware of overscheduling. Don't feel that to fill *out* a schedule you must fill *up* a schedule by packing activities so tightly that you leave no room to breathe. After the first week you will either see your mistake or you will

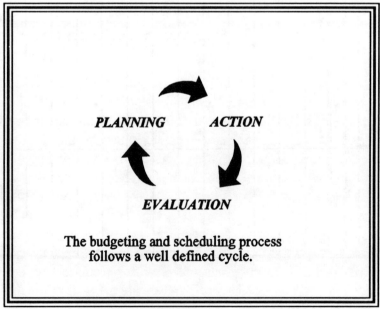

PLANNING   **ACTION**

EVALUATION

The budgeting and scheduling process
follows a well defined cycle.

Figure 6.4 The Planning Cycle.

112

become discouraged when you see that you can't possibly accomplish even a small part of what you have planned. To avoid overscheduling, become realistic. Don't expect drastic improvements in your time-use habits the first week. It is easy to write down on a planner all the things you feel you should be doing, but there is no magic in writing them down. Actually, the written plan only gives you direction and momentum. You have to supply the sustaining force.

The best method of beginning is probably making plans with one eye on your current actual performance and the other eye on your values and goals. As you practice your scheduling, you will find where strengths and weaknesses lie. Expect more of yourself but avoid expecting "the moon" and nothing less. All of this boils down to one thing: planning will not guarantee accomplishment. Over time, however, practice will bring you to the point that what you plan is very close to what you carry out. It will take commitment and stick-to-itiveness.

Observe yourself as you go through the week. If your weekly schedule has a place where you can write "accomplished" or check off finished activities, use it. Check off even fixed activities. If you cannot check off a planned activity because you did something else during that time, write whatever else you did during that time. This observation and recording activity is very important because you will use this information at the end of the day and the week in your evaluation.

Evaluation

Once you have planned your week and put your plan into practice, you are ready to evaluate. Evaluation should be done at the same time that you do your next planning, either at the end of one week (Saturday or Sunday) or at the beginning of the following week (early Monday morning). Evaluation should also be done daily, either at the day's end or its beginning. Effective evaluation should help you make the changes in your next plan that will most usefully lead you toward your goals. To make evaluation as effective as possible, you should ask questions like these: Does my plan help me adequately achieve my desired goals and objectives? Is the plan consistent with my values? If not, why not? What can be done to make my plan serve *my* purposes better? Do my goals and priorities accurately reflect what I really want? Do I need to change them? Where are the weak spots during the week? Are there certain days when I have trouble keeping with the schedule? Why am I having trouble? Is it my values, my goals and priorities, my schedule, or just me? Am I spending too much time on any of my projects, or not enough time? And so on . . .

Remember that your weekly schedule should help you reach your goals. If it isn't doing this, it is of no value to you. That is why evaluation is so important. Take time for an effective evaluation. This keeps your schedule up to date, and it keeps you in charge of your time—which is in charge of your life.

Two Hours That Make the Whole Week Worthwhile

All this valuing, goal setting, planning, acting, and evaluating sounds formidable, maybe impossible. It is not! Except for the periodic review of values and goals, all other planning should take you no more than two hours out of the 168 hours available in a week. Sunday night just before going to bed, for example, use a weekly schedule similar to the form found in Figures 6.3 and 6.4 and sit down in the soberness of the day and the hour and write a priority list and budget for the coming week. Then schedule your fixed items for all week and your flexible items for Monday. That should take you thirty minutes. Review also last week's activities as an evaluation.

Monday through Saturday, as your last activity of each day, take fifteen minutes to evaluate your day and enter your flexible items for the next day. That is your planning and evaluating, done in two hours for the entire week. Once this routine is habit, you will love the other 166 hours because they will be doing what you want them to, to meet your goals. You will love your life because it is yours—planned, acted, and evaluated—reflecting your values and leading to your goals in your own time frame.

114

1. Review the case of Rex in this chapter (p.95). Follow through his values and long-term goals. Then list what would be reasonable goals in an intermediate sense from his freshman year to graduation. List specific goals for him in the following areas: (1) career; (2) educational; (3) social; (4) personal; (5) spiritual. Be prepared to defend your goals on the basis of Rex's values and lifetime goals.

2. Critique Rex's semester schedule on the basis of probable semester goals and on the ten basic scheduling guidelines in this chapter.

3. Set your own values and goals. List the overriding values in your life today. Based on your values, set goals at three levels: lifetime, intermediate (to graduation), and short-term (this term or semester). Use the following areas for goal-setting at all three levels: (1) career; (2) educational; (3) social; (4) personal; (5) spiritual. Next, for each short-term goal list the weekly or daily activities that you will carry out to accomplish the goals.

4. Using a copy of the Weekly Planner located in the suppliment section in this text, make a personal weekly schedule that indicates all fixed activities for the coming week. Prepare a to-do list that lists all your known flexible activities for the week, and prioritize those activities using Lakein's A-B-C system. Hand in a copy of this to your instructor at the beginning of the week. Follow your schedule through for the week, changing priorities when needed, adding new to-do items, checking off completed items, scheduling flexible items at available times each day, and evaluating your progress daily. At the end of the week, evaluate your experience by submitting to your instructor a used schedule, to-do list, and evaluations of your time planning.

5. Once you understand goal setting and time planning, follow a planned schedule for the rest of the semester or term. Your instructor may want you to hand in your plans and evaluations at the end of each week's experience.

References

Dever, S. M. "It's Later Than You Think," Listen, September 1971, p. 18.

Glade, E. J. "Let Time Be a Friend," Instructor, December 1959, p. 401.

Lakein, A. How to Get Control of Your Time and Your Life. New York: Signet (The New American Library, Inc.), 1973.

Nightingale, E. A Worthy Destination: Set Your Goals--and Reach Them on Schedule. Audio tape and accompanying pamphlet by Nightingale-Conant Corp., the Human Resources Company, 1972.

Olney, C. W. Where There's a Will There's an "A." Paoli, PA: American Educational Publishers, Inc., 1988.

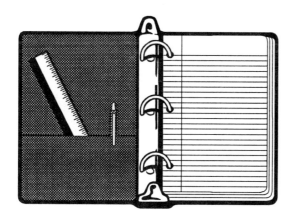

Chapter 7

Noting What You Hear

How can you become a more active listener? What effective listening skills do you practice? Does listening style relate to learning style? How can your notetaking system encourage a deeper approach to learning?

How important is good listening, anyway? The following story illustrates what can happen when you simply fail to listen. Stuart Levine and Michael Crom (1993), authors of <u>The Leader in You</u>, tell the story of how Hugh Downs (host of ABC's **20/20**) learned about the importance of listening. Back in the early days of radio, when Downs was getting started as an on-air interviewer, he remembered listening to a colleague interview a man who had escaped from a Kremlin prison in the thirties. Downs recalled the following:

This guest was telling him how, for months, the prisoners had been trying to tunnel their way out of there. They'd dug and dug. They'd eaten the dirt. They'd arranged to have a saw smuggled in. And when they figured their tunnel was outside the prison walls, they began digging up. It was quite a dramatic story. Then this one midnight, they were finally ready to break loose. They had already sawed through a wooden platform above their heads. But when this one prisoner stuck his head out, he was shocked by what he saw. "When I got up," he told the interviewer, "I realized I was right in the middle of Josef Stalin's office." And do you know what this interviewer said next? (p. 84)

Before you find out what the interviewer actually said, what do you think you would say if you were the interviewer? Wouldn't you be sitting on the edge of your seat wanting to know what happened next? You would if you were a good interviewer who was listening intently to your guest. As the story goes, the interviewer actually replied, "Do you have any hobbies?" Unbelievable, but true! Obviously the interviewer was not listening attentively.

Listening is an important communication skill for anyone who expects to communicate effectively with others.

Listening as a College Student

What some freshman students like most about their lower-level classes, such as Biology 100 or History 101, is the chance to get "lost in the crowd" among the hundreds of other students, exploiting opportunity to go unnoticed or unbothered by questions from the professor. Some students may think, "Good, all I have to do is sit here, listen and take notes," as if the task of listening requires little effort and involvement on their part at all. Maybe you have thought this yourself, or maybe you have experienced leaving a lecture, scratching your head, wondering why it is you do not remember what was just said. Or while looking over your notes later on in the day, you have found a lot of fragmented thoughts that do not make sense, and you feel confused because you thought you were listening and taking good notes. Most students, to one degree or another, have experienced these scenarios. You may have come away from such experiences believing you should not be attending college, when all you may need to know is how to really listen and take good notes.

How much time do you think the average college student spends listening in class? Thirty, forty, sixty percent? Would you believe that about 75 percent of your student time is spent listening? If this percentage seems high, consider the many lecture classes offered on the college level. Most of your classes will require you to sit and listen. Since most of your time is spent listening, it is imperative that you know how to listen effectively. Good listening will keep you involved and interested in your own learning and education.

118

How Do You Become a Good Listener?

> Good listening begins with your ***approach*** to learning.
> Good listening is enhanced by being an ***active listener***.
> Good listening requires identifying your good and bad ***listening habits***.
> Good listening is achieved by practicing effective ***listening skills***.

Good listening begins with your approach. A *surface* or *deep* approach to learning will influence your approach to listening. If your learning approach is surface, you will tend to focus on the task of listening. The task of listening is primarily seen as passive. The instructor is expected to tell the listener what is important to know. The task of listening centers mostly on accumulating and memorizing facts and ideas. There is more concern with what should be memorized to pass a test than with understanding the content and meaning of a lecture. In the surface approach, good listening constitutes coming away from a lecture with a few memorized ideas. The amount of information retained is measured, but not the quality of understanding.

In a deep approach to listening, the task is to understand the content and meaning of a lecture. Listening is viewed as an active process in which the listener accepts responsibility for figuring out what information in the lecture is important to learn and understand. For the person who has a deep approach to listening, good listening means leaving a lecture with a greater understanding of how separate facts and ideas fit together into meaningful wholes. The listener will also find personal meaning in what she or he learns.

Good listening is enhanced by being active. Merely hearing words does not constitute good listening. Understanding what has been said does. Good listening requires you to be actively involved and engaged in the listening process. You must be able to focus attention on others and their comments.

Good listening is not passive, it is a highly active. To be effective, you must deliberately work at thinking as you listen. Understanding the meaning of a lecture is the result of active mental processing, not mere absorption.

Attentive listening is encouraged and reinforced through a systematic approach called TQLR (Parker 1959, pp. 36-38). It is an active listening formula that stands for tune in, question, listen, review. It would be impossible to remain a passive listener while creatively using this formula. TQLR is presented here as a way to become a more active listener. The TQLR process is explained below.

TQLR

Tune in. Tuning in means focusing your attention. Simply recalling what you know about the speaker's topic before he or she begins a presentation will help you tune in and be attentive. This can occur moments before a lecture begins, or if you know in advance the topic of the lecture, you may want to think ahead on all you know about the topic. For a college class you will want to read related material in your textbook *before* the lecture.

Question. Asking questions that guide your listening will keep you mentally involved in a lecture. Your questions should help you understand the main points and organization of the lecture: "What point is the speaker making?" "How does this point relate to the point made earlier?" "How might these different points come together?" Coming into a lecture, you may have some questions already formed as a result of recalling what you know about the subject. Most of your questions, however, should be formed as you listen to the lecture. The questions are to guide your listening, not to be a distraction. They may be best answered during lulls or breaks in the lecture.

Listen. Your objective is to hear the basic message and to listen for the answers to your questions. Remember, though, that during a lecture your mind stays on the lecturer's topic, not on your questions. An active alertness and full concentration are required to accomplish this.

Review. Reviewing consists of evaluating periodically the message in relation to your questions, summarizing ideas, and fitting ideas together. You may wonder how to do all of this and still stay tuned in to the lecture. Sometimes extra thinking time is available between comments of the lecturer and can be used for reviewing. Your reviewing will most likely generate further questions, helping you to remain tuned in and attentive.

Good listening requires identifying your listening habits. By the time you reach college you may have developed several listening habits that interfere with good listening. (See Figure 7.1) For instance, you may have the habit of distracting yourself by doodling while listening; you may be easily distracted by things in your immediate environment, such as an attractive

		Yes	No	Sometimes

Directions: Read each statement and decide how the habit reflects your listening. Answer "yes" if you use the habit over half of your listening time, "no" if you don't use the habit very much at all and "sometimes" if you use the habit periodically.

		Yes	No	Sometimes
1.	Do you often doodle while listening?	_____	_____	_____
2.	Do you show attending behaviors through your eye contact, posture and facial expressions?	_____	_____	_____
3.	Do you try to write down everything you hear?	_____	_____	_____
4.	Do you listen largely for central ideas as opposed to facts and details?	_____	_____	_____
5.	Do you often daydream or think about personal concerns while listening?	_____	_____	_____
6.	Do you ask clarifying questions about what you do not understand in a lecture?	_____	_____	_____
7.	Do you frequently feel tired or sleepy when attending a lecture?	_____	_____	_____
8.	Do you mentally review information as you listen to make connections among points?	_____	_____	_____
9.	Do you often call a lecture boring?	_____	_____	_____
10.	Do you recall what you already know about a subject before the lecture begins?	_____	_____	_____
11.	Do you generally avoid listening when difficult information is presented?	_____	_____	_____
12.	Do you pay attention to the speaker's nonverbal cues?	_____	_____	_____
13.	Do you often find yourself thinking up arguments to refute the speaker?	_____	_____	_____
14.	Do you generally try to find something of interest in a lecture even if you think it is boring?	_____	_____	_____
15.	Do you usually criticize the speaker's delivery, appearance, or mannerisms?	_____	_____	_____
16.	Do you do what you can to control distractions around you?	_____	_____	_____
17.	Do you often fake attention to the speaker?	_____	_____	_____
18.	Do you periodically summarize to recapitulate what the speaker has said during the lecture?	_____	_____	_____
19.	Do you often go to class late?	_____	_____	_____
20.	Do you review the previous class lecture notes before attending class?	_____	_____	_____

The odd numbered items are considered ineffective listening habits, while the even numbered items are considered effective listening habits. If you have answered the item with "sometimes", determine how often and under what circumstances you find yourself responding this way.

Figure 7.1   Listening Questionnaire.

person sitting next to you or noises in the classroom which interfere with your listening. It is possible to come to class so fatigued that you sleep through the lecture. Your task as a listener is to manage or eliminate the various habits that interfere with your ability to listen efficiently.

Changing your listening habits starts with being aware of your effective and ineffective habits and then identifying the habits that perpetuate passive or inefficient listening. Figure 7.1 is a subjective questionnaire designed to help you get a sense of how well you listen and what you need to improve on.

Good listening is achieved by practicing effective listening skills. Now that you have a better idea of what habits you need to change, let's discuss how to change them. To rid yourself of unwanted listening habits, you must launch yourself into changing by practicing new ones. Stay committed to changing your habits by putting yourself into situations that require and encourage you to act in new ways.

Ralph G. Nichols, a former professor at the University of Minnesota, conducted a study of the 100 best listeners and the 100 worst listeners in the freshman class on the University of Minnesota campus. Nichols' (1976) findings are the basis of ten guides to improved listening. As you read through the skills, use the suggestions to help you change and improve any ineffective listening habits you identified through taking the listening inventory. Do not be the one who just reads about changing listening habits—do it!

1. **Avoid labeling a subject uninteresting; find an area of interest and use to you**. Within the first five minutes of a lecture, one usually decides if the topic of discussion is boring or not and whether it is of value to him or her. Listeners who call a subject boring have decided the subject has no personal use. They immediately tune out the lecture. Good listeners, although they may admit a subject is dry, will look beyond the words to meanings that may have personal value and use to them.

2. **Concentrate on gathering all you can from the content, and do not worry about how it is presented**. A speaker's mannerisms, personality, or delivery may be bothersome; however, *what* he or she is saying—he content of the lecture—should be judged, not the way it is presented. A good listener is most interested in finding out *what* the speaker knows that the listener does not.

3. **Refrain from getting overstimulated by specific points in the lecture; first hear all the speaker has to say.** Often exciting and stimulating things are said in a lecture, making it easy for the listener to get overinvolved in rejecting (or supporting) the speaker's point. An ineffective listener will immediately want to enter into the argument by thinking up some point that will refute what the speaker is saying. Often a win/lose attitude builds up in the mind of the listener, who enters into competition with the speaker and wants to come out the winner. The consequence is that subsequent information goes unheard. A good listener, on the other hand, will withhold evaluation until the speaker's point is understood completely and then wait for a time until it is appropriate to present an alternative viewpoint.

4. **Focus on central ideas, relationships among various points, and meanings that tie facts together.** Knowing how to discriminate between main ideas and facts is important to effective listening and learning. A deep approach to listening encourages the integration of information, not mere memorization of fact. Good listeners learn to identify central ideas by recognizing the organizational patterns, the transitional language, and the speaker's use of recapitulation in a lecture.

5. **Be a flexible notetaker rather than trying to make an outline out of everything.** Lectures are not often presented in a distinctly organized manner that allows the listener to write down information in succinct outline form. The listener who gets overly concerned with writing down every morsel of information or becomes too preoccupied with putting the information in outline form could end up feeling frustrated and missing important points. Notetaking should not detract from but should enhance learning. Good listeners learn to adjust their notetaking to the content and organization of a lecture. They also learn to discriminate between important and unimportant information. Learn to adapt and be flexible!

6. **Pay genuine attention; do not fake it.** If you make the effort to go to class, you might as well invest in listening by paying attention. Good listeners communicate that the lecture is important through their attending behaviors. By maintaining eye contact, assuming a posture that looks alert, and showing facial expressions that reflect back to the speaker that the listener is tuning in and understanding, the speaker is reinforced. By being genuine about the listening stance, the listener benefits from the clearer communication he or she has helped the speaker to achieve through showing interest.

7. **Learn to resist and manage distractions**. One of the authors had a professor who, when he presented his lectures, had a very distracting habit of stretching his mouth with his fingers as he talked. It was extremely difficult to concentrate on the lectures as he distorted his mouth, but there are some distractions one simply must learn to ignore in order to stay focused and concentrated. Other distractions can be managed by moving to another part of the room if the person next to you is talking, closing a door or turning off the T.V. if there is too much noise, or asking the lecturer to speak louder. Good listeners tend not to tolerate bad conditions that get in the way of effective listening. They learn to adjust to, manage, or resist interfering distractions.

8. **Expand your mind by sticking to difficult and challenging material**. When lecture material gets too technical or difficult, often the temptation is to stop listening by convincing yourself that the information is too hard to learn or by telling yourself that you will read the textbook later (actually, it is a good practice to read the textbook before the lecture, whenever possible). Good listeners tend not to evade difficult material but stick to listening even if it is hard. Also, good listeners are more apt to seek out and attend learning situations like forums, debates, and serious lectures that provide stimulating intellectual thought.

9. **Remain open-minded while listening by not letting emotion-laden words get in the way.** Trailing off on a divergent mental pathway from what the speaker is following is sometimes the result of reacting to a word or phrase that carries some emotional meaning for you. Depending on the context, you could be susceptible to responding emotionally in a lecture to words and phrases like **Commie, mother-in-law, sex, landlord, nuclear war, gay community, IRS,** or **abuse** (there are many more words that could be listed). Nichols refers to emotional-laden words as deaf spots which interfere with one's ability to perceive, understand, and concentrate on what is being said. Good listeners will try to recognize such listening traps and postpone thinking about them until after the lecture.

10. **Use extra thinking time to think about what you are learning.** There is a lot of excess thinking time between comments, examples, or topics within a lecture that can be used rather than wasted. Thought speed is generally believed to be at least four times as fast as speech speed (Nichols, 1973). Parker (1959, p. 40) even estimates thought speed to be as fast as 60,000 words per minute. Instead of daydreaming during a lecture, try to think about what the speaker is saying by anticipating what he or she will say next or identifying and summarizing ideas. A good listener will use his or her surplus thinking time to enhance understanding and comprehension of the speaker's topic rather than divert to extraneous ideas.

124

Learning style refers to the way a person goes about learning naturally. You have developed a learning style that emphasizes certain learning preferences over others. How you listen or respond to messages may reflect your learning style. For example, how you answer the question "Do you enjoy listening to and learning from lecture-type classes?" provides information about your learning preferences. Some individuals learn more effectively from listening to lectures because of the way they prefer to process information. What you listen for in a message may also indicate your learning style; do you listen to analyze, to interpret, or to evaluate a message?

Let us relate David A. Kolb's four learning styles (diverger, assimilator, converger, and accommodator) to listening style. An individual who is a diverger or an assimilator would tend to prefer a reflective approach to learning. Learning situations like lectures are generally preferred because divergers and assimilators like to be impartial, objective observers in gathering information. For them, listening to lectures facilitates learning in a way that being involved in hands-on action does not. Convergers and accommodators, on the other hand, will tend to be active in processing information by getting involved in learning situations that require "doing" or in practical application of ideas. More passive learning situations like lectures are not seen as very helpful. The accommodator and converger may more likely get tired or bored in a lecture-type class without the opportunity to be active in the learning process.

William Perry's theory of cognitive development suggests that individuals at different levels of development perceive and process information and values in different ways. A person at the dualistic stage classifies information into absolute categories, so as to reduce the ambiguity of the information. In the relativistic stage, a person realizes that knowledge is relative and that there may not be absolutes. A person at the commitment stage in relativism decides that personal commitment is important for growth and identity. At any Perry stage, information processing appears to be incomprehensible at a cognitive level more than about one position above the prevailing level of the learner (Finster, 1988, p. A40). "What students understand to be demanded of them in a learning situation will be dependent on the limits of their intellectual development and so delimit how they will tackle learning tasks" (Gibbs, 1981, p. 85). Given that individuals in each stage think differently, how will one's cognitive approach affect the way he or she listens and responds to information? How differently might persons at the dualism, relativism, or commitment in relativism stages each approach listening?

125

How helpful are your notes as a source of study? Do they tend to be useful or useless? Can you confidently refer back to your notes to help you review a concept or clarify an idea? Good notetaking is important in the learning process because most people cannot easily remember all the information that comes through the speech medium. Retention rate generally increases as material is written down because it is less difficult to remember what you read than to remember what you hear. Of course, writing notes does not in itself ensure retention of information. The study and review you exercise after the lecture give your notes their usable value.

An important criterion for determining the value of any notetaking system is the availability of built-in review. *Reviewing is the rehearsing of material, the going over of information in such a way as to encourage the understanding of relationships between ideas as opposed to mere memorization.* Reviewing or rehearsing is a most important memory process because it reinforces retention of information. How one rehearses, combines, relates, and evaluates information determines the level of depth in learning and how quickly knowledge is transferred to the long-term memory.

A notetaking system by itself cannot implement a surface or deep approach to learning. Your attitude toward reviewing will determine if deep learning occurs. If you review your notes the way good review was defined above, your learning will be more meaningful.

The notetaking technique presented here has been developed to encourage a deeper approach to learning by using the concept of whole or balanced learning. You will remember David Kolb's (chapter four) definition of an effective or balanced learner as being a person who personally gets involved in a learning experience (feeling), reflects on the experience (understanding), evaluates how the experience relates to other similar experiences (thinking), and applies what he or she has learned to making decisions and solving problems (doing) when a learning situation requires it. This notetaking technique is designed to encourage you to review or rehearse lecture material by asking **questions** that guide you to think holistically and completely about the material. If you approach the system seriously, with the intent to review the material, you will experience more meaningful learning.

Experiential Note Review Technique

Class Notes. While taking notes in class, do not be overly concerned with the organization of your notes. You want to focus on writing down the content accurately. Be discriminating as you listen. Your objective is not to write down everything you hear, because not every point may be pertinent information. Main points and subpoints may be distinguished as you go over your notes later.

First Review: Reading to identify and learn main points. After the lecture, you will want to read through your notes to add additional thoughts or make any incomplete sentences complete. During this first review, identify the central ideas of the lecture and highlight them in some way so that they are easily identifiable. You may also want to identify supporting points that correlate with the main ideas.

Often the next step in the process of notetaking is to go over and over the material by reading your notes again and again with the intent to memorize. Here is your opportunity to go beyond the ordinary by exercising your mind beyond mere memorization. The following steps in this notetaking system provide you with the opportunity to expand your thinking in a deeper, meaningful way.

Second Review: Summarizing. Having already reviewed your notes, you understand the main points of the lecture. The second review consists of reciting the important main ideas of the lecture by summarizing in your own words. The summary can be verbal or written or both. Summarizing by reciting forces you to think from memory, in your own style and word choice, what you have just learned.

Third Review: Question and answer. After you summarize and recite the main points of the lecture, your next step is to ask specific questions about the lecture which encourage you to think more holistically about the information (see figure 7.2). The questions and the answers to the questions should be written down to be easily accessible for review. Below are examples of the general types of questions you may want to ask in order to address your note content completely. You will notice that the questions require you to go beyond just asking for main ideas, facts, and details, or even how the separate points and ideas relate to each other.

---

1. *Get personally involved in the information.* The following questions help you develop a personal attitude toward the information and facilitate your personal expression of feeling, opinion, and values in relation to the information.

   How does this relate to me?
   What is my reaction or opinion about this?
   How do I feel about this?
   Does this fit with my values?

---

2. ***Reflect on the information.*** These questions help you understand more fully the relationship between concepts, facts, and details and to stimulate divergent and different ways of thinking.

How does this compare or relate to what I learned last week?

How might this compare to future ideas that I anticipate?

How important is this concept relative to . . . ?

How can I relate this to my other classes?

3. ***Think about and draw conclusions from the information.*** This type of question focuses on learning and drawing conclusions from the content of the lecture to help you clarify ideas, master concepts, and form hypotheses.

What is(are) the main idea(s)?

What are the supporting ideas?

How do the various ideas relate to each other?

How does this idea compare with . . . ?

What can be deduced from this?

What generalizations/hypotheses can be formed?

4. ***Apply the information.*** These questions stimulate further interest through practical application of the information. The questions should guide you to think about information in a practical sense.

Why is knowing this important?

How can this be used in everyday living?

What are some practical examples of how to apply this?

What is a practical application that is different from the context in which I learned this?

The above questions will help guide you to ask specific questions that directly relate to your note content. Obviously, you could spend several hours thinking up related questions, but that may be impractical in view of other study responsibilities you have. Learn to be selective in the questions you ask, because your time is limited. You may also find it impractical to cover one or two of the areas because of the class content or the learning expectation of the instructor. For example, in a math class, it would probably not be essential to address your feelings about math (unless you are experiencing math anxiety to the point that it interferes with your learning), but it would be extremely helpful to quiz yourself on how the Pythagorean theorem relates to what you learned in economics, or to explore other practical uses for it.

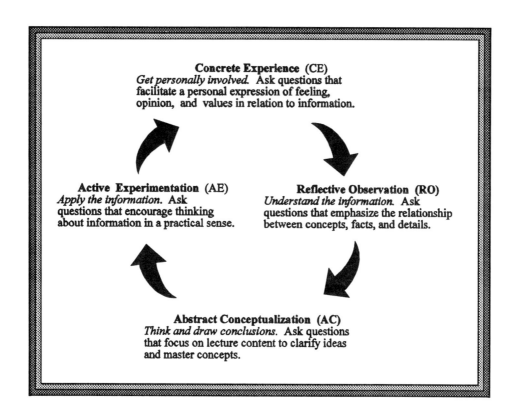

Figure 7.2 Questions Using David Kolb's Learning Cycle.

What your instructor expects you to learn will also determine where you will place emphasis. The common expectation of most undergraduate professors is that the student understand the main ideas and concepts or the facts and details from a given lecture. However, do not let that deter you from the opportunity to learn beyond the content, to link the information with other subjects, and to apply the information in a practical sense. Thinking in diverse and complete ways reinforces retention and comprehension of information.

Expect this approach to notetaking to take longer than you are used to—first, because you are going beyond mere memorization of material, and second, because new habits take time to learn and get used to. Eventually the system will become less demanding as you develop efficiency.

Example of The Experiential Note Review Technique

The following is an illustration of the Experiential Note Review Technique that is based on Kolb's Experiential Learning Theory.

129

<u>Adolescence: Choice or Confusion</u>

- Major issue of this stage: Process by which adolescents separate themselves from the rest of the family and achieve a sense of independence. The primary task for teenagers is to gain some independence from their parents.

- A family encapsulates the child. Encapsulates means to provide experiences and a version of what life means.

- Somewhere along pathway of life the child discovers that there are things that their parents didn't tell them about.

- All adolescents have their own experiences which parents can't regulate. Kids who make their own choices are more likely to get in trouble and are more vulnerable to groups who accept them and make decisions for them.

<u>4 methods of separating</u>

1. Overconforming — child readily accepts parental authority views, morals and decisions seen as good, however, no ability to make choices or decisions; will not be able to make choices until mid-life.

2. Co-dependency: parents are dependent on kids and kids on parents; prevents separation.
   Two forms: (1) parent indulgent and child helpless   (2) parent is excessively controlling and child resistant

3. Shared decision making: both work toward increased independence: share in decision making; recognizes the perception of freedom is not achieved by relaxing parental control, but by increasing ability of child to make choices.

4. Defiance — adolescent who runs away or parent pushes child out; a lot of emotional wounds.

Factors that contribute to positive separation

1. Self awareness — comes at moment of making a choice or having your own opinion
2. Distinct, identifiable activity of choosing
3. Opportunity to act and see their choices cause consequences
4. Have to achieve a high level of satisfaction from making choices
5. Making choices produces a strong sense of responsibility to ourselves

After taking your lecture notes, reviewing and summarizing, the final step in the Experiential Note Review Technique is to ask specific questions about the lecture. Sample questions for the lecture in Child Development are listed below:

Child Development

Concrete Experience (Feeling)

—How was my autonomy nurtured in my home?

—Which method of separating was reinforced in my home?

—What decisions have I made that reinforced my independence or positive separation?

Reflective Observation (Understanding)

—How does the method of overconforming relate to Perry's dualistic stage?

—In relation to Erikson's adolescent stage on identity development, how would insufficient separation affect a person's personal identity development?

—How does achieving a sense of independence relate to Perry's relativism and commitment stages?

Abstract Conceptualization (Thinking)

—What are the factors that contribute to positive separation?

—The four methods of separating are?

—The primary task for teenagers is?

—What would happen if parents forced autonomy or independence too soon in their child's development?

Active Experimentation (doing)

—Understanding the importance of independence and choice in personal development, how might I enhance others development in my interactions with them at school, work, church, etc?

—Why or how is knowing about independence helpful or important?

131

Forty years ago, Walter Pauk (1989) developed what is known as the **Cornell notetaking technique** to help Cornell University students better organize their notes. Today, Pauk's notetaking technique is probably the most widely used system throughout the United States. The Cornell notetaking system is presented as a second example to encourage a deeper approach to learning.

The Cornell notetaking technique emphasizes a distinct format system. A piece of paper is divided into three sections (see figure 7.3). Lecture notes are written in the wide, six-inch column. The narrow column (to the left of the wide column) is used to write cue words or questions that relate back to the information in the notes. At the bottom of the note page is a two inch single block for a summary.

Pauk outlines six steps in the Cornell notetaking system: **record**, **reduce** (or question), **recite**, **reflect**, **review**, and **recapitulate**.

Record. Simply record as many facts and ideas as you can in the six-inch column. Do not be concerned with getting every word down that the lecturer says or with writing your notes grammatically correctly. Learn to write telegraphic sentences or a streamlined version of the main points of the lecture by leaving out unnecessary words and using only key words. To ensure that your notes make sense weeks later, after the lecture is over, fill in blanks or make incomplete sentences complete.

Reduce or question. After you read through your notes, your next step is to reduce important facts and ideas to key words or phrases, or to formulate questions based on the facts and ideas. Key words, phrases, and questions are written in the narrow column left of the six-inch column. The words and phrases act as memory cues so that when you review them, you will recall the ideas or facts. The questions help to clarify the meanings of the facts and ideas.

Recite. Recitation is a very powerful process in the retention of information. Reciting is different from rereading in that you state *out loud* and *in your own words* the facts and ideas you are trying to learn. It is an effective way to learn because hearing your thoughts helps you to sharpen your thinking process; and stating ideas and facts in your own words challenges you to think

CORNELL NOTETAKING SYSTEM

2 ½"	6"

2. Reduce or Question (After Lecture)	**Classroom Notes**
● write key words, phrases or questions that serve as cues for notes taken in class	**1. Record (During Lecture)** *● write down facts and ideas in phrases* *● use abbreviations when possible*
● cue phrases and questions should be in your own words	**(After Lecture)** *● read through your notes* *● fill in blanks and make scribbles more legible*
3. Recite *● with classroom notes covered, read each key word or question* *● recite the fact or idea brought to mind by key word or question*	**4. & 5. Reflect and Review** *● review your notes periodically by reciting* *● think about what you have learned*

6. Recapitulation (After Lecture)
● summarize each main idea
● use complete sentences

Figure 7.3 Format of the Cornell notetaking system. (Based on Pauk, Walter. <u>How to Study in College</u>, 1989.)

out the meaning of the information. When reciting, cover up your notes in the six-inch column, while leaving the cue words and questions uncovered and readily accessible. Next, read each key word or question, then recite and state aloud, in your own words, the information. If your answer is correct, continue on through the lecture by reciting aloud.

Reflect. Reflection is pondering or thinking about the information you have learned. Reflecting is a step beyond learning note content. It reinforces deeper learning by the relating of facts and ideas to other learning and knowledge. Questions like the following enhance reflecting: How do these facts and ideas fit into what I already know? How can I apply them? How is knowing this important? What is the significance of these facts and ideas?

Review. The way to prevent forgetting is to review and recite your notes frequently. A good guideline to follow is to review your notes nightly or several times during the week by reciting, not rereading. Brief review sessions planned throughout the semester, perhaps weekly, will aid more complete comprehension and retention of information than will cramming the day before a test. It will cut on stress too!

Recapitulate. The recapitulation or summary of your notes goes at the bottom of the note page in the two-inch block column. Taking a few minutes after you have reduced, recited, and reflected to summarize the facts and ideas in your notes will help you integrate your information. The summary should not be a word-for-word rewriting of your notes. It should be in your own words and reflect the main points you want to remember from your notes. Reading through your summary(ies) in preparation for an exam is a good way to review. There are three ways to go about summarizing:

1.   Summarize each page of notes at the bottom of each page.
2.   Summarize the whole lecture on the last page.
3.   Do both 1 and 2, in combination.

Having read about the Cornell system and the system presented earlier in the chapter, what similarities and differences do you find between the two? What advantages and what changes or adaptations would you make?

Notetaking techniques that encourage a deep approach can be helpful catalysts for learning to learn. By using either of the notetaking systems presented here (or others like them), you can better understand and conceive what learning really consists of. There is more than one "right" way to take notes. Whatever technique or system you choose to use, keep in mind that the principles of reciting and reviewing are vital to any good notetaking system and successful learning.

134

Learning Applications

1. Take the listening questionnaire, if you haven't already. Identify your ineffective listening habits (odd-numbered items) and consider how these habits interfere with your learning. Decide how you will change your ineffective listening habits.

2. To become a more active listener, practice using TQLR (tune in, question, listen, review) while listening to a lecture. What do you like about this listening formula? What don't you like? If you had difficulty applying TQLR, how might you adapt it to fit your needs?

3. As you listen to a lecture, practice using the notetaking system based on Kolb's Experiential Learning Theory or the Cornell notetaking technique. You will need to practice either technique at least five times before you can use it with greater speed, ease, and confidence.

4. Remembering that an important criterion for a good notetaking system is built-in review for rehearsal of material, design your own notetaking technique.

References

Finster, D. C. "Freshmen Can Be Taught to Think Creatively, Not Just Amass Information." The Chronicle of Higher Education, July 13, 1988, p. A40.

Gibbs, G. "Changing Students' Approaches to Study Through Classroom Exercises." In R. M. Smith (ed.), Helping Adults Learn How to Learn, no. 19. San Francisco: Jossey-Bass, 1983.

Gibbs, G. Teaching Students to Learn: A Student-Centered Approach. Milton Keynes, England: The Open University Press, 1981.

Levine, S. & Crom, M. The Leader In You. New York: Simon & Schuster, 1993.

Myers, I. B., and McCaulley, M. H. Manual: A Guide to the Development and Use of the Myers-Briggs Type Indicator. Palo Alto: Counseling Psychologists Press, 1985.

Nichols, R. G. "He Who Hath Ears to Hear," Audio Tape of Brigham Young University Forum Lecture, Provo, UT: BYU Media Marketing, 1973.

Nichols, R. G. "Listening Is a 10-Part Skill." In J. I. Brown. Efficient Reading: Revised B Form. Lexington, MA: D.C. Heath and Company, 1976.

Parker, D. A. Instructor's Handbook, SRA Reading Laboratory, IVa. Chicago: Science Research Associates, Inc., 1959.

Pauk, W. How to Study in College. Boston: Houghton Mifflin, 1989.

Stewart, J. and D'Angelo, G. Together: Communicating Interpersonally. Reading, MA: Addison-Wesley Publishing Company, 1980.

Yeakley, F. R. "Communication Style Preferences and Adjustments as an Approach to Studying Effects of Similarity in Psychological Type." Research in Psychological Type. 1982, 5, 30-48.

Chapter 8

Noting What You Read

How can a systematic approach to reading help you as a student? Why is visual notetaking such a powerful memory aid? Do you know how to mark your reading material in a useful way that identifies the important information?

Have you ever considered the countless hours you spend reading textbooks and other materials for class assignments? If you are like the average college student, you will spend most of your study time reading. Suppose you spend twenty-five hours a week reading. For the duration of a typical college school year, that would calculate out to 800 hours a year. That is a lot of time to spend reading. Yet how strong is your ability to read meaningfully and effectively for understanding? Undoubtedly, you have had the experience of reading through a chapter or an article and on reaching the end realizing that you remember very little. What a frustrating feeling to spend the time and energy reading, just to find out you have wasted it! If this is a common experience for you, or if you find you are not gleaning meaningful information from your reading, your *approach* to reading may need some serious evaluation.

What is Your Approach to Reading?

Can you describe how you go about reading a textbook? Do you browse through the book to get some idea of its organization before you begin to read? Is your purpose in reading to accomplish the task of reading a certain number of pages? Do you read to memorize, or do you try to comprehend the implications of the information? Do you accept the literal meaning of the information or do you attempt to interpret what the information might mean? Reading is supposed to be easy, right?! Well, kind of! Reading is supposed to include thinking. How you approach your reading will determine the level of your understanding and the depth of your comprehension.

In his work with Harvard freshman students enrolled in a reading improvement course, William G. Perry Jr. observed that freshman students were not understanding the meaning of what they were reading—not because they lacked mechanical skills, but because they lacked **flexibility** and a sense of **purpose** or approach in their reading. Perry (1959, p. 195) had this to say:

> Year by year it has become more apparent that what the students lack is not mechanical skills but flexibility and purpose in the use of them—the capacity to adjust themselves to the variety of reading materials and purposes that exist on a college level. What they seem to do with almost any kind of reading is to open the book and read from word to word, having in advance abandoned all responsibility in regard to the purpose of the reading to those who had made the assignment. They complain consequently of difficulty in concentrating and feel that they have "read" whole assignments but are unable to remember anything in them...We have found that if they can be persuaded of their right to think, even though reading, they can then develop a broader and more flexible attack on the different forms of study and put their skills to meaningful use.

That was said about students of 35 years ago. Do you think Perry's comment still has application for the college student of the 1990s?

Your Right to Think

Believe it or not, it is possible to read and not to think. Do you read with your thinking cap on or off? Too often, students approach their reading simply as a task, and so read aimlessly and without focus. This kind of knowledge getting is passive. Passive readers usually learn information superficially. To really learn, you have to think about what you read.

Lewis Carroll (1907) wrote a humorous essay entitled "Feeding the Mind," in which he likened the feeding of the mind to the feeding of the body. He had this to say about the relationship between thinking and reading:

> And then as to the mastication of the food: the mental process answering to this is simply thinking over what we read. This is a very much greater exertion of mind than the mere passive taking in the contents of our author — so much greater an exertion is it, that, as Coleridge says, the mind often "angrily refuses" to put itself to such trouble—so much greater, that we are far too apt to neglect it altogether, and go on pouring in fresh food on the top of the undigested masses already lying there, till the unfortunate mind is fairly swamped under the food. But the greater the exertion, the more valuable, we may be sure, is the effect; one hour of steady thinking over a subject is worth two or three of reading only.

Reading With Flexibility and Purpose

Ineffective reading habits are hard to break. But why not give it a good try? Take Dr. Perry's advice and practice being more **flexible** and **purposeful** in your reading. To be a flexible reader means to be capable of modifying your approach—to have the courage to change convenient habits by developing a broader approach. For example, think about how you might approach an assigned reading task differently than what you are accustomed to. Instead of reading systematically, starting with page one and continuing straight through, why not start by glancing through the whole chapter first to get an overall focus. Or you might begin by first reading the summary, which could bring greater clarity to the factual information and detail.

To have a sense of purpose in reading means to read with a purpose in mind or to read with intent to guide your learning in a meaningful direction. You might ask yourself questions like "What is the overall meaning of what I'm reading?" "What do I want to learn?" "How can I apply this information to my life?"

As you evaluate your reading approach, remember to apply the principles of flexibility and purpose. Approach your reading thoughtfully, learn to be more flexible, read for meaning and strive to apply your knowledge. At the same time, be aware of the various factors that can influence your approach at any given time. Your reading approach may vary, depending on the level of reading difficulty of the text, the type of material you are reading, the learning demands of the course you are reading for, your level of motivation at the time of reading, or your interest or noninterest in the subject you are reading about. Any or all of these factors can affect how purposeful and flexible your reading approach will be.

Useful Reading Skills and Techniques

Although learning new reading techniques may not be as powerful a catalyst for learning as changing your approach would be, a change in technique accompanied by a change in approach would facilitate more effective learning. As you read through and try to adopt the following principles and reading techniques, keep in mind that the usefulness of the techniques depends on your ability to adjust the depth of your approach. If you persist in a surface approach to reading, any change in technique will continue to be of little learning value. If you change your approach as you change technique, the technique can improve your learning dramatically.

Study Your Textbook

Before you begin reading the chapters in any textbook, study your textbook first. You are probably thinking, "You've got to be kidding! Don't I have enough to do already?" But don't forget the first principle to any effective reading approach—be **flexible**! You might think it a waste of time to acquaint yourself with the book (and author) you will, undoubtedly, be spending several hours with. But in the short fifteen minutes it will take you to survey a textbook, you will better understand the content and organization of the book, the viewpoint of the author, and where to find important information. This will make your textbook more useful because you will know what is in it and where to find it. Don't forget the second principle of an effective reading approach, **purpose**. Survey your textbook with the intent to learn all you can in the short time you spend doing it.

Here is how you survey your textbook (adapted from Haburton, 1981):

1. Read the **title** and find out who the **author** is. The title will tell you about the material in the book. If there is a writeup on the author, read it. Background information is important in identifying the author's scholarly focus and his or her reputation in the field.

2. Out of curiosity, glance at the **copyright date** to find out when the book was published and how up-to-date the material is.

3. Glance through the **table of contents**—the outline of the book. It will tell you the specific areas covered and the relationship of each chapter to the others.

4. Don't skip over the **preface** or **introduction**! At least skim over these sections. You will usually find out about the overall scope and content of the book, as well as the author's purpose in writing the book.

5. Briefly peruse through each chapter. By reading each **chapter title**, each **section heading** and eyeballing the **text**, you will orient yourself to what you will be later learning in more detail. Have fun looking over the graphs, charts, pictures, and illustrations.

6. Discover if there is a **glossary** and where it is (usually in the back of the book). Consulting the glossary can be extremely helpful when you are trying to learn the meanings of words as the author uses them.

7. Are there **appendices**? This section consists of additional information related to the main body of the text.

8. Remember to refer to the **index** if you need help with a quick reference.

9. Look for a **bibliography**—a list of other books that relate in some way to the subject of the textbook. It can be a handy resource when writing a term paper.

SQ3R: The First Reading Skill Technique

Dr. Francis P. Robinson (1970) developed a systematic textbook reading skill technique called SQ3R (survey, question, read, recite, review). SQ3R was a uniquely different approach to studying, based on findings which showed that retention in learning was enhanced by surveying and questioning the material before it was read, reciting from memory after reading, and reviewing the material again for better understanding and retention.

The pioneer SQ3R became the model for other systematic techniques that arose in the 1960s and 1970s: PQRST (preview, question, read, summarize, test); OARWET (overview, ask, read, write, evaluate, test)—just to name a few. Like the SQ3R, these systems were developed to improve reading comprehension and retention.

The steps in the SQ3R are described below.

Survey. The purpose of surveying is to get a quick overview of the whole chapter and then to estimate what the chapter is about before you actually begin reading. It includes glancing over the chapter title, introductory paragraph, headings, subheadings, summary and any charts or graphs that will introduce you to core ideas. No more than a few minutes is necessary for this step. The idea is to gain a brief orientation to the chapter.

Question. Textbook chapters are conveniently organized into sections. Questioning includes turning each section heading into a question. By changing a heading into a question, you make a conscious effort to focus on the material for information. Usually the section heading relates or refers to the main point of the section. Asking the right question should lead you to the main point of the section. If, on reading the section, you find out that the question does not reflect the important point of the section, rephrase your question to fit the material. You may find that more than one question is appropriate for a section.

Read. You know what you want to learn when you begin reading with a question in mind. In this step you actively read, with an inquiring attitude, to answer your question rather than trying to remember everything in the section. Your aim is to organize your thinking around the question. Before answering the question, though, read through the entire section. In this way you will be sure your question reflects the important point to remember.

Recite. After reading the answer to your question, check whether you have comprehended the material by reciting the information in your own words *from memory*. You can recite by mentally reviewing the answer or by writing it down. If you write down your answer, do so briefly, in your own words, and only ***after you have read the whole section***. Notetaking habits like copying complete sentences from the book are not helpful practices in learning. Words or phrases that demonstrate that you know the topic act as cues for later review. You may want to recite the answer to your question a few times before moving on to the next section to ensure that you have retained the information. *Do the question, read, and recite steps cyclically for each section in the chapter, or for each subsection if you cannot keep a full section in mind at the time.*

Review. After you have finished reading the chapter, the review that follows immediately after should be brief but inclusive of all chapter notes. A way to review might be to cover your questions and recite the answers from memory. If you find you cannot recite the answers, keep studying until you can. You may want to go over the chapter introduction and summary again to make sure you understand the core points in the context of the organization of the chapter.

Advantages and Disadvantages of the SQ3R and Other Reading Techniques

SQ3R and other reading techniques suggest the mechanics of what a student should do to study most effectively. Yet most study techniques fall short, if not in the learning approach they encourage (surface vs. deep), then certainly in how students respond to the formulas. SQ3R and other study formulas are amenable to a deep approach to learning if *purpose, not formula*, is kept in mind.

In the past, the success of the SQ3R has been measured by an increase in a person's rate of memorization and retention of information. On a superficial level, SQ3R seems to encourage fixing facts, details, and concepts in memory. Comprehension at this level involves understanding the literal meaning of the material. Too often, one's aim in using the SQ3R tends not to be interpretation of the information but only memorization of it.

Benjamin Bloom (1956) defined how people approach and comprehend information at different levels of cognitive learning. According to Bloom's taxonomy of learning objectives (see figure 8.1), SQ3R basically encourages the two lowest levels of learning by emphasizing recall of information (knowledge) and demonstration of it through explanation in one's own words (comprehension). Knowing and comprehending the facts are important parts of learning, but they are at the lower level of learning, as opposed to learning at the higher levels—application, analysis, synthesis, and evaluation. Does this mean that the SQ3R is not a useful study technique?

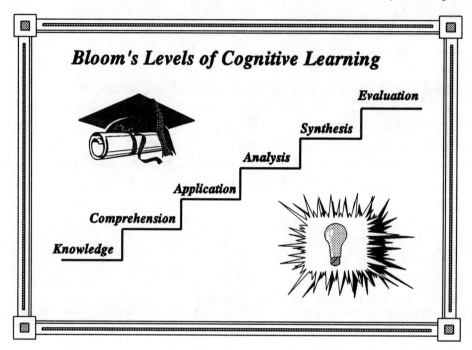

Figure 8.1 Bloom's Levels of Cognitive Learning.

If your ultimate aim is to learn at higher levels of cognition, SQ3R as it is described here will tend to be only preliminary to the higher levels of learning. Reading to interpret the meaning of information, as opposed to mere memorization, is vital to higher levels of comprehension and insight. However, memorizing information, and being able to recall it, are a part of learning. Higher levels of comprehension cannot take place unless the facts, details, and concepts are there from which to interpret and reason, make judgments, detect implications, and see applications. Undoubtedly you will be enrolled in classes in which you will be asked simply to memorize the literal meaning of information. In those instances, SQ3R would be a good technique to use; however, to receive the most from your efforts, the suggestion is that

144

you add to the review step of SQ3R Bloom's higher level cognitive processes. For instance, after completing a chapter, take additional time to reflect on how you could apply the information in a practical sense. Analyze how the separate facts and ideas join together to make a meaningful whole. Synthesize ideas by creating new insights or ideas based on the facts and ideas you read about. Critically evaluate the ideas in light of your already-existing knowledge. By using the higher-level mental processes of application, analysis, synthesis, and evaluation while you study, SQ3R will facilitate a deep approach to reading.

REAP: An Alternative Approach

Although some students will agree that their retention and recall improve after they use a systematic reading technique, most students will resist using such systems because studying in a systematic fashion feels unnatural to them, or the time required takes too long, or the approach seems too structured or rule-bound. Although not a panacea for the problems that beset most of the systematic reading skill techniques, REAP is a reading system that seems to address more the question of how a student actually does study. REAP could be described as the method that reaches students where they are at. It is a **flexible** approach that encourages opportunity for personal adaptation and at the same time encourages learning beyond a surface approach.

REAP (Westfall, 1978), which stands for read, encode, annotate, and ponder, was developed in 1976 by two University of Missouri professors. As you read through the explanation of REAP, notice how simple and flexible it is to use and how it lends itself to a deep approach to learning.

Read. Unlike other techniques that require you to survey, preview, question, or overview systematically before you actually begin to read, there is nothing complicated or mysterious about this step: you just read. You may decide to start from page one and go until page one-hundred, or read the summary first and then start with the introduction. How you prefer to sequence your reading is your decision; however, you must consider the type of material you are reading.

The organized format of a textbook chapter makes reading and identifying important points and ideas easier. Inevitably, however, you will be required to read material that is unheaded or even without an identified conclusion that summarizes the important points. You will be responsible for sifting through the material to find the major points and draw your own conclusions. When you are required to read unheaded material, you may need to consider ways to "precomprehend" the material before you actually begin reading. For instance, if an article has an abstract or short summary statement at the beginning, you may want to read it first. The important principle here is to do whatever leads you to read with comprehension, not merely to follow a mechanical process that fools you into thinking you are studying.

After you have taken into consideration the type of material you are reading, it is time to read. Read to comprehend the material. Ask yourself, "What am I aiming to learn by reading this?"

Encode. This is a fancy name for reciting what you have just read. What it really means is to put the author's ideas into your own words so that you demonstrate to yourself that you understand. Whether you encode page by page, concept by concept, or section by section does not really matter just as long as you are able to recall and rephrase the main ideas that are important to remember. The only requirement in this step is that you *immediately* encode what you have read and that you do it as much from memory as possible. This forces you to think actively about the material.

Annotate. Encoding may not be enough to remember material in the coming days and weeks, so you write down the ideas and concepts you want to retain and later review. Notes do not have to be extensive but should reflect the points and concepts that are important to remember. This is another form of reciting, but it also serves as a good source for later review.

Ponder. By now you are familiar with the steps read, encode, and annotate. Pondering, or thinking deeply about an idea or concept, however, may not be a routine practice in your studying process. Yet it is the key to meaningful learning. Because the load of information that students are required to digest is frequently overwhelming, they often get too narrowly task-oriented toward their studies. Too often students limit themselves to the facts on the page and do not take the initiative to be creative or to experiment with the new information. Knowledge is often too quickly compartmentalized, seen only in the context in which it was given. This is memorizing, not thinking. Pondering allows for and encourages thinking. The effort you spend encoding and memorizing information should at least be matched by pondering and reflecting on it. Finding the time and energy to ponder, philosophize, and be creative with your thinking can help you transform facts and ideas into knowledge that is useful and in context. Useful, contextual knowledge is the product of a deep approach to reading.

For some people, visual images imprint on the mind more easily than words alone. That is why **visual notetaking** can be a powerful memory aid. Visual notetaking or diagramming involves organizing information into a written visual format that reflects verbal or written thought patterns. Such diagramming is also referred to as **mapping**. A diagram or map is an effective way to organize and unite information with a visual symbol. It shows the interrelationships between ideas (giving a visual organization to a chapter or article) and activates better retrieval and recall.

Diagrams show direction and flow of material and can take any form wanted (see figure 8.2).

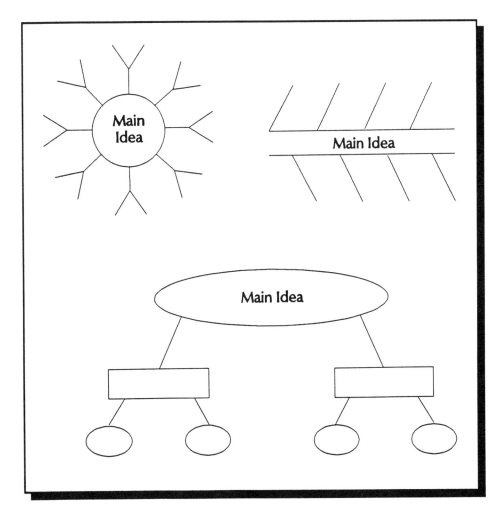

Figure 8.2 Sample Visual Diagrams.

It is important to consider the type of thought pattern when you choose a visual organizer to accurately display the content and to reflect the pattern of thought. The content of the material and how the author has organized the information may give clues to type of configuration or visual organizer to use. For instance, information that is presented so that one point builds on another may well be diagrammed in some type of format that shows sequential ordering or progression. Specifically, in reading about the events that led to America's involvement in WWII, one could use a visual diagram that maps the chronological pattern of the events as they happened (see Figure 8.3). Whatever diagram you choose, consider the following guidelines: (1) The thought pattern of the reading source should be reflected in your visual diagram. (2) State simply and concisely the main point(s) and subpoints in your own words. The idea is not to rewrite the whole article or chapter, but you do want to include enough information to make the diagram useful. Do not hesitate to include those facts, details, or examples that add to your understanding of the subpoints and main idea(s). (3) Show in your diagram how the subpoints relate or link to the main point(s). (4) Reflect in your mapping how all points and ideas fit together as a whole.

Visual notetaking requires that you go beyond mere memorization of concepts and facts by requiring the demonstration of interrelationships between ideas. This part of visual diagramming encourages deeper learning. In order to get the maximum value out of your learning, you may consider asking general types of questions that naturally arise from what you have just learned. Ask questions that encourage a personal expression toward the information, generate divergent ways of thinking, focus on understanding ideas and concepts, and stimulate interest through practical application of the information. Asking questions and pondering the answers to those questions will take you a step further in learning and will help you experience reading more comprehensively.

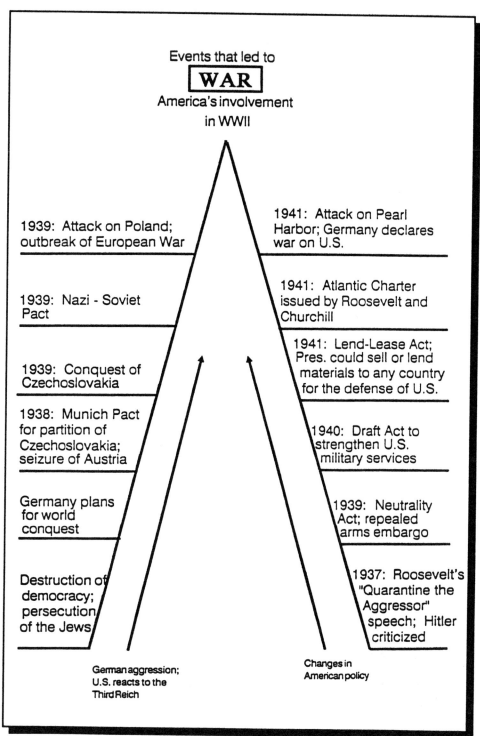

Figure 8.3 Visual Diagram: Sequential Ordering.

149

Marking Your Reading Material

If you are like most college students, money is tight. One way to cut down on your college expenses is to buy used books. The drawback to buying a used book, however, is the random, inept, and often sloppy marking of the text done by a previous book owner. This makes reading and identifying important information difficult. It may become your experience, if it has not occurred already, to open a textbook and find almost every sentence on a page highlighted as though each thought was as important as the next. A student who underlines material like this has probably not given much thought to what she or he has read. The random underlining becomes useless to the reader because it is difficult to distinguish the important from the unimportant information. Most students prefer to underline reading material rather than to take written notes because it is faster and seems easier. But do not let the ease of gliding your highlighter pen across the page fool you into believing you are capturing the important points or even understanding what you have just read. In fact, indiscriminate highlighting may be your substitute for thinking while reading. On the other hand, marking reading material can be an effective study method if it is done actively, with a purpose in mind, and selectively, making distinctions between significant and insignificant sentences. Active reading with purposeful marking is thinking as you read, followed by marking the information that is important to retain and understand.

Six Guidelines for Purposeful Underlining

For underlining to be useful it must be an active, thinking process rather than a mechanical exercise. These guidelines are merely a tool. If used only mechanically, they will not lend themselves to purposeful learning. Your approach and purpose in reading will determine the degree and level of how helpful these six guidelines will be.

Read to comprehend major points. A realistic goal in reading is to understand the overall meaning of the chapter or article you are reading and those supporting points which give greater depth to your understanding of the main ideas. Expecting that you must memorize every fact and detail is an unrealistic goal. Learn to generalize beyond immediate facts, to synthesize and integrate concepts into whole meanings.

Read first, underline later. Before determining what you want to underline, read the complete paragraph, section, or article first; then go back and underline what you think is important to retain and review later. Premature underlining often leads to highlighting unimportant information or highlighting excessively. Delay your underlining until you recognize what is important to remember. The main idea will more likely be identified and supported in this way. (Marking should be done during the recite step of SQ3R or the annotate step of REAP.)

Underline discriminately. Reading becomes such an arduous and tedious task for many students because of their overconcern with memorizing detail. You simply cannot remember everything you read, so it becomes extremely vital that you learn to mark or underline essential information selectively. Main ideas and major supporting points are most important to underline. Learn to identify and discriminate between them (if you need practice identifying main ideas from supporting ideas, the book Reading Well in College, by Paul B. Panes, 1986, can give you direction). The extent to which you underline details depends on your purpose and the demands of your instructor. If you are required to know minor detail, then selectively highlighting detail becomes important in underlining discriminately. Not all detail may be important.

Underline key phrases, not complete sentences. The frustration of reviewing reading material that has been overly underlined is that it becomes difficult to perceive quickly the important points and to give those points immediate attention. A page with occasional highlights, bringing attention to fewer items, is easier to review. When you underline, it may be best to refrain from highlighting complete sentences and instead to highlight important words or phrases within the sentence.

Use a marking system that shows the relationship between key points and supporting points. Underlining or highlighting alone may not be sufficient to distinguish quickly between main ideas and supporting points and to see clearly how they relate to each other. A marking system that uses symbols, numbers, letters, or lines will help you quickly identify relationships while you read and review. There are several ways to use a marking system. Following are some basic ideas: double underline or star the most important points, single underline supporting points, number or letter a list of points the author makes according to their importance, design a color coding system (using different highlighting colors for main and subpoints), use arrows to draw attention to connecting thoughts or to show cause and effect relationships, or jot down page numbers of points that are relevant to the point you are marking, to assure continuity to your learning. The marking system you adopt is up to you. The goal is to develop a method that enhances your learning.

Review your marked textbook. Before you review the main ideas and subpoints you have marked, it would be beneficial to test yourself on how well you have understood the overall meaning of what you have just read. Take a few minutes to summarize in your own words, on paper or verbally, the general message of the chapter or article, to determine whether you have really comprehended the meaning. A deep approach to reading facilitates the synthesis of separate facts and ideas into a whole, making summarizing a possible task. No matter how difficult the task of summarizing might be for you, stick to it until you feel confident that you understand and comprehend the content. After you have briefly summarized the general meaning, continue reviewing by reciting, in your own words, and committing to memory the main ideas and supporting points you have highlighted throughout the text or article. These are the points you decided were the most important to remember. As you recite these important main points, go a step beyond memorization to integrate your learning by thinking how each point relates to the other points.

Figure 8.4 illustrates one way to highlight effectively. Notice how focused and simple the highlighting is. **The main point is identified in bold.** *The two examples that illustrate the main point are identified in italics.*

The Scholar and Personal Responsibility

From the scholar perspective, we do not search for the meaning of life, we define it, we develop it, we create it. We don't seek out who we are. Our identity is not found by searching across the land. Our identity is something we decide. **Students expect someone else to define them; scholars accept the responsibility of defining themselves.** Students expect the textbook to have the answer, and they want to know whether it is A or B. I was intrigued recently in reading *Norman Cousins's book,* <u>Anatomy of an Illness</u>, where he describes how he *accepted the joint responsibility with his doctor for his own health.* He was told that his odds for getting better were 500-1 against, and he said when that announcement was made he decided he had to become a participant in this process in a way he had not considered previously. Norman Cousins, as the editor of the <u>Saturday Review,</u> had available to him a research staff. He sent his research staff out to do a survey of various medical findings, and he found that what his doctors were prescribing was not accurate. Norman Cousins did not blindly accept the diagnosis and prescriptions his

---

doctor had arrived at working with incomplete data. Norman Cousins took the scholar-leader role and asked why. He found that the prescribed medication and the hospital environment were inappropriate. He determined that what he really needed was some Vitamin C, some laughter, and a pleasant environment. He moved himself out of a hospital into a nice hotel room. He started taking Vitamin C and watching Laurel and Hardy movies and he got better.

Cousins became part of the healing process. He applied the power of the participant, rather than to sit back and defer to the expert doctor. Another example touches upon an uncomfortable and a difficult issue, but one that I find terribly compelling. *Victor Frankl in* Man's Search for Meaning, *describes the fate of people in the concentration camps in Nazi captivity. He argues that what was needed was a fundamental change in attitude.* Attitudes towards life, he said, had become too self-indulgent, too narcissistic, too self-serving, to really understand what was going on and to survive the brutality of the camp. In talking about the men in his camp, he said, "what was really needed was a fundamental change in our attitude towards life. We had to learn ourselves and furthermore we had to teach others that *the issue was not what we expected from life but what life expected from us.* We needed to stop asking what the meaning of life was and instead think of ourselves as those who were being questioned by life daily and hourly.

Figure 8.4 Example of highlighting. (Taken from Ritchie, J.B. and Thompson, Paul. "We Need a Nation of Scholar-leaders." In Organization and People: Readings, Cases, and Exercises in Organizational Behavior, 3rd Edition, 1984, pp. 13-18. St. Paul: West Publishing Co.)

In reviewing this section, the reader should be able to glance at the highlighted phrases and recite (in his or her own words) the meaning of the material. For example, "According to Ritchie, part of being a 'scholar' is taking responsibility for directing and defining one's life and not letting outside influences or circumstances do it for you. The life of Norman Cousins and Victor Frankl are used as examples of the power of personal choice in defining one's life."

153

Learning Applications

1. Take a few moments to evaluate your reading approach. What factors or personal habits prevent you from approaching your reading with greater depth?

2. Practice surveying a textbook. Write on a piece of paper the name of the textbook, author, copyright date; list if the book has a glossary, index, bibliography, etc.; after reading the preface and introduction and skimming the chapters, briefly explain the content of the book, the plan of the author, and his or her purpose in writing the book.

3. Choose a textbook chapter and practice using SQ3R or REAP. Approach the technique with purpose by incorporating Bloom's cognitive processes of application, analysis, synthesis, and evaluation in the review (SQ3R) or ponder (REAP) step. If you have trouble applying these mental processes, practice with another student in a class or ask your instructor for help.

4. To begin practicing visual notetaking, start with a reading assignment that is not overly complex or too difficult to follow. Simply and concisely state the main point of the article and then show in your diagram how the subpoints relate to the main idea.

5. Practice underlining a textbook chapter or article in the way it is outlined in this chapter, or try applying SQ3R to underlining by:

    *   surveying the chapter
    *   turning each section heading into a question
    *   reciting it in your own words and then highlighting only the answer to your question
    *   reviewing again the highlighted underlinings to get a picture of what the whole chapter is about

References

Bloom, B. S., Ed. <u>Taxonomy of Educational Objectives.</u> New York: David McKay, 1956.

Bruner, J. S. "Learning and Thinking." <u>Harvard Educational Review,</u> 1959, <u>29,</u> 184-192.

Carroll, L. Feeding the Mind. Chatto and Windus, 1907.

Gibbs, G. <u>Teaching Students to Learn: A Student Centered Approach.</u> Milton Keynes, England: The Open University Press, 1981.

Haburton, E. <u>Study Skills for College</u>. Cambridge, Mass.: Winthrop Publishers, Inc., 1981.

Panes, P. B. <u>Reading Well in College.</u> New York: Harper and Row, 1986.

Perry, W. G. "Students' Use and Misuse of Reading Skills: A Report to the Faculty. "Harvard Educational Review," 1959, <u>29,</u> 193-200.

Robinson, F. P. <u>Effective Study.</u> New York: Harper and Row, 1970.

Stein, H. "Visualized Notemaking: Left-Right Brain Theory Applied in the Classroom." <u>The Social Studies,</u> July/August 1987, <u>77,</u> 163-168.

Steinley, G. "Left Brain/Right Brain: More of the Same?" <u>Language Arts,</u> April 1983, <u>60</u>(4), 459-462.

Westfall, P. "Magical Memory Tour: The Unending Quest for a Study Formula That Words." <u>Insider: Ford's Continuing Series of College Newspaper Supplements,</u> 1978, 4-7.

Chapter 9

Demonstrating What You Have Learned

What levels of learning can teachers expect students to achieve? Can you predict what the teacher will ask? What can you do to prepare for the different type of questions that may appear on tests? Are there some secrets to successful test taking?

The most widely accepted classification system of educational objectives found in the current educational literature is Bloom's Taxonomy (Bloom, et al, 1956). This remarkable paradigm categorizes the levels at which you learn. The model includes six levels: (1) knowledge, (2) comprehension, (3) application, (4) analysis, (5) synthesis, and (6) evaluation. ***Your college instructors devise assignments, term papers, projects, and tests to teach you, and then measure your ability at these six discrete levels of learning. The aim of this chapter is to help you recognize these six levels and deal with them in the most effective ways possible.*** The assumption made by the authors is that you are striving to operate with a deep learning approach and that you will want to know more than just how to demonstrate knowledge. Therefore all six elements of Bloom's taxonomy of educational objectives will be reviewed to discover how students are tested. Following that review, you will receive suggestions for general study-review and some practical suggestions for handling specific test problems.

Learning and retaining knowledge often seems like a dualistic activity, most efficiently handled by routine, surface approaches to learning. But will

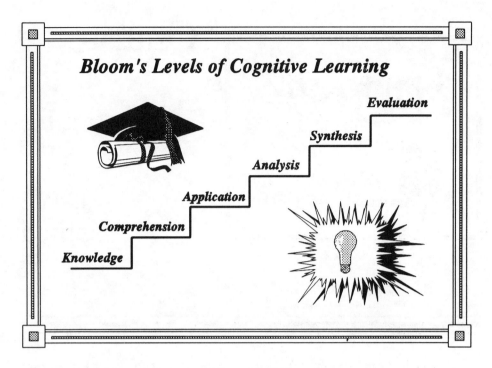

Figure 9.1 Bloom's Levels of Cognitive Learning.

surface approaches ensure knowledge in long-term memory? The most pursued learning level in most college courses is comprehension. How does a deep learning approach enhance comprehension? Professors pay lip service to application, but does one really apply knowledge to significant problems in the typical college course? Analysis and synthesis are complementary skills, often taught but seldom recognized by students who perform at a dualistic level of development or who learn from a surface approach. Finally, evaluation is too often seen as the instructor's province, not the student's. The student too often merely does what he or she is told while the instructor evaluates. Simply jumping through hoops for the teacher does not help the student learn to function at higher levels. The instructor must make an effort to raise levels and the student make an even more concerted effort to learn at higher levels. In fact, good learning, committed to higher levels takes a highly developed skill. Once students possess it, they can match the instructor's testing requirements with their own testing acumen.

Bloom's Taxonomy and Student Testing

With mastery of this chapter, you should be able to review your next course examination and understand what the instructor was trying to do when she or he asked you each examination question. Was your knowledge being tested? Your comprehension? Your application, analysis or synthesis ability? Were you asked to evaluate something? Chances are that whatever you were asked, you were required to use one or more of Bloom's levels of cognitive ability.

Testing Knowledge

Bloom (1956) defined knowledge as "little more than the remembering of the idea or phenomenon in a form very close to that in which it was originally encountered." Knowledge alone is of little value to one's education unless one is acquiring knowledge solely for some isolated activity, such as doing well on a quiz show. *Jeopardy* contestants, for example, display pure knowledge and little more. Even so, rightly or wrongly, knowledge is one of the most common educational objectives, and the wary student acquires stores of knowledge with the expectation of demonstrating that knowledge on tests. In fact, it is instructors' absolute insistence on specific knowledge that drives students into much of their cynical test preparation behavior which could be categorized as dualistic and surface. Students do not dare bypass the content knowledge in a course and do not find time or will to go beyond knowledge to higher level course and learning objectives. And so they memorize!

Content- and memory-oriented "knowledge" questions are the most basic part of every course; they are considered important enough to be asked more frequently than college teachers will admit. *Though knowledge is the lowest objective of instruction, it is the most frequently tested; consequently, your preparations must take knowledge questions into account.* Typical tests which emphasize the knowledge level are fill-in-the-blanks, matching, multiple choice, true-false, identifications, or listing. Any test item that requires a selection or response in terms of specifics, ways of dealing with specifics, or universal abstractions (principles, generalizations, or theories) is most likely a question of knowledge. These testing methods make you recall an idea or phenomenon essentially as you learned it. Even the famous equation $E=MC^2$ is mere knowledge as long as it is no more than recalled. On page 171 of this chapter is a section called *Testing Strategies.* It will give you techniques to use when you take "knowledge" oriented tests.

Testing Comprehension

Often in your classes you will be tested for knowledge when your instructor really wants to test you for your comprehension. Bloom defines comprehension in terms of three uses of knowledge: (1) translation, (2) interpretation, and (3) extrapolation. *Any test of your comprehension requires that you take information or knowledge and put it into your own words, and then incorporate it into one or more of these three activities.* To translate, you must summarize, abstract, or symbolically deal with ideas. If given the summary, abstraction, or symbol, you must illustrate their critical characteristics in concrete examples.

Knowledge is manipulated and transfigured in two directions: concrete to abstract, or abstract to concrete. For example, answer this possible test question: *"Given the textbook definition of the 'Surface' learning approach (Chapter 3), illustrate surface learning in three different classes that you have taken."*

Notice that when answering a "comprehension" question, the answers include "knowledge." Notice also that a comprehension question is harder for the instructor to write and the student to answer. It is interesting to note that if you were given three examples of "surface" learning in the lecture or the text, what was intended as a comprehension question could suddenly become a knowledge question. This happens simply because you could recall the idea—not think it through—and write it.

To interpret, you go one step beyond translation: not only do you abstract from detail or see detail from abstraction, but you interrelate ideas in a way that your thinking goes up to abstraction or down to concreteness plus across to relationships. Consider this test question as an example: " *A student writes his or her English theme in well organized fashion and with careful attention to grammar and punctuation, but dashes off a reaction paper for*

160

a sociology class with little attention to writing or mechanics. Describe this student's learning behavior in terms of deep and surface approach (Chapter 3) and locate the student behavior in terms of the Perry scheme (Chapter 2). Explain what elements of the deep/surface approach relate to the Perry scheme in this scenario."

Notice in this question that one task must be translated as an example of two learning-related concepts, and that the two concepts must then be interrelated. Full interpretation must take place, demonstrating comprehension of the concepts in the process.

Extrapolation, the third manifestation of comprehension, adds an extension of ideas beyond translation and interrelatedness. Figure 9.2 illustrates comprehension graphically, in all its manifestations of translation, interpretation, and extrapolation. ***Translation is using your own words to describe an idea in terms of abstract or concreteness; interpretation is explaining the difference between the abstract and the concrete; and***

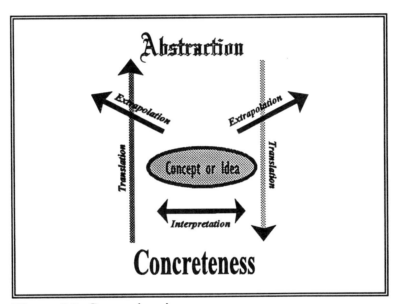

Figure 9.2 Comprehension

extrapolation is illustrating the effect of crossing the ideas into a new dimension of comprehension.

In extrapolation, the learner goes beyond data or idea manipulation to see connections between two or more identified ideas and an additional idea that is brought into the learning picture *by the learner*. Thus if the test item used above to illustrate interpretation had added to it the instructions, "Reverse the scenario for the sociology class and speculate how the reversed approach to writing in sociology would illustrate surface and deep learning and cause shifts along the Perry scale," the original explanation of the tightly compartmentalized view of the learner's writing skills would need to be extrapolated to a scenario that universalizes writing skills. This added effort would be extrapolated comprehension.

Comprehension can be tested most easily by the essay question. However, good essay questions are difficult to write and time-consuming to grade. Even bad essay questions though easy to write, are still time-consuming to grade. The result is that instructors, particularly of large classes, tend to restrict or dispense with essay questions when possible, some instructors using none at all. Multiple-choice questions can test comprehension, but too often multiple-choice questions designed to be comprehensive, are little more than tricky knowledge questions. It is no wonder that most test items, even in college, are really knowledge questions, at their best written to require searching recall of ideas planted in textbooks and lectures.

Testing Application

Keep in mind that Bloom's taxonomy of educational objectives is arranged in a hierarchy (Bloom, 1956). Comprehension requires knowledge, and application requires comprehension. The most complex aspect of comprehension, extrapolation, is very close to application itself, because in extrapolation, the student thinks beyond the given ideas to new, self-constructed ideas. The difference that makes application unique from comprehension is that in application the student deals with a *new* problem *without* the promptings inherent in comprehension. True problem solving skills are applications of knowledge that has been comprehended to the point of extrapolation and has been deliberately selected for use because it appears to the student to apply to the problem's solution. *That extra search-and-selection step for use makes the comprehended knowledge an application.* Bloom (1956) draws the distinction: "Comprehension shows that the student *can* use the abstraction. . . . Application shows that he or she

162

will use it correctly, given an appropriate situation in which no mode of solution is specified." Testing application is difficult, because even if the student knows and comprehends, the instructor must wait until the student is willing and able to act before the quality of the action (application) can be assessed.

In a general education class at a large university, the course subject was cross-disciplinary and included information on America history, economics and government. One of the text authors attended that class through a full semester. The course instructor and his colleagues tried desperately to help freshman students comprehend and apply knowledge. Issues of history, economics, and politics were presented deliberately for cross-content thinking, and application of concepts was constantly emphasized. For example, in a chapter on "The Role of Prices and Profits" (Fox and Pope, 1986) the textbook said:

Applications

The operation of prices and profits in a market system can best be seen by examining specific situations in which they are allowed to fulfill their function in the system, as well as situations in which, for one reason or another, the government has prevented prices or profits from functioning. The first example, involving the market system and American agriculture, illustrates how prices and profits reallocate resources. This example is strong evidence of the allocative power of a market system.

That introduction was followed by three specific application examples, highlighting farm labor, government intervention, and minimum wages in the market system. So far, so good: the course was geared to move students through knowledge and comprehension to applications. The flow in the process is predictable to someone who is familiar with the Perry scheme you learned in Chapter 2: a freshman course, with freshman students, largely dualistic behavior. The students tried to memorize the applications, and most of the students could not carry through a new scenario to its abstract meanings; consequently, testing application was largely beyond the student's capability. As soon as the instructors asked for more than knowledge or simple comprehension, the students missed the intent of the test question.

Sad but true, many college instructors discover this developmental problem and stay safely within mere knowledge testing. Because of the difficulties of teaching and testing higher levels of learning, they seldom go beyond comprehension testing.

Testing Analysis, Synthesis, and Evaluation

Thinking at the higher levels of Bloom's Taxonomy requires manipulation of ideas in such a way that their component parts are clearly seen, not only in their existence, but in the level of contribution their existence makes to the whole and in what value their contribution has for the whole idea under critique. Analysis, synthesis, and evaluation make up the ingredients of what most people commonly call critical or creative thinking.

Analysis is what logicians call deduction. It is a process of thinking in which one moves from the general to the specific, or in other words, examining the whole and drawing out the parts. Analysis goes beyond seeing relationships at the level of comprehension to become the basis for evaluation. An example of an analysis question from this text would be, "Review the studies of Morton, Saljo, and Svensson, and then determine the critical defining characteristics of deep learning." The idea is to be considered in the question is deep learning. The analysis is to determine the critical defining points. To list and describe the points would be an analysis, unless someone had already done the analysis and the student is merely recalling what was done; in that case the cognitive level would be knowledge.

If a testing requirement were given to determine which of the component parts of the deep learning approach was most important to learning, the idea of value would be added, and the analysis would merge into evaluation. Thus it is easy to move from analysis to evaluation, and if you, the student, are given analysis questions, you will likely also have elements of evaluation as well.

In synthesis, or what many logicians call induction, individual discrete ideas are examined with the purpose of identifying new concepts, unknown conclusions, and even new applications. This level of thinking borders on pure creativity, and it could be tested by asking the student to go beyond a set of data into a new thought or conclusion. Or it could be tested by asking the student to generate or brainstorm totally new ideas regarding a new concept.

164

An example of a synthesis question from this text would be "After reading chapters seven and eight, suggest your own unified method for learning information from textbooks and lectures." The answer involves synthesizing the ideas from chapters seven and eight and developing new, creative ways of gathering information from textbooks and lectures.

To move from synthesis to evaluation, this test question would need to require some form of value judgement. It could be reworded as follows: "Develop a theory of information intake based on reading and listening techniques given in chapters seven and eight. Identify components of the theories that you chose and that you rejected, and explain the basis for your decision." In this version of the question there is added inquiry which requires a response that includes a personal value judgment. Consequently, the question moves to the level of evaluation.

Summary of Testing, Based on Bloom's Taxonomy

Analysis, synthesis, and evaluation have been viewed together because of their combined relationship to higher order or critical thinking. Critical thinking is a universally recognized educational goal given only sporadic attention. Bloom was one of the first to focus on higher order or creative thinking, and after more than 30 years, the educational trends are favoring higher-level thinking with increased attention. For this reason, you have been shown examples of how analysis or synthesis might be included in your college testing. You have also been shown how evaluation is commonly combined with either analysis or synthesis when instructors construct their tests. Remember that analysis and synthesis testing requires essay-type questions that call for rather involved answers. Instructors will often design term papers and projects to assess your analytical, synthesizing, and evaluative skills. They probably will use the term paper/project approach to test your application skills as well. That leaves exams primarily to test knowledge and comprehension.

You will be assessed for all of Bloom's objectives in any good college course. The summary of Bloom's levels of thinking which follows on the next two pages will give you some ideas of the way students think on the various levels and also how instructors ask questions. Pay close attention to the descriptive words that instructors use. Your job will be to anticipate where, when, and how these assessments will take place. Do not overlook the obvious: if you want to know where, when, and how, ask your instructor!

SUMMARY OF THE BLOOM'S LEVELS OF THINKING

LEVEL OF THINKING	*WAY OF THINKING*	*SAMPLE QUESTIONS*
1. KNOWLEDGE	Memorize facts or recall information. (list, define, tell, recall, identify, copy)	List all the Great Lakes. Place a set of events in order.
2. COMPREHENSION	Tell in your own words. (understand, configure, discuss, explain)	Explain what the author meant in this passage. Summarize the chapter.
3. APPLICATION	Solve a problem in a given situation. (demonstrate, model, draw, manipulate, illustrate, apply)	Describe how to set policy in a business setting. Organize the facts and present them to the group.
4. ANALYSIS	Break information into parts and identify relationships. (compare, defend, support, divide, pattern)	Analyze the impact of the President's policy on business. Compare the decisive battles of the civil war.
5. SYNTHESIS	Bring concepts together and rearrange into creative new ideas. (alter, predict, modify, recombine, design)	Organize ideas into a new story. Design an experiment to prove the hypothesis.
6. EVALUATION	Make a value judgment and give reasons to support it. (critique, rate, standardize, appraise, justify)	Which concept is better for the poor? Support your answer. Tell why you have taken a stand.

166

DESCRIPTIVE WORDS FREQUENTLY
USED IN TEST QUESTIONS

Knowledge Questions

collect
complete
copy
count
define
duplicate
find
identify
imitate
label
list
mark
match
name
note
omit
order
place
point
recall
repeat
select
state
tally
tell

Comprehension Questions

code
configure
explain
indicate
interpret
perceive
recast
record
relate
rephrase
represent
restate
transform
translate
understand

Application Questions

apply
assemble
calculate
construct
demonstrate
describe
display
draw
estimate
illustrate
make
model
present
produce
show
solve
support
teach

Analysis Questions

analyze
associate
categorize
classify
compare
conclude
connect
defend
differentiate
discriminate
dissect
distinguish
divide
group
isolate
order
organize
separate
subtract
summarize
support
systematize
take apart

Synthesis Questions

add to
alter
assume
change
connect
design
develop
discover
expand
extend
formulate
generate
hypothesize
infer
interpret
maximize
minimize
modify
predict
propose
rearrange
reconstruct
rename
reorder
reorganize
simplify
substitute
vary

Evaluation Questions

argue
appraise
assess
conclude
criticize
decide
judge
justify
rate
surmise
standardize
symbolize
validate
value
verify

The time to begin preparing for your final examination is the first day of class (unless you picked up your text early). Start by reading the course syllabus and planning a time schedule to accomplish all course requirements *before* they become crises.

Divide your study into at least two types: first-time study and review study. To give you an idea how the idealized scenario may be accomplished, look at a hypothetical three-unit course, Biology 100. It meets three days per week, has three midterms and a final, and requires one major term paper. The textbook has 700 pages , which includes 47 chapters in 7 sections. Your job is to organize the course for effective, study. Figure 9.3 represents a time-line and plan for Biology 100. Study it to gain some idea of the planning phase to succeed in the course.

The first important principle illustrated in figure 9.3 is that first-time study (FST) is separate from review study (RS). FST should occur as soon as possible after the lecture (within 24 hours). Five important activities should take place during FST. There are spaces on the study plan sheet to mark the date and time the study was completed.

FIRST TIME STUDY ACTIVITIES

1. *Finalize your lecture notes* by completing the unfinished sections and placing them in the desired format (the Cornell system described in Chapter seven or something similar).

2. *Complete your required reading.* It is preferred that you take notes as you read, as illustrated in Chapter eight. At a minimum, class reading should be completed and the important parts underlined and marked.

3. *Write down knowledge questions that you perceive the instructor may ask on exams.* It is important to get a feel for the type of examination the teacher will use. If the test is objective, you should make at least three or more questions from a small chapter or a single lecture.

4. *Draft comprehension and application questions from the notes and reading material.* Several sample questions should be created to help you understand the more difficult questions the teacher may ask.

5. *Compose creative essay questions which the most demanding instructors would ask on exams.* It is helpful to write questions which correspond to the analysis, synthesis, and evaluation levels of Bloom's taxonomy. Write these questions even if you perceive that the teacher will not test on these levels. Doing so will help you get into deep learning habits, and it will also help you learn principles that your memory will retain longer.

SIX UNIT STUDY PLAN

Name _____ Target Content Course _____ Grade Expected _____

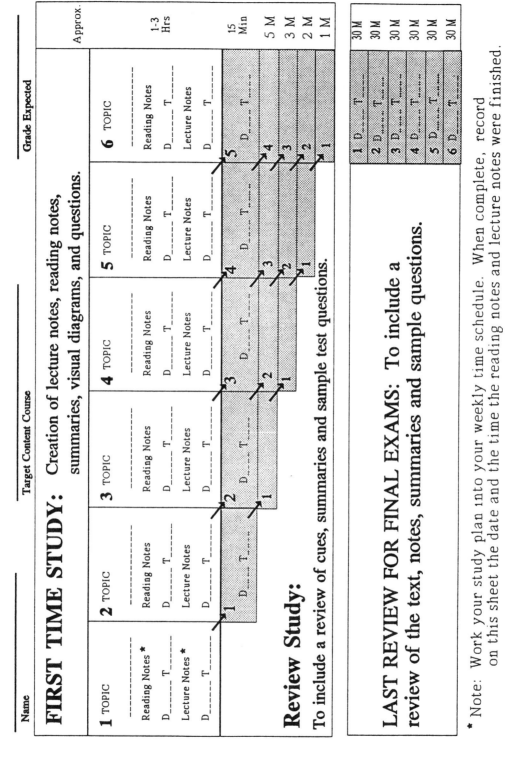

FIRST TIME STUDY: Creation of lecture notes, reading notes, summaries, visual diagrams, and questions.

Review Study:
To include a review of cues, summaries and sample test questions.

LAST REVIEW FOR FINAL EXAMS: To include a review of the text, notes, summaries and sample questions.

* Note: Work your study plan into your weekly time schedule. When complete, record on this sheet the date and the time the reading notes and lecture notes were finished.

Figure 9.3 Six Unit Study Plan.

169

By the end of your first-time study session you should have completed your lecture and textbook notes, a minimum of three knowledge questions, several comprehension/application questions, and at least one of the advanced-type questions. This is a model for excellent preparation; there are many ways to reduce this preparation, but they all lead to reduced readiness.

The second principle that guides the study plan is that review study is cumulative. The study plan includes important activities for review study. These activities take place after each FTS session, as indicated in Figure 9.3.

REVIEW STUDY

1. *Review the lecture notes, and reading materials you covered in the previous study sessions.* As shown in Figure 9.3, this is cumulative study that needs less and less time. Note how after study session two you review the materials from session one, after session three you review the materials from sessions one and two. By the time you finish six sessions the review may only take a minute or two. You may also think you know it so well that it is no longer necessary. Note: This is just the time when it will become fixed in your mind and clear for the test.

2. *Pay particular attention, during these reviews, to the lecture note summaries (Cornell) and the reading note (SQ3R) summaries.* Many times a student will wait until just before tests to do these reviews. Generally, the student who waits to do the reviews is re-learning most of the material and when the test comes will be less prepared.

3. *Answer the questions you prepared in your first-time study.* After a week you will have memorized the answers. Consequently, you will need very little time to study in the days just before an exam.

The key to a successful study plan is to continue studying in a cumulative fashion. You will note as you look at the plan in Figure 9.3 that it can be used as a two-week study plan for a class that meets three times per week. If your class meets two times a week, it becomes a three-week plan. Start over with a new study plan sheet every two weeks (or three weeks) until the exam comes, then plan some time for test review, as shown on the bottom of Figure 9.3.

Following the last midterm exam, you should bring back all your accumulated study materials and review everything. This complete review is done assuming that the final exam will be comprehensive in nature and will cover the last segment of the course. (Check that out with your instructor.)

Additional *must do principles* not shown in the study plan should be taken into consideration.

1. ***Extra credit is an opportunity, DO IT!*** Realize that there is no such thing as "extra-credit" in a college course. Your job is to learn as well as get a good grade. "Extra-credit will enhance both."

2. ***Arrange your projects and papers to come due at your convenience, not your instructor's.*** The only way to do that safely is to move your deadline ahead of your instructor's, unless the deadline happens to suit your own schedule well. Term papers should be done in advance so that you have time to prepare for final exams.

3. ***Take the time to determine what is most important to study for each test.*** You have many resources to help you identify key materials. Always ask your instructor, lab assistants, and classmates what they think is important to learn and remember for the exams. Anything legitimately learned can be legitimately used.

Strategies for the Master Test Taker

It is important to understand that there is no substitute for effective study. However, having an effective strategy can help when you actually take the test. The last part of this chapter includes a series of suggestions that have been used successfully by college students for the better part of this century. You would do well to pay close attention to these proven techniques.

General Guidelines for All Tests

1. *Arrive early and take a moment to relax and reduce your anxiety.* This brief time period will boost your confidence and give you time to think positive thoughts and focus your mind.

2. *Listen attentively to last minute instructions given by the instructor.* The teacher will almost always give you some valuable information just before handing out the test. Don't miss them because your anxiety causes you to talk to a classmate.

3. *Read the directions very carefully, looking for specific instructions on how to proceed.* Watch for details. You may find that more than one answer may be possible on multiple choice or that you only need to answer three out of the five essay questions given.

4. *Plan how you will use the time for the test.* Estimate how many minutes you will need to finish each test section and finish in the total time allotted. Bring your watch and pay close attention to the passing time. Follow your own pace and do not let the pace of others cause you to become nervous. Be confident in your plan for completing the test on time.

5. *Determine which test sections will receive priority.* It is generally best to do the section that is easiest for you especially if it has a high point total. It is not a good idea to do the most difficult section first. Often, a student following this method will not leave enough time for questions that would have been sure points. Leaving essay and sentence completion questions for last can often be beneficial because you find answers among the already completed objective questions. However, if essays are left for last, be sure to leave enough time to outline your thoughts, and then write the answer clearly.

6. *Keep a steady pace and do not let more difficult questions affect your attitude and steal your valuable time.* Students often cloud their minds by lingering over difficult questions. Moving on and finding success with other questions is a better method. If you are not penalized for wrong answers, guess and move on.

7. *Rely on your knowledge and don't watch for patterns.* Noticing that the last four answers are "c" is not a good reason to change an answer. One cannot be sure that the teacher varied the answers. It is better to trust knowledge to help you answer the questions.

172

8. *Change answers only when you are certain.* The answer which comes to mind first is often correct. Reviewing with an anxious mind and changing answers when you are not certain can do more harm than good.

9. *When you have completed your test, use the remaining time effectively.* Review the difficult questions you left. Proofread your essays. Check your grammar and spelling. Make sure you answered all questions. More that one student has turned in a test and received only 50% because there were questions on the back side of the paper.

10. *Learn from your tests!* When tests are returned, go through them thoroughly and see if your plan worked. Look at each section to identify your fault patterns. Do not be a defeatist. Consider every test a practice session. Do you need to pay more attention to multiple choice facts? Talk with the teachers regarding essay questions and find out how to describe your ideas, provide examples or be more clear. Test taking is an art, one which needs refinement. One can not refine the art without practice and serious thought.

Guidelines for Answering True-false Questions

1. *There is no substitute for the truth.* Many concentrated hours of study to force facts into your memory is the best way to prepare true-false questions. Teachers, however, often try to test your memory of the material by slightly altering it. In this case, practice and some test-taking skill will help.

2. *When you do not know or can't remember information to determine the truth of a statement, assume that it is true.* There are generally more true questions on true-false exams than false questions because instructors tend to emphasize true questions. If there is specific detail in the statement, it may also tend to be true. For example, the statement "There are 980 endangered species worldwide" has specific detail and is likely to be true.

3. *Carefully read each question, looking for any factor that will make it false.* It is easier for the instructor to add a false part to an otherwise true statement. Students often read the question and see some truth and assume that the entire statement is true.

4. *Look for extreme modifiers that tend to make the question false.* Extreme modifiers, such as always, all, never, or only make it more likely that the question is false. A more complete list of extreme modifiers follows.

all	none	best	absolutely
always	never	worst	absolutely not
only	nobody	everybody	certainly
invariably	no one	everyone	certainly not

5. *Identify qualifiers that tend to make the question true.* Qualifiers (seldom, often, many) make the question more likely true. A more complete list of often used qualifiers follows.

usually	frequently	often	sometimes
some	seldom	many	much
probably	a majority	apt to	most
might	a few	may	unlikely

6. *Watch out for negative words and how they may affect the truth.* Statements containing negative words may be true or false but **you** must see them to make that determination. The prefixes (un-, im-, miss-) will alter the meaning of the statement. Double negatives make the statement true. For example "not uncommon" actually means common. Don't let this language dilemma cause you to make a mistake.

7. *Questions that state a reason tend to be false.* Words in the statement that cause justification or reason (since, because, when, if) tend to make the statement false because they bring in a reason that is incorrect or incomplete.

1. ***Read each question with the intention of answering the question without the alternatives which follow.*** Focus on finding an answer without the help of the alternatives. This will increase your concentration and help you read the question more clearly.

2. ***Use the process of elimination when you do not know the answer for sure.*** Eliminate two alternatives quickly and then make the decision between the two remaining. This increases your probability to 50/50. Another helpful method of elimination is to use the true-false methods described in the previous set of guidelines. When you can determine a likely false alternative, eliminate it. The true-false elimination method is particularly helpful when more that one answer is possibly true.

3. ***When numbers are in each alternative, choose the numbers that are in the middle range, not the extremes.*** For example, if the height of Cascade Mountain is requested, eliminate 20,000 feet, and 3,000 feet. Then choose between 8,000 feet and 11,000 feet. Remember, the best results are obtained when you have studied and know the exact answer is 11,000 feet.

4. ***Choose answers that are longer and more descriptive.*** These answers stand out from the others. Instructors will often give you descriptive detail to help you identify the truth.

5. ***When two very similar answers appear, it is likely that one of them is the correct choice.*** Test makers often disguise the correct option by giving another option that looks very much like the correct one.

6. ***Watch out for negative words in the instructions or in the main question.*** You may have been told to select an option that is **not true**. Remember to reverse your procedure and eliminate truth, not falsehood. When looking for negative options look for extreme modifiers that make them false (always, never, all, etc.)

Guidelines for Answering Matching Questions

1. ***Examine both lists to determine the types of items and their relationships.*** The test maker uses many terms or a large number of facts on a matching type test to discover if you have mastered a subject. There are usually two lists that need to be matched. Take a look at both lists to get a feel for the relationships and build your confidence.

2. ***Use one list as a starting point and go through the second list to find a match.*** This process organizes your thinking. It will also speed your answers because you become familiar with the second list and will be able to go straight to a match that you saw when looking through the lists a previous time.

3. ***Move through the entire list before selecting. a match.*** If you make a match with the first likely answer, you may make an error, because an answer later in the list may be more correct.

4. ***Cross off items on the second list when your are certain that you have a match.*** This seems simplistic, but it helps you feel confident and stay organized.

5. ***Do not guess until all absolute matches have been made.*** If you guess early in the process, you will likely eliminate an answer that could be used correctly for a later choice.

Guidelines for Answering Sentence Completion or Fill-in-the-blank Questions

1. ***Read the question with the intent to give an answer and make the sentence grammatically correct.*** In this process it is important to focus on how the sentence is written. For example, if the blank is preceded by the article "an," you know the word that goes in the blank must start with a vowel.

176

2. *Concentrate on the number of blanks in the sentence and the length of the space.* The test maker is giving you clues to the answer by adding spaces and making them longer.

3. *Provide a descriptive answer when you can not think of the exact word or words.* The instructor will often give you credit or partial credit when you demonstrate that you have studied the material and can give a credible answer, even when you have not given the exact words.

Guidelines for Essay Questions

1. *Read each essay question with the intent to identify the verbs or words that give you direction.* These are the verbs that describe the task you are expected to complete. Circle the direction verbs in the question to make sure that you are focusing on the desired task. Sample direction verbs or adjectives, and their generally intended action or task, are listed below.

Direction *verbs* that ask you to *review an idea or concept* in your own words:

   summarize, survey, discuss, explain

Direction *verbs* that ask for a *set of items or ideas* that were presented in lecture or reading. These action words generally require more precise wording of items by giving numbers or steps:

   trace, outline, list, diagram, solve

Direction *verbs* that ask you to *speak in favor* of a concept or give the reasons why it should be accepted as valid:

   defend, argue, debate, contend, justify

Direction *verbs* that ask for a *specific meaning* or picture of a concept:

   define, clarify, describe, depict, illustrate

Direction *verbs* that ask you to show *differences* in several ideas or situations:

   contrast, compare, distinguish, differentiate,

Direction *adjectives* that ask for *specific information* the instructor considers important:

   significant, critical, key, important, major,
   principal, essential, vital

2.   *Write your answer clearly, so the reader will be able to decode your writing and understand your ideas.* Without clearly written words your chances of a good grade are severely diminished. Write or print clearly, using a dark-colored erasable ball point pen. Avoid crossing out words or sentences, and don't smudge your paper.

3.   *Organize your thoughts before you begin to write.* A short outline on a separate piece of paper will improve your thinking. There is usually a main idea or issue, several supporting issues and examples to illustrate the issues.

4.   *Use the principles of good English composition when answering all types of essay questions.* Form a clear thesis statement (statement of purpose) and place it as near to the beginning as possible. Provide supporting issues to back up the main concept you present. Underline or highlight the main and supporting issues. Examples will improve your answers and set them apart from other students' answers. Remember to save some space for a brief but adequate summary.

5.   *Paraphrase the original question to form your introductory statement.* This benefits you in two ways. First, it helps you get the question straight in your mind. Second, it may protect you from the teacher. If you have re-phrased the question, the teacher can see how you understood the question. Perhaps you understood it to mean something other than the teacher intended. If so, the teacher may give you credit for seeing another perspective.

A Final Note on Testing

The first part of this chapter described testing in terms of the levels of learning that the instructors may be approaching. Occasionally there are students who could earn high grades in high school, but in college become totally frustrated. Usually the problem was traced to the ability to memorize and repeat without the ability to comprehend, apply, or analyze the information. In college, your instructors should generally demand more than comprehension. If you study to prepare for exams as outlined in this chapter, you will begin to move to deep approaches.

178

Hopefully, an understanding of the higher levels of learning or cognitive development will help you improve your performance in those courses and with those instructors who are testing your advanced learning skills.

The second part of this chapter gives you a sample study plan to prepare for tests. The concept of first-time study and review study is presented. Your test preparation is vastly improved when you use the accumulative nature of study in your study plans.

Finally, test taking is a skill: some would say it is an art. Some students come by the skills naturally, but most of us need practice. As you take tests, pay particular attention to the skills and strategies presented at the end of this chapter, and you will see the principles become increasingly valuable to you.

Learning Applications

1. Set up a *two-week study plan* using the skills you have learned in chapters six through nine. Use the following steps to organize your plan. (Copies of the study plan are in the suppliment section in the rear of this text).

   a. Select a *target content course* to use for your study plan. This course should be a course that requires class notes and textbook reading. The study plan will pertain to this course for two weeks.

   b. Prepare a *detailed* weekly schedule for three weeks. *Remember to include your goals and itemized priorities for each week.* The plan should also include the time you scheduled and the details for the use of the time. Include all fixed events and flexible activities. The blocks of study time for your target content course should be highlighted.

   c. Take detailed class notes using the Cornell Notetaking System, as discussed in Chapter seven. All three major parts should be included: (1) recorded ideas or concepts, (2) key words or phrases in a column on the left, (3) a summary of main ideas.

d. Read the text and prepare notes from the reading as discussed in Chapter eight. The notes should include the text material covered in the two-week period.

e. Include a diagram or map of class or text notes for at least three lectures or chapters that were studied.

f. Submit a study plan to your instructor which includes first-time study for each class period, and review study for previous class periods as explained in Chapter nine. The project should include an illustration of your two-week study plan. Your time schedule, class notes, reading notes, and study questions will demonstrate how effectively you followed your study plan.

2. For one of your concurrent courses, analyze each test item from the most recent test on the basis of Bloom's taxonomy. How many questions fit each of the six objectives?

3. Develop a practice exam for a concurrent course in which you write 50 percent knowledge questions, 20 percent comprehension questions, 20 percent application questions, and 10 percent analysis, synthesis or evaluation questions. Label what objective each question fits. Answer the questions.

4. Develop a practice exam based on Chapters 6, 7, 8, and 9 of this textbook. Write 100 questions, dividing the question types up in the same proportions as in application exercise 3 above. Answer the questions.

5. Analyze an examination in one of your concurrent courses on the basis of your level of success. What test preparation principles were followed well and what principles were too much ignored? For the next exam, what will you change? How and why?

References

Bloom, B. S. et al. (eds.) Taxonomy of Educational Objectives: The Classification of Educational Goals, Handbook 1, Cognitive Domain. New York: David McKay Company, Inc., 1956.

Fox, F. W. and Pope, C. L. America Heritage: An Interdisciplinary Approach, 3rd edition. Dubuque, IA: Kendall/Hunt Publishing Co., 1986.

Wallace, R. A., King, J. L., and Sanders, G. P. Biosphere: The Realm of Life. Glenview, IL: Scott, Foresman and Co., 1984.

Chapter 10

Thinking Your Way Through College

Where does the college student begin the process of serious thinking? How can you systematically organize the ideas of scholars? Is critical thinking simply being negative to all ideas and playing "devil's advocate" in the classroom? How can you develop Socratic questioning skills?

desire
⬇
give place for planting
⬇
good seed
⬇
cultivate
⬇
growth
⬇
nourishment
⬇
root
⬇
fruit

There is a story of a young boy and his early experiences in school. At the age of five he began kindergarten. The boy was excited about his new experience. As his first day of class began, the class quickly embarked on its first exercise in learning. They were to draw a picture using the paper and crayons that were handed out. The little boy's mind filled with the possibilities of what he might be able to put down on the paper to show the others. He thought of airplanes, fire engines, and cars. He saw his house and all the toys he could draw. Breaking his thoughts, the teacher gave instructions: they were to draw a flower with one long green stem, two green leaves, and a red bud at the top with five petals and a small yellow spot in the middle. It was to be a certain size and the only thing on the paper. The boy didn't understand why everyone had to draw the same picture, but he set about doing as he was told because the teacher knew best.

A year passed and the little boy's family moved away to a new city and a new school. He missed his friends, but as on his first day of kindergarten, he was excited and enthusiastic about the new experiences he would have. The young boy went into class and after some brief introductions the teacher and the class started a learning experience. Paper and crayons were handed out and the class was instructed to draw a picture. The boy sat silently awaiting instructions until the teacher walked over and told him to draw anything in the world his mind could imagine. He quickly began to draw and produced a single flower, with a long green stem with two leaves attached. At the top of the stem was a bud with five petals and a small yellow spot in the middle.

Adapted from *Flowers Are Red,* A song by Harry Chapin, 1988.

The Learning Process

The learning process is one in which the mind can either be freed and taught to think in terms of the many possibilities, or it can be limited until nothing new will be produced in the thinking process. At that point the learner might only see what others have taught him or her to see.

Thinking is a natural act. Children and adults who have never been to school think everyday. Within each person is a natural ability to be curious and to think about experiences. In your childhood you were curious about everything; you were a poet and a philosopher exploring life. In American society, it seems, that children are taught while growing up to be content to imitate their elders. As young adults, students often become content to have the same thought patterns, opinions, and behavior as the authorities around them.

Dr. Thomas G. Plummer (1990), a professor of Germanic and Slavic languages, articulated his thoughts on thinking in an address to college students entitled "Diagnosing and Treating the Ophelia Syndrome."

In Hamlet, Act 1, Scene 3, Laertes warns his sister, Ophelia, to avoid falling in love with Hamlet, whose advances, he claims, are prompted by fleeing, youthful lust. He cautions her against Hamlet's "unmastered importunity" and counsels her that "best safety lies in fear." Then her father, Polonius, begins to meddle. He knows, he tells Ophelia, that she has

desire
truth
informal/ formal education
cultivate
deep learning
application
blessings

184

life long learning [& service]

responded to Hamlet's attention and then informs her that she "does not understand (herself) so clearly." He asks if she believes Hamlet's affections are genuine, to which Ophelia responds, "I do not know, my lord, what I should think." Polonius answers "I'll teach you. Think yourself a baby..." In this scene Shakespeare has given us the essence of what I call the "Ophelia Syndrome." It requires two players: a Polonius and an Ophelia. It is condensed into these two lines: "I do not know, my lord, what I should think," and "I'll teach you. Think yourself a baby." Ophelia does not know what to think, and Polonius, reducing her to the stature of a baby, presumes to tell her. Polonius pontificates. He purports to know the answers when he has none. He claims to have truth when he himself has obscured it. He feigns expertise by virtue of his authority.

Dr. Plummer's intuitive and insightful analogy on thinking illustrates how students can suffer from "The Ophelia Syndrome" and have been conditioned to do so throughout their lives. In the earliest stages of education students like the little boy or girl in the kindergarten class are taught what to think. Like Ophelia, you can give up your stature as independent thinker to assume the role of a child, waiting to be told how to think. What effect has education and culture had on you? Do you express your opinions to others you accept as authorities?

A Discussion of Critical Thinking

Thinking is a process that needs to be cultivated and developed. It is often biased, distorted, partial, uninformed, and prejudiced. Without interventions to help you develop the process, your thinking can become dependent and naive. *The quality of life, the excellence of government, and the productivity of the corporation depends on the thinking skill students learn and develop in schools.*

In his extensive writings on critical thinking, Richard Paul (1992) gives a thorough explanation of critical thinking and the need for it in our schools. The following discussion of critical thinking and the reasoning process is adapted from Paul's publications and from materials presented in workshops of the "Foundation for Critical Thinking" founded by Dr. Paul.

Critical thinking is a process wherein the thinker uses an organized structure to examine his or her own reasoning and the reasoning of others. This procedure uses key elements, inherent in the reasoning process, to probe into information intended to convince people that certain facts, data, or thoughts have a specific meaning or intention.

Critical thinking is not intended to be negative where anything and everything is questioned. It is a process that seeks to question material that might be taken for granted or quickly rejected. Critical thinking can lead the thinker to agreement with as well as the rejection of ideas. The process can lead into a systematic analysis and foster new creative dimensions.

The Elements of Reason

Thinking that is to be purposeful or productive needs structure to become effective. *The eight elements in a well developed reasoning process are illustrated in figure 10.1. The upper four areas of the circular model help the thinker analyze the basic components (elements) which the reasoner or presenter is using as a foundation for the reasoning. The lower four elements in the model guide the thinker to examine the information or proof being used to justify the direction the presenter wants the thinker to follow.* When concentrating on these elements, students move into more complex ways of thinking.

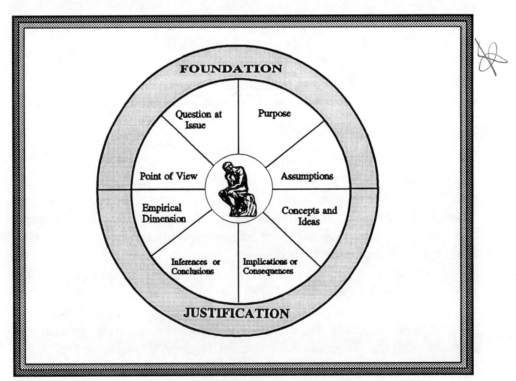

Figure 10.1 The Elements of Reason (Adapted from Paul, 1992).

186

Critical thinking should consciously involve the following elements of reason.

---

*(1)   **Purpose, goal or end in view**: Reasoning is used to achieve an end, to satisfy some desire, or fulfill some need. If the goal is unclear, unrealistic, or confusing, the reasoning used to achieve it will be cloudy and obscure.*

*(2)   **Question at issue (or problem to be solved)**: Reasoning always has at least one question at issue, at least one problem to be solved, or there would be no need to begin. A clear description to the issue or question is at the core of the reasoning process.*

*(3)   **Point of view or frame of reference**: Reasoning must originate from some point of view or frame of reference. Any defect in the point of view or frame of reference is a possible source of problems in reasoning. The point of view may be too narrow or too parochial, may be based on false or misleading analogies or metaphors, may not be precise enough, may contain contradictions, or in other ways be defective.*

*(4)   **The empirical dimension of reasoning**: Any defect in the experiences, data, evidence, or raw material upon which the reasoning is based is a possible source of problems. One must actively decide which of a myriad of possible experiences, data, or evidence will be used.*

*(5)   **The conceptual dimension of reasoning**: All reasoning uses some ideas or concepts as a foundation. Any defect in the concepts or ideas (including the theories, principles, axioms, or rules) will lead to difficulties.*

*(6)   **Assumptions— the starting points of reasoning**: All reasoning must begin somewhere, must take some things for granted. A reasoner or presenter always takes something for granted, even if it is that someone will listen. Thinking is based on assumptions that are at the origin of one's thoughts.*

*(7)   **Inferences**: Reasoning proceeds by steps called inferences. One says that since "B" follows "A," there are similar situations which are also true. "Because this is so, that also is so (or probably so)." Any defect in the inferences made while reasoning may lead to false conclusions. Information, data, and situations do not determine what one shall deduce from them; reasoners create inferences through the concepts and assumptions which are brought to the situation.*

*(8)   **Implications and consequences—where the reasoning leads**: All reasoning begins somewhere and proceeds somewhere else. No reasoning is static. Reasoning is a sequence of inferences that begin somewhere and lead to an end. All reasoning has implications or consequences beyond those the reasoner has considered.*

Adapted from <u>The Elements of Reason</u>, published by The Foundation for Critical Thinking (Paul, 1992).

Application of The Elements of Reason

Figure 10.2 is a worksheet which you can use to organize your critical thinking. For example, if a student were assigned to think critically about a beer advertisement, he or she might begin by reasoning in this manner. Recognizing that the *purpose* of the advertiser is to sell a product, the student may reason that the advertiser may be more interested in selling a product than in the health or well-being of the customer. The student continues on to look at the *issues* being presented and observes that the advertiser wants the listener to focus on the need for youthful pleasures or entertaining activities, without considering questions or issues about the behavior being illustrated. Eventually a critical thinking student will come to recognize a not so subtle *inference* that beer or a certain brand of beer is a catalyst that brings beautiful people and fun into life and that without the catalyst (beer) life will be dull. Is it true that beer must be present for the activity to be fun? Was the reasoning complete? Further thinking might bring the student to understand that no *consequences* for adopting this product or behavior have been presented. Are there other *points of view*? Was factual *evidence* presented? Is the sponsor *assuming* that children, teenagers, and adults will all be fairly influenced by this reasoning?

The Elements of Reasoning Worksheet

The objective for which reasoning has taken place.

The reasoning started somewhere and took something for granted.

The theories, axioms, principles, or rules used while reasoning.

The place or end to which the reasoning leads.

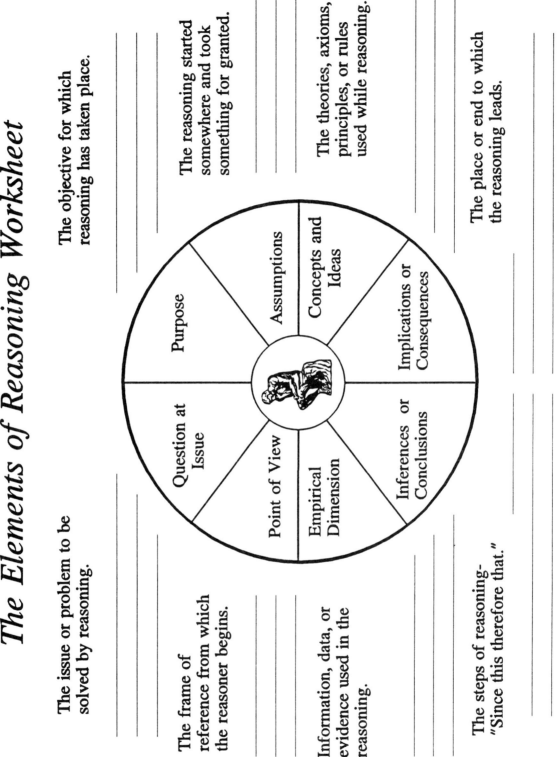

The issue or problem to be solved by reasoning.

The frame of reference from which the reasoner begins.

Information, data, or evidence used in the reasoning.

The steps of reasoning- "Since this therefore that."

Figure 10.2   The Elements of Reasoning Worksheet (Adapted from Paul, 1992).

189

Intellectual Standards

When using the elements of reasoning and developing thoughts, it is important to have a way to measure the quality of thinking. In every domain or mode of thinking (mathematics, biology, physics, humanities, history, etc.), there are unique differences. At the same time, the elements of reasoning apply to each domain. The elements of reasoning become a universal language of thought that allow students to transform various modes of thinking into a value-centered core of knowledge.

Teachers and students alike should have patterns to follow when they are assessing their own thoughts or the thoughts of others. When reviewing a person's ability to compare and evaluate issues, the teacher or student should judge whether he or she has made the evaluations in a *relevant* and *consistent* way. Moreover, the thinking and logic should have paid attention to *accuracy*, *fairness*, and *completeness*.

When describing each point of view, idea or concept there should be a degree of *precision* appropriate to the topic. To assist in assessing the quality of thinking, a set of standards has been developed. It matters not what subject has been studied or what conclusions have been reached. The standards help by giving a way to ask if the thinking has been thorough or objective. A universal group of intellectual standards is shown in Table 10.2 . You may want to go through the standards and evaluate your last term paper. Try using the standards in some subjects as diverse as history, physics, or drama.

190

Intellectual Standards That Apply to Thinking in Every Subject	
Clear	Unclear
Precise	Imprecise
Specific	Vague
Accurate	Inaccurate
Relevant	Irrelevant
Plausible	Implausible
Consistent	Inconsistent
Logical	Illogical
Deep	Superficial
Broad	Narrow
Complete	Incomplete
Significant	Trivial
Adequate	Inadequate
Fair	Biased

Table 10.2 Intellectual Standards (Adapted from Paul, 1992).

Using standards (Figure 10.2) each student should examine the elements that have been used to defend a position. A worksheet is provided in Figure 10.3 to facilitate this process. To demonstrate depth of thinking, you should move from point to point in the worksheet taking time to carefully review the information and opinions presented in each of the elements. For example, to judge your skill at recognizing the *frame of reference*, you would want to judge whether you could see *relevant* alternatives and identify *accurate* evidence to support a frame of reference. You would look closely to see if the answer was *deep* rather than *superficial*, *clear* rather than *vague*,

191

and *fair* rather than *biased*. Intellectual standards can be applied to many modes of thinking, such as politics, science, literature, poetry, and everyday living.

Critical thinking can be fostered by applying intellectual standards in a process (see Figure 10.3). Standards are more useful to students if they are made explicit by teachers. If students see standards used in classroom interaction and use them in required exercises, they begin to refine their thinking while taking tests. Students begin to use a full range of ideas, and self-imposed standards become common place. For example, when assigning a paper, teachers would remind students of the need for a well defined, clearly written *purpose*. Students would instinctively know that they would need three or four main *significant issues* to explain. In the search for information students would strive to find *empirical evidence* that is *accurate and relevant*. When the student developed the paper he or she would search for *conclusions* that were *logical and fair*.

Wouldn't it be surprising to see this type of learning spread beyond the classroom into the political arena. Imagine a political candidate realizing that his or her constituents will evaluate the campaign using critical thinking elements and holding the candidate to intellectual standards. If candidates were required to present other *points of view* for every issue or illustrate their proposals with *empirical evidence* rather than slogans, wouldn't elections become refreshing. Imagine television commentators asking candidates to be *consistent, relevant, complete or fair* in their presentations. What if the public demanded intellectual standards and the media responded by insisting that all candidates comply.

Teachers and students alike should develop patterns (Figure 10.3) to follow when they assess their own thoughts or the thoughts of others. When reviewing a person's ability to compare and evaluate issues, a student should make a judgement as to whether the information received is *relevant* and *consistent*, with attention to *accuracy, fairness*, and *completeness*. When describing each point of view, idea or concept, there should be a degree of *precision* appropriate to the topic.

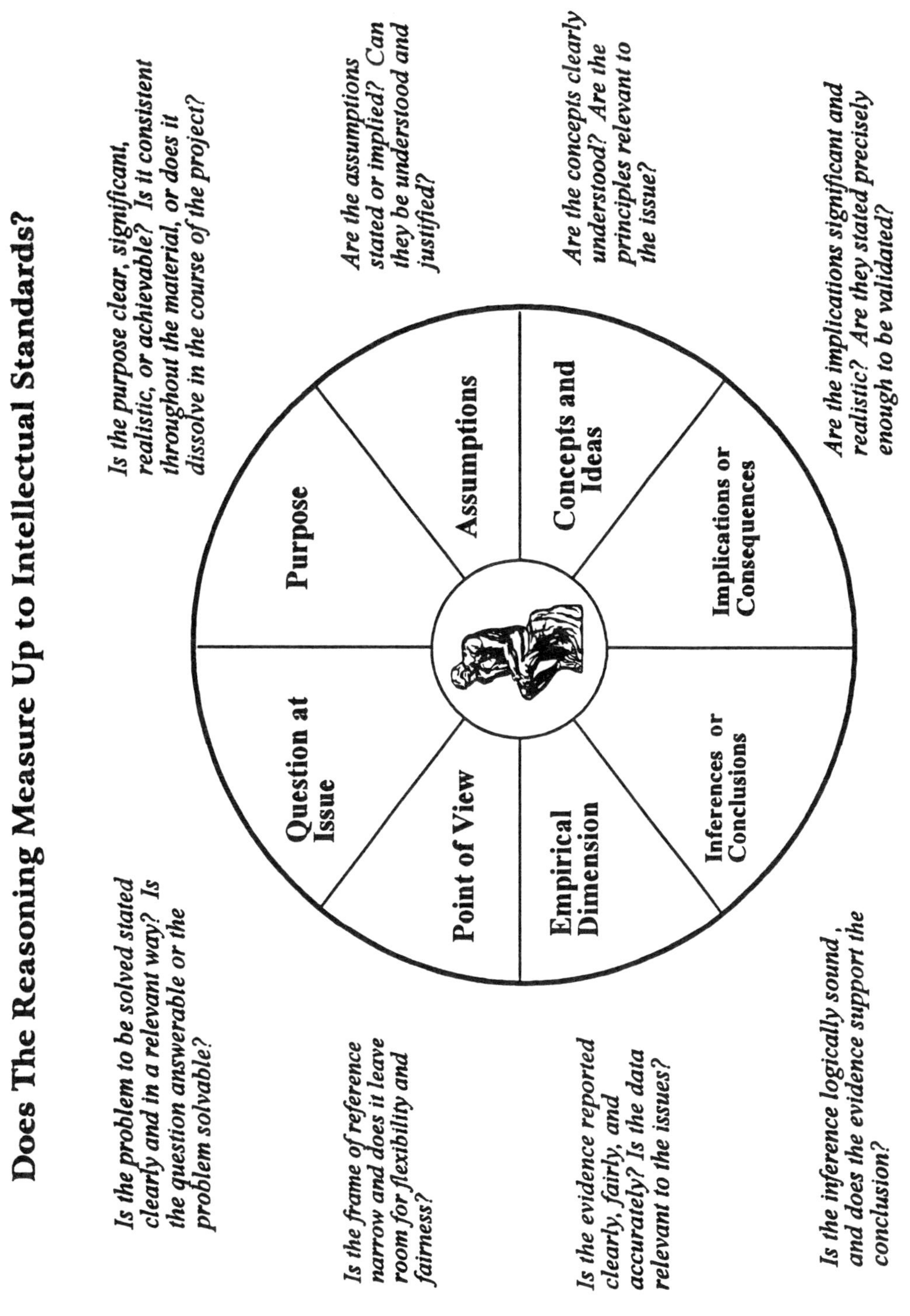

Does The Reasoning Measure Up to Intellectual Standards?

Is the purpose clear, significant, realistic, or achievable? Is it consistent throughout the material, or does it dissolve in the course of the project?

Are the assumptions stated or implied? Can they be understood and justified?

Are the concepts clearly understood? Are the principles relevant to the issue?

Are the implications significant and realistic? Are they stated precisely enough to be validated?

Purpose

Assumptions

Concepts and Ideas

Implications or Consequences

Question at Issue

Point of View

Empirical Dimension

Inferences or Conclusions

Is the problem to be solved stated clearly and in a relevant way? Is the question answerable or the problem solvable?

Is the frame of reference narrow and does it leave room for flexibility and fairness?

Is the evidence reported clearly, fairly, and accurately? Is the data relevant to the issues?

Is the inference logically sound, and does the evidence support the conclusion?

Figure 10.3 Intellectual Standards (Adapted from Paul, 1992).

193

Summary of The Elements of Reason

To summarize the discussion of the elements of reason, it should be noted that *when you use the elements of reason and intellectual standards, you can move into higher-order thinking.* The process begins by getting a deeper understanding of college material while using the elements of reason. You will then make significant discoveries as you challenge the quality of your own thinking and the thinking of your instructors. The discoveries start when you find that there is at least one goal in every developed thought, which may only be to get you to see things from the presenters point of view. There is always at least one question involved—it needs to be understood. There is always a point of view to be recognized. All thinking is done from some base of information or data. What is it? Is it simply random observation or a more credible source? Are some fundamental concepts being used or taught? Most reasoning and thinking rely on some basic assumptions which lead to logical inferences. After all is said and done, you have to ask yourself, what is at stake here? What is implicated here, and what are the consequences of this reasoning?

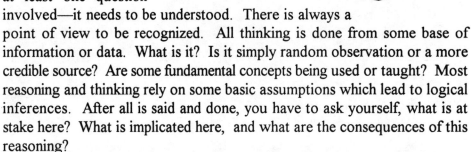

From here intellectual standards will govern the evaluation of your thinking. As you look at the elements you will automatically want to know, for example, if the concept's purpose has been clearly stated, if the empirical evidence is relevant and accurate, etc. The standards are used as a structured method to ensure that you are evaluating information at a significantly high measure of quality.

If students are to cultivate the process of critical thinking, and do it well, intellectual virtues need to be integrated into their daily lives. These virtues, illustrated in figure 10.4, are basic traits of mind and character essential for appropriate action and thinking. *Virtues are what distinguish the narrow-minded, self-serving critical thinker from the open-minded, truth-seeking critical thinker.* Without these traits, a student trained effectively in reason may be inclined to be arrogant, manipulative, or unwilling to use information that he or she has analyzed in a fair way.

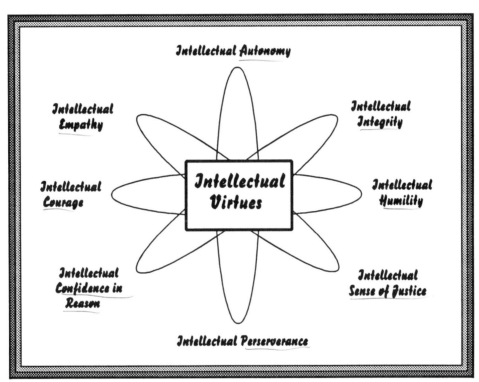

Figure 10.4 Intellectual Virtues (Adapted from Paul, 1992).

Virtues cannot be imposed on students through lectures or reading; they can be cultivated only by living examples and encouragement. Because the traits are interdependent, they need to be approached as a whole and not developed in a step-by-step fashion. Often times, in order to put into practice any one of the traits, it will be necessary to do so simultaneously with some of the others.

***Students can come to deeply understand and accept the importance
of virtues by analyzing their experiences with them.*** For example, a student
may seek facts from an unfamiliar source and discover that his or her thinking
is incomplete. Also, the student may have an essay returned that has been
shown to have an unclear purpose, or a conclusion was not significantly
realistic. If the student has learned an appreciation of virtue it will be easier
to generate the humility to accept criticism, or the courage to try again.

Reflecting back to Chapter two and Perry's model of Intellectual and
Ethical Development, can you see how seeking virtue would help students
move out of dualism and into the higher stages of relativism. Perry said he
saw few students at the upper levels. How would the study of intellectual
virtue increase the percentage of college students at the higher levels of
Perry's model? Could it be that experience with life and virtue bring higher
levels of maturity in the phases of life following college?

A description of the virtues you can seek follows:

---

*Intellectual Autonomy: Having rational control of one's beliefs, values, and
inferences. The ideal of critical thinking is to learn to think for oneself and
to gain command over one's thought processes.*

*(Intellectual) Confidence in Reason: A conviction that humankind at large
will best be served by encouraging people to come to their own conclusions
by developing their own rational faculties. Confidence in reason is developed
through experiences in which reason is used to solve problems and develop
the skills of persuasion.*

*Intellectual Courage: To be fair and aggressive in assessing ideas, beliefs,
or viewpoints when one has not been given a serious hearing. Intellectual
courage comes into play when one has been treated unfairly. It is necessary
because truth can be found in some ideas one considers dangerous and
absurd. Ideas long held to be true may also be discovered to be untrue.*

*Intellectual Empathy: Understanding the need to put oneself in the place
of others to genuinely understand them. This trait requires that you
remember occasions when you were wrong, despite an intense conviction that
you were right. It is that trait which requires the reasoner to look at other
points of view to have compassion and sensitivity.*

*Intellectual Humility: An awareness of the limits of one's knowledge and the
recognition that no one should claim more than he or she knows. This trait
makes it possible for one to know that one's native beliefs may be self-
deceptive. It does not imply spinelessness or submissiveness but is evidence
of a strong inner spirit that prevents arrogance and conceit.*

196

Intellectual Integrity: Recognition of the need to be consistent in the intellectual standards one applies and to hold oneself to the same rigorous standards of evidence to which one holds others. This trait leads one to practice what one advocates for others, and to honestly admit discrepancies and inconsistencies in one's own thoughts and actions.

Intellectual Perseverance: A willingness to pursue intellectual insights and truths despite difficulties, obstacles, and frustrations. This includes a firm adherence to rational principles despite irrational opposition of others.

Intellectual Sense of Justice: A conscious effort to entertain all viewpoints fairly and to weigh all viewpoints with the same intellectual standard. This trait makes it possible to make judgments without reference to one's own feelings, vested interests, or the interests of one's friends, community, or nation.

Adapted from virtues published by The Foundation for Critical Thinking.

Paul, Critical Thinking, 1992 pp. 651-653.

Socratic Questioning

Probably one of the easiest ways to achieve a skill-based learning environment such as the one described above is to avoid traditional learning and seek out the atmosphere in which both the teacher and the student participate in the learning process. The format of dialogue and questioning goes back to Socrates and the writings of Plato. The environment is one in which the teacher probes the students by asking questions to get them to participate and offer up their thoughts on any given subject. *The principal concept of Socratic questioning is that probing by the teacher will stimulate responses that lead to a dialogue in which teacher and student can practice using the "elements of reason" and cultivate "intellectual virtues."*

This type of thinking and questioning is based on the idea that all thinking is founded on some type of logic. The format requires the teacher to become an example of all the aforementioned traits by thinking and wondering out loud while using the elements of reason. The students in turn develop the patterns of thinking they have seen the teacher exhibit.

197

This approach requires students to try on other beliefs and probe their own thoughts and opinions until a good understanding is reached. The idea is to go from the *unclear and vague* to the *clear and precise* understanding of the concepts being shared. For teachers, the main idea of a Socratic method is to avoid telling students the way things are and what they should think.

The questioning process should stimulate freedom of thought. Used effectively, this method of instruction will lead you to a self-correcting process. In each of your classes, you should be willing to correct yourself through questions, answers, and feedback.

The idea of the Socratic spirit is not entirely unfamiliar. Socratic questioning is a dialogue you engage in informally without conscious recognition. The average person engages in Socratic questioning while sitting around the lunch table with friends, or around the dinner table with family. It usually begins with a single question or statement, followed by a series questions that involve the group in discussions related to a broad topic. Most often, because people are not aware of what is actually occurring, they don't attempt to move to any disciplined form of dialogue or standard similar to the "elements of reason." Consequently, the informal thinking that goes on is generally limited to narrow data and personal observations.

In the classroom, the instructor should function as a role model by asking an initial question and then asking the students to pose additional questions. Are you prepared to challenge your college professors? There are six questioning areas which help you engage in topics and move in the desired direction of critical thinking.

SOCRATIC QUESTIONING

QUESTIONS OF CLARIFICATION

What do you mean by____?

What is your main point?

Could you give me an example?

Could you put that another way?

How does this relate to our discussion?

QUESTIONS THAT LOOK AT ASSUMPTIONS

What are you assuming here?

What is Tom assuming here?

If I understand you correctly, you are assuming_____?

You seem to be assuming_____. How do you justify that stance?

QUESTIONS THAT PROBE REASON AND EVIDENCE

How do you know?

What would be an example?

Could you explain your reasons to us?

What led you to that belief?

QUESTIONS ABOUT VIEWPOINT OR PERSPECTIVE

You seem to be approaching this from ____perspective?

Can/did anyone see it another way?

What is an alternative approach?

How would other types of people or groups respond?

QUESTIONS THAT PROBE IMPLICATIONS
AND CONSEQUENCES

What are you implying by that?

What effect would that have?

If this and this are the case, then what else must also be true?

What is an alternative?

QUESTIONS ABOUT THE QUESTIONS

Is this the same issue as_____?

Is the question clear?

Can we break the question down at all?

Adapted from Richard Paul (1992), Critical Thinking , pp. **367-368**

By using these questions and engaging in meaningful dialogue, you can see how to work through the various elements of thought. Probing questions in study groups and class discussions can help you make logical thinking a naturally stimulating process. You and your fellow students will find it natural to modify positions as you progress through your discussions. The end result should be a much clearer understanding of the original issues. Moreover, the use of Socratic discipline helps you move into much broader and deeper subject matter. The discussion group actually uses the process to stimulate and entertain themselves far beyond the traditional lecture, which simply disperses information.

An example of Socratic discussions is called a *fishbowl*. In the fishbowl members of the class surround a small discussion group that has been given a relevant topic to openly discuss. The class is expected to reflect on what they would say if they were part of the group—how they could improve the interrelationships and transactions that occur. The teacher would be there mainly as a mediator or guide if the discussion starts to lose its intensity and direction. Another example of Socratic discussion is when the class breaks into small groups to discuss a topic and form conclusions. The groups then appoint a spokesperson to pass the conclusion on to the instructor and the other groups.

It is imperative that you determine how you will prepare yourself to use Socratic methodology. Practicing the Socratic questions previously given will help you learn to form effective questions and probe topics at a deeper level. The techniques listed below will also give you additional Socratic skills to use in discussion groups.

* *Listen carefully to what is said.*

* *Take seriously what is said.*

* *Look for understanding and clarification.*

* *Look for evidence and reason involved.*

* *Seek examples, analogies, metaphors, etc.*

* *Distinguish knowledge from beliefs.*

* *Take the other person's point of view for a moment.*

* *Maintain a healthy sense of skepticism.*

* *Be willing to look deeper; play devil's advocate.*

Adapted from Richard Paul, Critical Thinking, 1992, p. 370.

Examples of Socratic Questioning

Children provide us with a microcosm of most theories. In this case it is helpful to see how children naturally use Socratic methods. The following is a spontaneous dialogue that takes place between two nine-year-old children that demonstrates the mind's ability to reason in terms of issues at an early age.

Jane:	Isn't that great music!
Sue:	Yeah, I like rock music. It sounds neat. Listen to that country song.
Jane:	I hate country music!
Sue:	Why?
Jane:	My sister plays it all the time, and I'm sick of it.
Sue:	I kind of like it. My dad plays it in the car. His music must be different.
Jane:	Must be. Come on, let's go play computer games.
Sue:	I'm tired of computer games.
Jane:	Don't you like them any more?
Sue:	Yes, but I spent too much time doing it yesterday.
Jane:	What shall we do now?

Sue agrees that rock music is great, but she reasons that country music is not so great because her sister plays it a lot. Jane reasons that country is good because her dad likes it. Note how the Socratic questions follow a statement of opinion. Can you find them in the dialogue? The questions are naturally more curious than accusative. Can you see how this helps the two youngsters sort out the issues? Another natural conversation by children might be as follows:

Tom:	I saw a neat show on television today.
Jim:	About what?
Tom:	About people blowing things up and fighting.
Jim:	So what?

Tom: They were showing all these neat things like spears and guns.

Jim: Yeah, so what?

Tom: Well, if I could throw spears like that it would be great.

Jim: You want to hurt people?

Tom: No, I just want to throw spears.

While the conversation seems elementary, there are profound elements of thinking. Who is being Socratic? What could parents learn from these conversations? In both of these conversations, two willing participants hear each other quite well and question each other's assertions. The following actual high school classroom discussion (Paul, 1992) is a little more advanced.

Teacher: This is a course in biology. What kind of subject is that? What do you know about biology already? Kathleen, what do you know about it?

Kathleen: It's a science.

Teacher: And what's a science?

Kathleen: Me? A science is very exact. They do experiments and measure things.

Teacher: What other sciences are there besides biology? Marissa, could you name some?

Marissa: Sure, there's chemistry and physics.

Teacher: What else?

Blake: There's botany and math.

Teacher: Math...Math is a little different from the others, isn't it? How is it different from the others? Blake, what would you say?

Blake: You don't do experiments in math.

Teacher: And why not?

Blake: I guess because numbers are different.

> Teacher: Yes, studying numbers and other mathematical things is different from studying chemicals or laws in the physical world or living things and so forth. You might ask your math teacher about why numbers are different or do some reading about that, but let's focus our attention here on what are called the life sciences. Why are biology and botany called life sciences?
>
> Peter: Because they both study living things.
>
> Teacher: How are they different, Jennifer?
>
> Jennifer: I don't know.
>
> Teacher: Well let's all look it up and read together.
>
> Jennifer: It says. . . .

This dialogue is an example of how the teacher can assist students in a Socratic discussion. In this case the discussion leads the class right into the course material so that they are active participants and partners with the teacher in the learning process. This allows the class to be self-correcting and at the same time allows the instructor to control the direction and quality of the discussion.

As you learn to think and participate in this type of discussion you will learn at a faster rate with a minimal amount of guidance from instructors. You will want to watch for opportunities in the classroom to use Socratic questions and participate with your teacher and fellow students. Remember the deep and surface approaches to learning that were covered in Chapter three? Socratic questioning is a technique to help you develop a deep approach to each classroom situation. Can you see how personal meaning can be developed through questions? The relationships between you, your teachers, and your classmates will be strengthened by thoughtful but probing questions.

In your college experience you should find teachers who do not give you the answers. Rather than spoon feed you, teachers will become involved in the kind of discussion that goes past the mundane and routine to a stage which requires more complex thinking. Hopefully, instead of using rote memorization, you will become actively involved in the course material and become Socratic in your approach to the teacher and other students.

Summary

Learning to think critically is a natural process that can be enhanced by using a disciplined organized approach. When you begin to look at subjects in light of *the eight elements of reason,* the depth and breadth of the subject is naturally expanded. Imposing *intellectual standards* helps you, in the learning process, see the necessity of being clear, relevant, complete, etc. Instructors will use intellectual standards in measuring the progress of students, and to become more specific in the assignments given. *Intellectual virtue* is extremely important to help you develop critical thinking skills. Without virtue, a trained critical thinker can become manipulative and cruel to those with less intellectual discipline. Finally, the tools of *Socratic questioning* come into the process. The questioning process helps the instructor probe deeper into subject matter, and helps you, as the student, expand the issues being presented.

The thinking of every student and the progress of the school system would be helped with the use of the tools included in this chapter. The success of all organizations—from families to huge corporations—is enhanced when people think more deeply.

Learning Applications

1. Analyze a recent college subject that was presented to you in class, using the elements of reason. (Copies are in the supplement section at the rear of the text.)

2. Examine a recent essay which you have written in light of the elements of reason. Intellectual standards could be a part of this process: see if your purpose was clear, if your issues were relevant, and if your data was accurate, etc.

3. Write your next college paper using the elements of thinking while you outline the material to address in the paper.

4. Using the elements of reason, look at a classical piece of poetry and search for deeper meaning.

5. Teach your classmates in a study group how to use Socratic questioning. Then attend one of your classes and use Socratic questions to expand the discussion or challenge the instructor.

6. Critically examine one of the readings in the last section of this text. Use the elements of reason and the standards to take a long, hard look at the information presented. Return to class and give a presentation based on your thinking about one of the essays.

References

Chapin, Harry. "Flowers Are Red," Gold Medal Collection (Album), 1988.

Paul, Richard. Critical Thinking: What Every Person Needs To Survive in a Rapidly Changing World. Sonoma, California: The Foundation For Critical Thinking, 1992.

Paul, Richard, and Alec Fisher, and Gerald Nosich. "Workshop on Critical Thinking Strategies," Sonoma, California: The Foundation for Critical Thinking, 1993.

Plummer, Thomas G. "Diagnosing and Treating the Ophelia Syndrome," Delta Phi Alpha Faculty Lecture, the German Honor Society, Brigham Young University, Provo, Utah. April, 1990.

"Conference on Critical Thinking and Educational Reform," Sonoma State University: Center for Critical Thinking and Moral Critique (Proceedings, August, 1992)

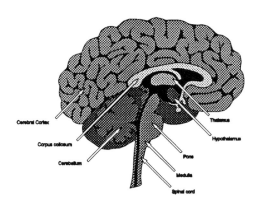

Chapter 11

Making Your Learning Stick

How is learning related to your memory? Are there methods you can use that will improve your ability to remember facts? Can you reduce the amount of time it takes to study and retain information? Is there a way to store information in your memory for a longer time?

All of the specific techniques suggested in this text are practical applications of accepted psychological principles of memory and learning. But these are not the only available applications. As an effective learner, you will probably develop applications of your own. You may also adopt good study skills gleaned from other sources. The learning methods you ultimately choose will depend largely on factors of personal preference—your cognitive and ethical development or your personal preferred learning style. Your learning approach will go deep or stay on the surface, depending on how you view the world of learning and how you interpret your place in it.

In this chapter you will review psychological principles of memory and see how effective study skills are devised to apply psychological principles of memory. You will also consider a very simple theory of development that shows how learning development can best occur. ***The purpose of all this is to help you summarize your selection of skills and techniques to get the most out of your learning approach and to make information stick.***

Involvement Theory

The theory you are asked to look at here, postulated by Alexander Astin (1984, 1985), is most often referred to as "involvement theory." Basically Astin's theory is common-sense psychology: students learn by becoming involved. Upcraft (1989) has summarized Astin's ideas into five basic postulates:

INVOLVEMENT THEORY

1. Involvement refers to the investment of physical energy in various "objects." The objects may be highly generalized (the student experience) or highly specific (preparing for a chemistry examination).

2. Regardless of its object, involvement occurs along a continuum. Different students manifest different degrees of involvement in a given object, and the same student manifests different degrees of involvement in different objects at different times.

3. Involvement has both quantitative and qualitative features. The extent of a student's involvement in, say, academic work can be measured quantitatively (how many hours the student spends studying) and qualitatively (does the student review and comprehend reading assignments, or does the student simply stare at the textbook and daydream?)

4. The amount of student learning and personal development associated with any educational program is directly proportional to the quality and quantity of student involvement in that program.

5. The effectiveness of any educational policy or practice is directly related to the capacity of that policy or practice to increase student involvement.

[handwritten margin notes:]
Physical Involvement
Continuum
qualitative & quantitative features
quality & quantity
capacity of policy or practice

208

A question now naturally arises, "What is the best way to practice academic involvement and get the information I study to stick in my brain?" This question will be answered by reviewing the psychology of memory, and discovering the relationship between study skills and improved memory.

The Psychology of Memory

As you applied ideas and techniques from earlier chapters, you may have wondered such things as "Why must I wait until after I read to record notes or to underline key phrases?" Or "Why should I bother to reorganize lecture notes within twenty-four hours of a lecture?" You may have thought it a bit too much to use the SQ3R or REAP formula to read textbooks, or to worry about visual notetaking or marking your reading material. After all, those techniques take precious time, and you are already loaded with too much to do. Just when you became the busiest, you were told to do more as you study. Yet all these practices are good advice; a study of memory will give you the reasons why.

While much of the concept of memory is accepted only as a theory, memory is believed to function at two distinct levels: short-term memory (STM) and long-term memory (LTM). Each level has specific characteristics that must be exploited to ensure memory of the important ideas or skills that become parts of new learning.

Short-term Memory

For the purpose of our study here, the fact that memory is preceded by sensory registration and outside stimulation will be accepted as fundamental. More simply stated, you must see or hear or smell or taste or feel something before you can remember it. While you don't generally smell or taste your subjects in college, the study skills you learn are, to a great extent, methods to increase the sensory stimulation.

Short-term memory is a temporary storage facility for the stimuli recorded by the sensory system. Stimuli, once caught by one of the senses, are either immediately dropped from recognition because they are deemed unimportant, or they are passed on to STM. This usually occurs in a fraction of a second.

The first limitation of STM is its inability to hold memories without frequent rehearsals. Actually, this limitation is probably fortunate, because minds would become hopelessly cluttered if everything that entered short-term memory stayed there. Can you imagine the strain if all pleasant and unpleasant smells remained vivid in one's memory?

The second limitation of short-term memory is its inability to hold large numbers of separate stimuli in memory at the same time. Research by Miller (1956), and later by Broadbent (1975), suggests that a total of six or seven distinct items can be briefly held in STM. This limitation is like a long bench with no arm rests at either end. It will seat exactly seven occupants. Once filled, it will hold no more; if an eighth person crowds in at one end, the unfortunate occupant at the other end gets squeezed off. Likewise, the least rehearsed bit of information in short-term memory gets crowded out of memory when the STM gets overloaded.

With its two major limitations, STM must serve a limited function in the human memory system. Klatzky's (1975) analogy of the use of short-term memory is helpful because it illustrates at once the limitations and the usefulness of short-term memory. STM is seen as a workbench on which a carpenter is building a cabinet. In the workroom are shelves and storage spaces for many tools. On the workbench are only those tools currently being used. The workbench has limited capacity for storage, but it does accommodate immediate work needs without cluttering the work space or hampering the job. Once the workbench is loaded, the carpenter must put the least needed tool away (or push it on the floor) in order to select an additional tool from the storage shelves. The short-term memory (workbench) serves immediate needs well, while the long-term memory (storage shelves) must be relied upon for expanded activity. The only thing wrong with the analogy is that disuse of the carpenter's immediate tools on the workbench would not cause decay (rusting, etc.) nearly as rapidly as disuse of the items in STM. Without long-term memory, the learner or user must constantly use what is there or rapidly lose it.

210

The long-term memory makes it possible for humans to store vast amounts of what mankind has discovered and recorded. The LTM is a vast storehouse, complex in nature, remarkable in capacity. Daily life is enhanced by the use of LTM. Many simple things, like the streets in our neighborhood and more complex concepts, like mathematics come back automatically.

While very little about LTM can be stated as absolute fact, psychologists have postulated a number of useful notions that have held up after much theoretical consideration and numerous practical studies. Some of the more important ideas are below.

CHARACTERISTICS OF
LONG-TERM MEMORY

1. *Information can be entered into LTM by the use of sound (auditory), sight (visual), or semantics (meaning).*

2. *Information coded into LTM must come through the STM first.*

3. *LTM is arranged (encoded) in a precise retrievable order rather than in haphazard disarray. Retrievability is affected by the circumstances of encoding and the associations made at the time.*

4. *LTM seems to be made up of two classes of memory: (a) semantic memory—all meaningful associations and concepts; and (b) episodic-memory—all sequentially associated memories (time-sequence related).*

5. *LTM is essentially permanent. It remains in storage waiting for retrieval.*

6. *LTM is almost unlimited in capacity. It is hypothesized that humans use a very small percentage of the brain's memory capacity.*

[Handwritten margin notes:]
- Entered by sound, sight or semantics
- Comes thru STM 1st
- Arranged in order
- 1. semantic 2. episodic
- Permanent
- Unlimited

The Processes of Memory and
Related Study and Learning Techniques

To this point, our consideration of human memory has emphasized the structure of memory: (1) sensory registration (a condition prior to memory), (2) the nature of STM, and (3) the nature of LTM. How these three structures function is the consideration of memory processes; it serves to show why the many specific study skills work. One such process, rehearsal, has already been mentioned. Rehearsal needs further explanation, however, and other processes need to be added to the list.

Rehearsal: The Most Important Memory Process

Practically speaking, rehearsal is exactly what is implied in the nontechnical sense: practicing what is sensed (seen, heard, etc.) over and over again until it is more easily remembered. Technically speaking, rehearsal runs information through the memory cycle. The first major result of rehearsal is to hold information in STM. The second major result is more significant, transferring information from STM to LTM.   The effects of rehearsal are simple: the more effective the rehearsal, the more effective the retrieval from LTM.

Rehearsal is critical to memory, and the study techniques that require rehearsal are key to the successful use of memory. Rehearsal techniques are included in many of the preceding chapters. Notice how the techniques are using rehearsal to enhance memory.

STUDY SKILLS AND REHEARSAL

SQ3R or REAP (Reading Study). To complete the SQ3R scheme for reading a textbook, the reader rehearses the chapter multiple times: the student (1) surveys the ideas, (2) turns headings into questions, (3) reads, (4) recites a section at a time, and (5) reviews the complete chapter. In the REAP reading scheme, the reader rehearses the chapter in a slightly different way: the student (1) reads, (2) encodes, (3) makes notes, and (4) thinks about meanings.

212

> *TQLR (Listening).* The listener rehearses the lecture mentally by (1) tuning in, (2) periodically questioning, (3) listening, and (4) frequently reviewing. In addition, if the listener keeps notes, a fifth rehearsal takes place in the form of notetaking, and a sixth rehearsal takes place when the listener revises and organizes the notes.
>
> *Study Plans and Test Preparation.* If one sets up an effective study plan and review schedule, the frequent rehearsals strengthen the memory. When a student consolidates all notes the last few days before a test, writes a sample exam, and answers it, rehearsal again strengthens memory.
>
> *Last-Minute Preparations.* Yes, cramming is rehearsal, but as the sole rehearsal effort it usually is unsuccessful because it fails to move information from STM to LTM. But cramming as a final rehearsal, following prior spaced rehearsals, sharpens the retrieval process as well as places the information into long-term memory.

A Final Rehearsal on Rehearsal

The entire study process—from reading and listening to taking exams—includes constant rehearsal. The psychological term for this memory process is *rehearsal*; the study skills term is *review*. This technique moves STM items to LTM if sufficient rehearsal is done over sufficient time. Remember, information in STM is subject to crowding out and almost instant loss. Experiments on memory, for example, show that sheer rote rehearsal maintains information in STM, but often fails to move information to LTM. *Rehearsal, properly used, is the most important principle of memory as memory relates to study and learning.*

Mediation: A Process That Links STM and LTM

A more focused form of memory processing, called *mediation,* is an enhancement to rehearsal. *Mediation is a process wherein the learner successfully transfers information from STM to LTM as a result of various strategies the learner uses during rehearsal to change, relate, elaborate, and understand the information being rehearsed.* Again, the process is an application of Astin's involvement theory. Mediation is almost always a part of the rehearsal process. *During mediation, two important phenomena occur: (1) the learner draws on the LTM to decide how to rehearse, and (2) the information in STM is matched with related information in LTM.* The quality of the rehearsal strategy and the mix of the new and old information (the involvement) have a lot to do with the rapidity of transfer from STM to LTM and with the strength of the addition to the memory bank.

During rehearsal, mediation of some kind takes place either consciously or unconsciously. *Study techniques generally are devised to increase the learner's conscious efforts to mediate new learning as efficiently as possible.* Any of the techniques studied so far could be used as examples of forcing mediation, but only two are selected in the following illustration.

STUDY SKILLS AND MEDIATION

The Cornell notetaking system. You will recall, that the Cornell system requires a routine of taking raw notes first, followed by an early revision of the notes, a narrow column of cue notes, and a summary. The raw notes, taken in class, are well spaced, with one idea per line These notes are revised and completed after the class. After having revised the notes, the student places topics in a two-and-a-half-inch side column. Meaningful summaries are completed at the end of each section. *Note how the Cornell system rehearses and mediates the information by mixing the new information with cues that are short, simple, and related to (old) language already stored in LTM.* Moreover, the summaries organize material so that it can be more easily categorized for storage and retrieval from LTM. The Cornell strategies and mix of new and old words are a well planned mediation scheme.

Critical Thinking. Recall next the framework used in Chapter 10 to organize information so that it can enhance critical thinking. When applying the model, the student initially uses the *elements of reason* to organize the material. *As the new material is organized into an old framework (purpose, questions at issue, points of view, etc.), mediation begins.* The subject matter is categorized and prepared for LTM through the organization process. The mediation experience is enhanced by creating a relationship of new information to (old) elements. The same process occurs when intellectual virtues are explored and the student must test the new information against established (old) virtues. Forced intermingling of material in both short- and long-term memory brings involvement, rehearsal, and mediation into play. Finally, an evaluation experience takes place as the student learns to question issues and topics through the use of Socratic techniques. The entire critical thinking process enhances the learner's memory through rehearsal and mediation.

214

Only the Cornell notetaking and critical thinking techniques are treated here. You might, as an exercise, however, satisfy yourself that SQ3R, TQLR, and all other formulated techniques ensure systematic, conscious mediation during the rehearsal process. The writers constantly have encouraged what they term active thinking—active use of mental processes—as the key to effective study. Psychologists speak of the processes of rehearsal and mediation as being required in both renewal of STM and transfer to LTM. Astin calls the process *developmental involvement*. Activity, work and involvement in this context are all the same thing.

Chunking: A Method to Simplify Memorizing

A third process involved with the structure of memory is called *chunking*. In this process no more than six items (chunk) become the focus of rehearsal. This chunk can then be more effectively sent on to the LTM. Handling more than six items without chunking is not only difficult but extremely frustrating.   For example, memorize the following six letters: b—q—f—a—x—l. As presented, they go almost to the STM limit.

Here is a longer group of letters to test your ability to memorize: d—o—g—j—o—b—m—a—n—r—u—n—c—a—t—c—a—n. There are eighteen letters, too many to remember in a series. Note: If you chunk them into smaller groups, it is easy: dog—job—man—run—cat—can. You had these letter sequences in long-term memory and pulled them into short-term memory to help you remember the eighteen letters, which are now, for you, six words. By chunking, related ideas can be grouped for working purposes. Chunking is usually the principle by which experts in a field seem always to have vast quantities of information on the tip of the tongue.

Chunking is a mediating process that enables learners to expand their working capacity. Mnemonics and mnemonic devices are often used to enhance the process of chunking. By attaching a letter or familiar word to a chunk, you have used a *mnemonic*, and made it easier to remember.   For example, the mnemonic device (SQ3R) not only helps you remember (survey, question, read, recite and review), it helps you recall an entire reading-study system within four symbols. Can you describe the system and apply them from the mnemonic cue? Chunking helps you do that.

Forgetting: Why Me?

The last process of memory is forgetting. Forgetting is the opposite of remembering, and the forgetting process is a definite part of the memory system. Technically defined, forgetting is a loss of information from the memory system. It occurs primarily in two forms: (1) passive decay, a simple loss from the system, or (2) interference, a circumstance that squeezes the older information out with newer, competing information. Both types of forgetting occur while information is still in STM. Whether or not forgetting information occurs in LTM is not as clear. *Theoretically, information in LTM is not forgotten. Practically speaking, most people seem to lose data from LTM. The theorists hedge on this issue by claiming that "forgetting" from LTM is really failing to access the information properly. It is a problem of how to retrieve what is there somewhere in the memory bank.* Some interesting experiments using hypnosis and brain probes tend to support the poor-retrieval-mechanism theory of "forgetting" material that is rooted in LTM.

For most students, forgetting happens rapidly, which is support for the assumption that the information never got out of STM.   By the end of twenty-four hours most of what is learned is gone. After that, what is left tends to be quite stable. Now think of the study techniques recommended in this book. How many of them emphasize early review for retention?

Rehearsal, mediation, and chunking are clearly processes that combat forgetting. If you can get information into LTM, you probably have it on deposit for later withdrawal. Hence the phrase *memory bank* is quite appropriate to describe data that has been worked on long enough to transfer it from STM to LTM. And the study skills recommended are the orderly deposit slips, bank books, and withdrawal forms. The study skills processes tend to increase the systematic nature of long-term storage and ensure ready access when information is to be withdrawn from the "bank."

What to Remember About Forgetting

Forgetting, as it relates to LTM, is a lack of easy and orderly access. Remembering, on the other hand, results from careful, systematic learning skills that deposit information in a retrievable order. Again, study skills give a system to the learner that makes the "memory bank" work.

216

Kenneth Higbee, a noted expert on memory, has discussed ten common myths of learning in his book <u>Your Memory: How It Works and How to Improve It</u> (1988). The ten myths of memory follow.

MYTHS ABOUT MEMORY

1. Memory is a thing.
2. There is a secret to a good memory.
3. There is an easy way to memorize.
4. Some people are stuck with bad memories.
5. Some people are blessed with photographic memories.
6. Some people are too old (or young) to improve their memories.
7. Memory, like a muscle, benefits from exercise.
8. A trained memory never forgets.
9. Remembering too much can clutter your mind.
10. People only use ten percent of their memory potential.

For a thorough description of the fallacies of these memory myths, you are referred to Higbee's book. The point to be made here is that a leading national expert on memory viewed these common sayings about memory as neither true nor defensible. Briefly, Higbee's discussion comes down to two basic contentions. *First, memory is not a thing.* Knowing this, one should be actively involved to improve the memorization process. *Second, there is no secret to a good memory.* Understood this way, one can proceed to apply effective memory techniques and improve one's memory.

217

Astin's theory of involvement supports the essence of Higbee's meaning. If memory is active, the involvement will enhance memory, and hence enhance learning. Since involvement varies from individual to individual as well as from task to task, memory and learning will also vary. Applying sound principles of learning will help intensify involvement, which in turn will increase memory and learning.

Some Further Principles of Learning

In this chapter the authors have tried to convince you that learning and memory are synonymous and that memory is strengthened by systematic application of useful study techniques. Taking into consideration the memory system and its processes, certain principles of learning emerge. As you apply study techniques, remember that the mechanical aspects of going through study techniques will never make you a good student. Only when you understand the memory system and its processes—and apply the techniques accordingly—will you learn. It is a true case of "the letter killeth, but the spirit giveth life." The learning principles that follow are additional mediators (to use a memory system term) between the "letter" of the technique and the "spirit" of true learning.

Interest: A Passion for Learning

No matter how intelligent or how slow-witted a student may be, learning can happen if there is interest. Conversely, a student who has a lifeless zeal for a subject will not learn effectively. Without interest, the student will seldom get the information registered in his or her senses. Interest is a form of self-motivation that is illustrated when the student gets involved. Without getting involved one won't even find the memory bank; and making a deposit will be virtually impossible.

Selecting and Rejecting: Helpful Decisions

Since no one can learn everything about everything, you will have to pick and choose what you learn. This is especially true within a course, a lecture, or a textbook. Your constant challenge will be to sift wisely and choose what seems most relevant to your goals. The following suggestions may help, because true education is as much learning what to leave out as what to include.

Principles of Selecting and Rejecting

1. *Select and reject material to study and remember according to criteria you set.*

2. *Realize that the selecting and rejecting process requires active thinking: your personal involvement in your education and the processes of memory.*

3. *In selecting, learn to differentiate main ideas from details, central issues from side issues, and related points from unrelated points. In short, learn to be a critical thinker.*

4. *Read thoroughly and widely as a matter of habit.*

5. *In the typical lecture course, use the clues in the instructors lectures to guide what you want to remember.*

Intent to Remember: A Heart That's in It

If you do not intend to remember something, chances are good that you won't. You won't register it in your senses, or you won't enter it in your short-term memory, or you won't rehearse if it gets there. Have you ever forgotten an appointment? On the other hand, have you ever forgotten a date with your favorite person of the opposite sex? What did intent to remember have to do with either? To learn, you must go through the steps of learning. How often the authors have heard students claim they have not the time to use SQ3R! Did they intend to remember what their texts told them? If you do not intend to remember, you can attend, listen, or read as haphazardly as you wish. And you'll get your wish: you won't remember.

Pay Attention

Relate material

Actively Understanding

+--+
| **The Principles of "Intent to Learn"** |
| |
| 1. Pay close attention to new information so that it registers clearly in |
| your senses. |
| 2. Make sure that what you register is complete by thinking how the |
| material relates to you. |
| 3. Strive actively to understand. (This means you call on related memories |
| in your LTM to mediate the new learning, and place it in a logical |
| pattern for easy storage and retrieval.) |
+--+

Background Memory: Making Connections

To carry out an intent to remember you call on several principles of learning. *The mediation process begins when you call up old memories that might relate to the new learning.* For example, when the authors use the phrase *memory bank*, they expect you to think of a place where money is kept and to understand that memories can be similarly deposited, stored, and withdrawn when needed. Your background with banks helps you understand the memory storage system. (To complete the metaphor, the monetary interest is earned when you draw the stored information out and expand it into a new realm that is greater than the new or the old information alone.)

It is almost impossible to understand new learning without drawing references from old backgrounds. Your study techniques ensure quality comparison of the new information and the old stored memory.

Organization and Meaning: Putting It Your Way

Meaningful information is much easier to remember. A person inflicted with cancer is much more likely to remember a television spot about new cancer cures than a noncancer inflicted person will. Remember chunking, a process by which you organize your new information into meaningful small groups or chunks so that you can handle them in your short-term, working

220

memory. Meaningfulness is increased when you place things in categories and make associations. The transfer from STM to LTM is enhanced by the ways you organize and attach meaning to new data. Repetition of ideas in your own words—a practice of several study techniques—creates this meaningful organization that transfers ideas from STM to LTM. Thus organization and meaning play an important part in the memory process.

Recitation: Studying Out Loud

Recitation is sheer rehearsal, done verbally. Once organization is sought and background memory is recalled, recitation becomes a serious key to memory storage. This point was made earlier when rehearsal was identified as the most important process of memory. If you intend to remember, recite. How much you recite depends on you and what you are learning. But organized, meaningful recitation is a legitimate part of almost all learning.

Distributed Practice: Variety Spices Your Study

Distributed practice is a learning process by which the student distributes the learning applications at well spaced intervals. The work associated with learning can be fatiguing even when learning is pleasant. As time of rehearsing goes on, fatigue and other distractions become more possible. At some point (the point varies for people, tasks, and situations), interest and intent are overpowered by fatigue, boredom, or other concentration factors. At that point rehearsal becomes mechanical, meaningless, and useless. Since learning stops, the study application might as well stop too. It is better to space learning over several shorter sessions of greater efficiency than to try to cram everything into a few massed practice sessions.

Since avoiding fatigue is mentioned here as a reason for distributing practice over several practice sessions, it is important to note that most student fatigue is really boredom. Often a break or a change of approach to the same task will take the edge off the boredom and allow the student to continue some kind of useful study. The distributed-practice principle thus becomes one of the reasons for goal setting and time scheduling that allow for a variety of activities at appropriate times throughout the day.

221

Real mental fatigue seldom happens to students. Students who stay in good physical condition and schedule wisely can push themselves beyond the first signs of so-called fatigue to a sort of "second wind." By this persistence, students can stay at a task and accomplish much learning otherwise thought impossible. The moral is this: Distribute practice judiciously, but do not distribute as a cop-out for not persisting in important tasks.

Roediger and Crowder (1974), in a study of spacing rehearsals of lists in free recall, discovered that often a kind of spontaneous learning increase occurred during a break between rehearsals of lists. For no apparent reason, subjects seemed to improve during the break between rehearsals when no actual practice took place. Psychologists have named this almost mystical memory phenomenon, *consolidation. In this resting or consolidation period, new learning that has been rehearsed during a previous period seems to soak in.* Its meaning and relationships are often not immediately apparent during the active rehearsal, but later—after some ruminating time—the meaning appears spontaneously.

Consolidation is a second reason for distributed practice. The time between rehearsals has a function as well as the rehearsals themselves. Consolidation is the principle underlying the final review in SQ3R. Take note: Consolidation is another reason why cramming is an unproductive practice. Time is required if consolidation is to take place.

Concentration: How to Avoid Distractions

Concentration cannot be pinned down directly as a principle of learning because it represents neither a structure nor a process of memory. Moreover, it is not a product of memory, but rather a by-product of sound learning principles. The nearest statement of principle might be that concentration results from conscientious applications of learning principles to the processes of memory. *Whenever concentration is broken, the learning principles of interest, selection and rejection, and intent to remember are impeded.* The resulting breakdown creates a distraction to study, and learning is inhibited. The distractions can be external or internal, but the break in concentration is real either way.

222

External Distractions

1. A noisy or cluttered study location
2. Inadequate materials for study
3. Improper lighting
4. Loud background music
5. Temperature too hot or too cold
6. Too much or too little to eat
7. Fatigue from too little sleep
8. Illness

Internal Distractions

1. Study goals and activities that don't match
2. Worry about projects or studies (studying one subject but worry about another)
3. Worry about personal problems (home, roommates, finances, etc.)
4. Desire for play over work

If you find yourself troubled with poor concentration, it is doubtful you will have much success with direct attacks to study in spite of the problem. Such remedies do not seem to work. It is better to search for causes of the distraction. Once you think you know your distraction, take care of it. Then get back to work. If you can't take care of it, try to override it by setting a time when you will take care of it and go back to work. Knowing you have scheduled a time to work on your problem should lower anxiety.

Paper and Pencil

Pauk (1984) calls the pencil his secret technique: "Whenever working to learn, always study with a pencil in hand." In high school and college, one of the authors always found himself doing his math assignments first. It wasn't that he liked math that much, but with paper and pencil at hand, he could go directly to work and stay at the task until it was done. It took many years into college before he realized that he could do the same thing for history, psychology, biology, and any other subject. Somehow that paper and pencil focused attention on the task and signaled when the task was done. It enhanced concentration, helped rehearsal, recorded organization, and established a directory for continuing distributed practice. In short, it increased involvement.

You can use your paper and pencil in a similar way. Notetaking is one of the important steps in SQ3R and REAP, in the Cornell system, and in just about all other specific learning techniques. Always keep paper and pencil at hand while studying—and use them.

Learning Applications

1. Develop a system for memorizing Higbee's ten memory myths. Then memorize them. Defend the efficiency of your system.

2. Illustrate the following learning and memorizing phenomena from experience in a class in which you are currently enrolled:
   a. Short-term memory
   b. Long-term memory
   c. Mediation
   d. Chunking
   e. Forgetting

3. Select a memorizing technique from Higbee's <u>Your Memory: How It Works and How to Improve It</u> or another source, and practice it until you are able to demonstrate it to your class or study group.

4. Explain one of the following learning techniques in terms of principles discussed in this chapter:
   a. REAP
   b. TQLR
   c. Cornell Notetaking System

References

Astin, A. W. "Student Involvement: A Developmental Theory for Higher Education." Journal of College Student Personnel, 1984, 25 pp. 297-308.

Astin, A. W. Achieving Educational Excellence: A Critical Assessment of Priorities and Practice in Higher Education. San Francisco: Jossey-Bass, 1985.

Broadbent, D. A. "The Magical Number Seven after 15 Years" in Kennedy, A. and Wilkes A. (eds.), Studies in Long-Term Memory, 1975.

Higbee, K. L. "What Can You Expect From Your Memory? Some Facts and Some Fallacies," Tape #1, Audio Tape Series, Your Memory. Provo, UT: Your Memory Inc., 1979.

Higbee, K. L. Your Memory: How It Works and How to Improve It, 2nd edition. New York: Prentice Hall Press, 1988.

Klatzky, R. L. Human Memory: Structures and Processes. San Francisco: W. H. Freeman and Co., 1975.

Miller, G. A. "The Magical Number Seven Plus or Minus Two: Some Limits on Our Capacity for Processing Information," Psychological Review, 1956, 63, pp. 81-97.

Pauk, W. How to Study in College, 3rd edition. Boston: Houghton Mifflin Co., 1984.

Roediger, H. L. III and Crowder, R. G. "The Spacing of Lists in Free Recall." Journal of Verbal Learning and Verbal Behavior, 1975, 14, pp. 590-602.

Upcraft, M. L. "Understanding Student Development: Insights from Theory." In Upcraft, M. L., and Gardner, J. N. (eds)., The Freshman Year Experience. San Francisco: Jossey-Bass, 1989.

Part Three

Supplemental
Readings
And Worksheets

Reading # 1   **Learning and Teaching**

Concepts developed by Walter Gong. Adapted from unpublished workshops and papers presented to the BYU faculty, Provo, Utah, August 15, 1979.

*As you read about Walter Gong's approach to learning, pay attention to how he ensures learning that goes far beneath the surface. Gong used teaching as a vehicle to learning in a way that can easily be formalized and formula-ized. That, however, was not his purpose, nor should it be yours. Gong's approach also is not **the** way to develop a deep approach, but it is **a** way.*

Walter Gong, a biology professor at San Jose State University, developed his concepts into a fully integrated theory of learning and teaching. His psychological and pedagogical experimentation capped seventeen years of intensive work with programs that enriched learning processes, first in biology, and then in many subjects from a wide variety of academic disciplines. His goal has always been to develop a learning process by which students could assimilate and retain 100 percent of the essential content of the original learning source.

The purpose of this account is to give you an overview of the Gong system. The system is no panacea—it offers no substitute for hard work and deep thinking—but it does offer a way to learn and remember, even to continue to learn beyond the organized pedagogy of classroom and college, which by definition is a deep approach.

Love the Doctrinal Base

The Lord said . . . . *Thou shalt love the Lord thy God with all thy heart, and with all thy soul, and with all thy mind. This is the first and great commandment. And the second is like unto it, Thou shalt love thy neighbour as thyself. On these two commandments hang all the law and the prophets.* (Matthew 22:37-40)

In Christianity this scripture places all human beings in a divinely sanctioned love relationship with all other human beings and with God. It is also the foundation for all other commandments of God and for fulfillment of all other commandments by God's children. It serves as the doctrinal base for learning and teaching, a normal extension of the principle of love. Note who is involved in love as the Lord sees it: love God; love yourself; love others as yourself. That is three persons: God, self, others. Just as perfect love on a three personage basis is essential to eternal salvation, applying the three-person model to learning and teaching is essential to perfect knowledge, which is knowledge at the "eternal salvation" level of understanding.

Before glossing over the above analogy too quickly, take a second look. If your goal is seriously to learn what you can in college and learn how to go on learning beyond, understand and apply the two great commandments to all your learning efforts. That is the doctrinal base, and that is the reason Gong always talks of being a learner/teacher, not just a learner or just a teacher. Note the following change in the three person model: teacher--learner--others. Now place yourself in that model as the learner and apply the love principle.

What happens when you show your teacher respect, courtesy, attention, and obedience borne of love? Based on a genuine love motivation, how much of what the teacher knows can you learn? Do you bless your teacher by showing him or her love? By learning what the teacher teaches, do you bless both the teacher and yourself? This is akin to loving God: it involves loving the teacher and yourself.

Next, go the other way in the three-person model. If you love your neighbor as yourself, what must you do? You must bless your neighbor as you did yourself (and incidentally, as you did your teacher). But to love your neighbor, you shift your role, for when you bless your neighbor with the same thing you were blessed with, you teach him or her what you have learned. Thus in a Christian sense, no one can satisfactorily be a learner alone—he or she must be a learner/teacher, blessing and being blessed mutually in love of God, self, and others—to fulfill the two great commandments. Fulfilling these commandments in a learner/teacher context brings about the learning equivalent of eternal salvation, that is, expanded and expanding knowledge forever. Such learning and teaching are infinitely greater than the selfish hoarding that students do in their frantic attempt to cram everything in during the semester and grind it all out during finals.

Gong (1979) has distilled seven principles in solving what he has termed the "three-person problem," or accepting the scriptural challenge to fulfill the two great commandments. These seven principles, developed in three different academic settings, were finally integrated within a Christian framework during a period of four years as Professor Gong worked with teachers at Ricks College and BYU. The seven principles explain how a learner may learn well and how a teacher may teach well—for both are parts of the same larger process of learning and teaching in a context of love.

230

1. The General Case: The Three-Person Problem

As one solves the problem of learning and teaching as a fulfillment of the two great commandments, one solves the three-person problem. This is the doctrinal base for a learning/teaching system that shifts roles and activities, is lovingly unselfish, and accomplishes learning as (1) conscientious, diligent study and (2) deliberate, outward sharing. The world's store of knowledge is replete with specific cases of such knowledge diffusion, but the general case, the model, grows out of living the two great commandments.

2. The Learner/Teacher Role for Exponential Growth

The shifting role from learner to teacher to learner again is crucial to learning in two respects, one from the standpoint of the learner, and one from the standpoint of the theoretical potential number of learners, once love is the basis for learning and teaching. First, the learner/teacher grows exponentially in two ways: (1) his or her own specific content knowledge is placed in long-term memory context—a context that allows further learning in the future—and (2) his or her own ability to apply the learning/teaching system more and more efficiently expands as he/she has repeated learning experiences using the Gong system. Second, the learner/teacher, in fulfillment of a divine and love-inspired role as teacher (father, mother, brother, sister, fellow student, etc.) touches the lives of an exponentially expanding body of learners. Thus as more and more people learn by teaching, more and more others also learn.

3. The Four Essential Experiences

While working on an educational project for Lockheed Corporation, Gong and his colleagues found that study alone, no matter how conceived, did not provide the integrated command of knowledge that they wanted their learners to have. The learners needed to do more than merely capture information. Gong's solution led to a four-fold experience that each learner was expected to follow to ensure deep learning and long-term memory. *Students were asked (1) to capture the message to be learned (using a format that is the basis for principle number four); (2) to expand on the message from other sources, from personal extended thought, and from attempts to integrate the message into already-known concepts; (3) to teach others the expanded and rethought concepts; and, (4) to evaluate their own growth in learning as a result of the first three experiences.* Gong labeled this process "The Four Essential Experiences."

4. The Four Essential Knowledges

Knowledge comes in many types as well as in many disciplines. Cutting across the disciplines, Gong proposed four knowledge types that were essential to deep understanding of content. *Other knowledge can be usefully rearranged into the "Four Essential Knowledges": (1) purposes, (2) central messages, (3) validations and applications, and (4) values.* The learner attempts to rearrange knowledge to see what purposes the teacher (lecturer, etc.) has in mind in presenting it; what pattern of central messages the teacher gives; what support the teacher uses to validate the central messages and what applications the teacher has that grew out of the messages; and what values the teacher places on the messages' importance or timeliness. The teacher, on the other hand, tries to present the same knowledges for the benefit of the learner. Such a four-fold knowledge organization may seem constricted or constricting, but virtually all learning can be so organized to the benefit of both teacher and learner. Then, too, seeing content arranged in these four knowledge types helps both learner and teacher fulfill their shifting roles, whether in home, church, school, or society.

5. The Journey at a Glance

Gong's "journey at a glance" is a principle for abstracting a summary of content from its component parts and is the essence of a deep approach to learning. The many classes, lectures, topics, and units of a course, lecture series, or program generally are parts of a unified, interrelated content. Just as one solves the general three-person problem for specific lectures or classes, one can abstract to a higher topic or content level to see how everything fits together. The learner may do this abstraction of the four knowledges after several teaching sessions, but the teacher can help the learner very early in the course (lecture series, etc.) by providing a four-fold presentation of the whole course, the "journey at a glance," and help the learner construct a one-page capture sheet of the entire course or series. By thus seeing the "journey at a glance" early, the learner knows relationships from the beginning.

6. Reference Examples

The principle of reference examples is the basis for personal exponential growth of learning. It also is fundamental to deep learning. It may be the principle that supports Gong's own teaching procedure that best teaches his system by multiple, repeated, practical applications rather than by concentrated theoretical study. The principle of reference examples holds that many excellent instances of learning and teaching of the four knowledges will

232

accomplish two things. First, the learning of specific examples of content and concepts provides unifying structures by which new knowledge can be located, hence referenced. Second, the experience of "going through" a Gong learning/teaching cycle becomes a prototype for more learning. During the first few Gong experience cycles the learner/teacher gropes to learn and to fit learning into the system. As more reference examples accumulate, learning and teaching become easier, fuller, and more satisfying. Sufficient reference examples lead to 100 percent capturing ability of essential content. Failure to reach 100 percent capture usually reflects poverty of reference examples and represents difficulty with deep learning.

7. Application to Any Learning/Teaching Situation by Any Procedures

The application principle, according to Gong, simply means that learning/teaching problems may be solved by performing learning and teaching as a solution to the "three-person problem," i.e., by applying the two greatest commandments to the learning/teaching situation. Learning is showing love to a teacher and to oneself. Teaching is showing love to oneself and to one's neighbor. But a learning outcome, or product, is the natural by-product of love in three directions, and is what remains as a personal reward from first blessing at least two others in the three-person problem solution. The ultimate solution to the problem occurs when the number of people blessed from the aggregate of individual solutions increases exponentially.

The application principle allows the authors to dare view the Gong system as an example of a unified deep learning approach capable of integrating the best lecture listening techniques, reading formulas, notetaking procedures, and test review skills into a learning/teaching system that makes the learner a better student in the short run and a better person in the long run. For in the integration of techniques three persons are blessed, but especially the learner/teacher.

The Gong Principles in Practice

Professor Gong melds his seven principles into a teaching practice that emphasizes the four types of knowledge, the four essential experiences, and the shifting learner/teacher role within four broad role categories. The four knowledges that any learner/teacher should master are purposes, central messages, validations/applications, and values. The four experiences that any learner/teacher should undergo are capture, expand, teach/bless, and evaluate.

Finally, the learner/teacher role can function in the home, church, school, or society. (See Figure 1) All of these dimensions serve to accomplish the solution to the three-person problem, a solution that Gong sees as pure application of the two greatest commandments. In this system deep learning occurs; note, however, that such learning in the Gong model is ultimately a by-product of service borne of love. (A sample worksheet to use in implementing this system is on the following page.)

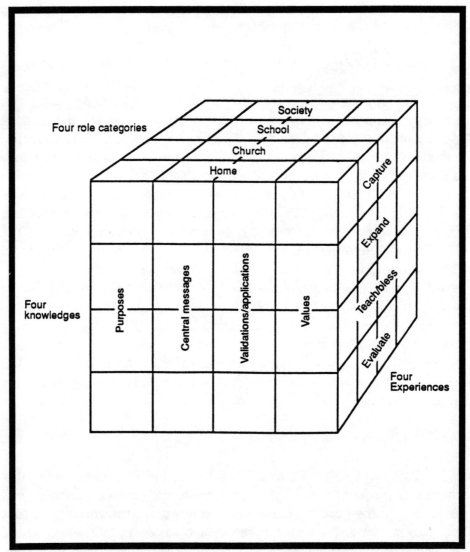

Figure 1 Dimensions of knowledges, experiences and role categories in the Gong learner /teacher method.

234

CAPTURE DOCUMENT

Name of Presenter _____   Name of Listener_____

1.   **PURPOSES:** What were the significant purposes (goals, problems, or questions to be answered.

2.   **CENTRAL MESSAGES:** What were the <u>central messages</u> (main concepts, significant solutions, vital procedures, or issues) presented?

3.   **VALIDATIONS** and **APPLICATIONS:** What were the <u>validations</u> (evidences or arguments) or the <u>applications</u> (uses, examples) given in support of the central messages?

4.   **VALUES:** What were the *values* (priorities, benefits, evaluations) expressed about the above three types of knowledges?

Reading # 2   Brain Dominance Theory

Material adapted from Ned Herrmann, The Creative Brain, Lake Lure, NC: Brain Books, 1988.

The idea of brain dominance, whether a person is more right brained or left brained, has become a popular way of explaining individual differences in thinking styles. Examine your own methods and study habits to see if this theory depicts you.

Ned Herrmann has probably done more than any other person to popularize the right and left brain idea. It was during high school that Herrmann first became aware of his duality of interests, realizing they fell in divergent directions. He greatly enjoyed math and science but was also a natural at singing and acting. In college he continued to pursue these dual interests and eventually graduated in both physics and music. Later, Herrmann got a job that emphasized his science background, but to balance his workload he actively continued his singing career.

His first interest in brain dominance came about quite unintentionally. A devastating illness which left him unable to sing caused him to redirect his artistic ability to painting. Much to Herrmann's surprise, he found he had natural talent for painting and sculpturing as well as for music. With a lot of diligence and hard work he eventually became a professional artist. His newfound creativity got him wondering about the workings of artistic creativity. As president of the Stamford Art Association, Herrmann encouraged a panel discussion to be presented on artistic creativity. In preparing for that discussion he came across various research on brain specialization, the most prominent being that of Dr. Roger Sperry. Herrmann's theory of brain dominance evolved from Dr. Sperry's research in the 1960's on split-brain.

The results of Sperry's work on end-state epileptics who had their corpus callosum (a thick nerve cable that connects the right and left cerebral hemispheres and serves as a pathway for memory and learning between the two hemispheres) surgically severed to help control intractable epileptic seizures revealed some major findings about the operations of the right and left brain hemispheres. Through a series of tasks given the epileptic patients, it was discovered that each hemisphere was specialized in mental activity. From earlier studies of people with damage to one hemisphere, it was already known that the right hemisphere specialized in nonlinguistic processes, while the left hemisphere specialized in language. Sperry's work confirmed these earlier studies: the right hemisphere specialized in spatial tasks, while the left hemisphere specialized in verbal tasks.

Herrmann's interest in Sperry's and others' work on brain specialization eventually molded his theory on how brain function affects individual behavior and preferences in learning. Herrmann wrote:

> *Brain dominance is expressed in terms of how we prefer to learn, understand, and express something. I call these cognitive preference, or preferred modes of knowing. Our preferred mode of knowing is the one we are most likely to use when faced with the need to solve a problem or select a learning experience. A left-brain approach to solving a problem would be fact-based, analytic, and step-by-step, favoring words, numbers, and facts presented in logical sequence. A right-brain strategy, by contrast, would seek out insight, images, concepts, patterns, sounds, and movement, all to be synthesized into an intuitive sense of the whole. So, our preferred mode of knowing correlates strongly with what we prefer to learn and how we prefer to go about learning it. (Herrmann, 1988, p.17)*

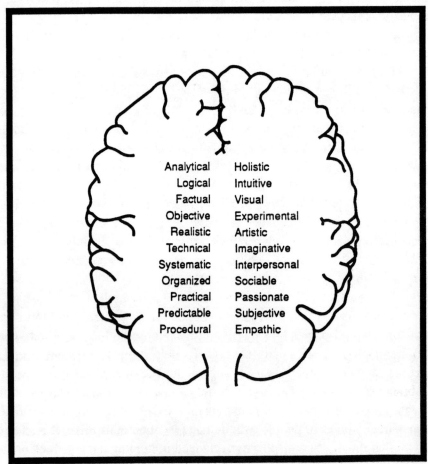

Figure 1 Right-mode and Left-mode Characteristics.

238

According to Herrmann, whether a person is right-brain or left-brain dominant influences mental processes and preferences and affects choices in learning activities, decision-making, and problem-solving. The left hemisphere tends to control mental functions needed for scientific thinking, while the right hemisphere tends to control functions used in what Herrmann termed artistic thinking. Perceptions of our environment and how we specifically deal with our experiences are also shaped by our preferred mode of knowing. Figure 1 lists a more complete description of right-mode and left-mode characteristics. As you look at the lists, ask yourself which set of characteristics best describes your perception of how you learn. You may find you prefer a combination of both, but most likely you will find you have a greater preference for either the left or right mode of knowing.

There has been some criticism of the popular hemisphere-dominant claims of Herrmann's theory. Jerry Levy , a biopsychologist at the University of Chicago, discounted the popular view that a person is either right-brained or left-brained. She had this to say about individual differences and brain function:

> *There is both psychological and physiological evidence that people vary in the relative balance of activation of the two hemispheres. Further, there is a significant correlation between which hemisphere is more active and the relative degree of verbal or spatial skills. But there is no evidence that people are purely ``left brained" or "right brained." Not even those with the most extremely asymmetrical activation between hemispheres think only with the more activated side. Rather, there is a continuum. The left hemisphere is more active in some people, to varying degrees, and verbal functioning is promoted to varying degrees. Similarly, in those with a more active right hemisphere, spatial abilities are favored. While activation patterns and cognitive patterns are correlated, the relationship is very far from perfect. This means that differences in activation of the hemispheres are but one of many factors affecting the way we think.*
>
> *(Levy, J. "Right Brain Left Brain: Fact or Fiction." Psychology Today, May 1984, p.44)*

Refining this thought further, Levy stated that each hemisphere makes a contribution to all cognitive activities. The two hemispheres do not act independently, such that one is involved and the other is not. The brain is designed to function as a whole. People do not have two brains that function independently from each other. Certain characteristics are not confined to a particular hemisphere; creativity and intuition may not be exclusively a property of the right hemisphere, and logic may not be the sole property of the left hemisphere.

239

Herrmann originally viewed his theory of brain dominance as physiologically based. The individual was thought to prefer thinking only with the more activated hemisphere when dealing with his or her environment. When further research on brain specialization concluded that brain function was more complex than Herrmann had supposed, and was not so easily dichotomized, Herrmann abandoned his original model. From a straight-line, left/right continuum model, Herrmann shifted to a metaphoric model, a pictorial representation of the whole thinking brain, emphasizing in one dimension the important selective thinking contributions of the left and right modes and in an additional dimension the cerebral (thinking) and limbic (feeling) qualities of mental functioning. Figure 2 shows the original left-right dimension with the newer cerebral-limbic dimension added to complete the metaphoric model.

The value in what Herrmann is saying is that along one dimension people tend to favor right or left brain activity; these preferences correlate with their learning patterns. Similarly, they favor thinking or feeling activity; these preferences correlate with a second dimension of learning patterns different from right or left brain involvement. Herrmann's theory is a way to describe the two sets of correlations, and for that purpose it gives valuable information in evaluating personal styles of learning. Understanding and evaluating one's strengths and weaknesses in relation to learning style is useful in one's development as an effective and efficient learner.

Herrmann Brain Dominance Instrument

Rather than merely scanning a list of characteristics as you did earlier, a more reliable way of determining your preference for learning in relation to left or right brain dominance along one dimension and cerebral and limbic preference along the other dimension is to take the Herrmann Brain Dominance Instrument (HBDI). The instrument may be available through the assessment center at your college. If it is not available, you may inquire how to go about taking the HBDI by writing Applied Creative Services, Ltd., 2075 Buffalo Creek Road, Lake Lure, NC 28746. You should be aware, though, that taking the HBDI and receiving an interpretation will cost you a fee.

240

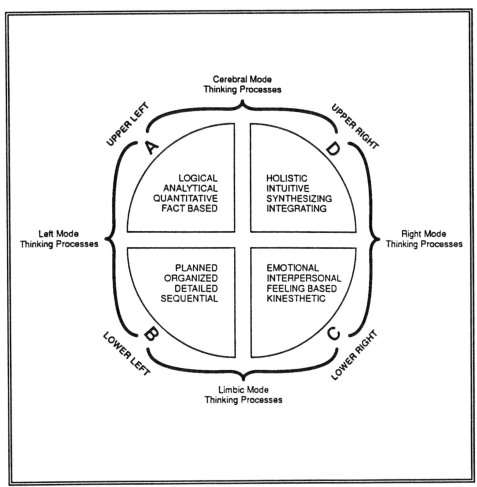

Figure 2 Herrmann's Brain Model. (Taken from Ned Herrmann: The Creative Brain. Copyright 1988.) Reprinted by permission.

The HBDI is intended to measure thinking patterns or the type of mental activity a person prefers to engage in. Results from the HBDI should not be interpreted simplistically or stereotypically. Results do not reflect ability or IQ. The test does not measure level of competence either. Neither are the learning preferences to be judged as right or wrong, good or bad, or any other value-laden connotation. Each learning preference brings its own contributions to living and learning; if you complete the inventory, you should view your learning style pattern as a way of comparing your style with the learning demands placed upon you. Scores are plotted on a profile which, remember, is only a metaphoric representation of the whole brain. The circular model is divided into four quadrants, referred to as modes of knowing. Each quadrant (labeled A,B,C,D) has specific preferences for acquiring and

241

processing information (see figure 2). Individual scores reflect the level of preference of each mental quadrant. A four-digit numerical code is assigned, each quadrant receiving a 1, 2, or 3, indicating whether the quadrant is a preferred, used, or avoided mode of knowing. Plotting the numerical code on the circular model creates a personalized visual metaphor of learning strengths and weaknesses.

Individuals rarely have just one primary or preferred mode in only one of the four quadrants. Most people's profiles will exhibit a multi-dominance, showing preferences in more than one mode of learning. Herrmann (1988, p. 63) found the majority of the participants in one study to have a double dominance; next in frequency were those with a triple dominance; then those with a single dominance; finally, a few showed quadruple dominance, in which each mode of learning was equally preferred. Read the following quadrant descriptions, as explained by Herrmann (1988), with the understanding that most people have more than one mode of operating. Glean from the descriptions the primary influences of each quadrant.

Quadrant A: "thinking" preference. Like Spock, the unemotional, logical Vulcan character on Star Trek, people who prefer this quadrant tend to be fact-oriented and logical. Being analytical thinkers, they are capable of breaking down complex thoughts into parts and seeing how ideas fit together. They tend to be good reasoners and to understand scientific and technical thought. Their choices will tend to be based on reason, not emotion. Decision-making or responding on a "hunch" or impulse would seem "illogical."

Quadrant B: "doing" preference. People who prefer quadrant B tend to be good organizers and thorough planners. They have a knack for arranging things, ideas, people, etc. in an orderly, manageable fashion. The slightest details are paid attention to and remembered. Problems are approached practically. Taking action will tend to be delayed until methods are first formulated. Responding safely to their environment, these people will tend to take few risks. In living and working they may appear restrained or controlled.

Quadrant C: "feeling" preference. People who enjoy interacting interpersonally with others will tend to prefer quadrant C. These individuals can be astutely sensitive to and aware of interpersonal dynamics: they pick up on nonverbal cues, recognize difficulties within a relationship, feel and understand emotional elements and respond accordingly. Others will often gravitate to them because of their empathic, altruistic natures. Their environment will tend to be perceived subjectively, causing their feelings to be easily stirred. Decision-making will most often be based on feeling.

Quadrant D: "seeing" preference. A person who prefers activities in quadrant D could be described as a visual or ``seeing" person. To understand

242

how something works they might first have to "see" it. For instance, when putting together an unassembled desk, they might carefully study the picture of the assembled desk and after "seeing" or visualizing how the desk is supposed to look, attempt to put it together without reading the actual instructions. Quadrant D learners tend to be skillful at understanding how individual parts and pieces fit into the larger whole. These individuals will tend to work well at integrating ideas and concepts and generating new and novel possibilities. Being divergent thinkers, alternative thinking patterns will be explored. They tend to be experimenters and risk-takers.

Having read through the quadrant descriptions, you now have a better understanding of the various learning preferences that influence individual learning style. Are you beginning to get an idea of your own learning preferences and the specific areas you tend to ignore or avoid?

Multi-dominant Learners

Among multi-dominant preferences some will be compatible with each other and some will not. For example, a person who has preferred scores in quadrants B and D (characterized by "safekeeping" and by "risk-taking") would most likely experience what Herrmann termed "pulls and tugs," or internal conflict due to the opposite nature of the quadrant characteristics. The conflict might be manifest by thoughts like "Do I play it safe or do I act impulsively? Would it be best to approach this assignment systematically or divergently? I feel like being spontaneous and creative, but it may be better if I act predictable and practical." The "tension" does not have to be problematic if one is aware of it and understands it. The "pulls and tugs" may even lend themselves to a tolerance of complex learning. However, if the conflict is too stressful, learning could be interfered with. Indecision could result as well. Those with triple or quadruple profiles could also experience the "pulls and tugs" created by diagonal opposites or be so evenly balanced in preferences that indecision or vacillation of performance will be manifest. A person with a double-dominant profile in the same hemisphere, either left or right, would tend not to feel the internal conflict felt by a person with a double dominant opposite profile. Rather, an internal harmony or integration would be felt. Double dominant primary scores in the same hemisphere tend to strengthen that mode of thinking.

243

An individual with a quadruple profile is referred to by Herrmann as "whole-brained," meaning she or he equally prefers all four modes of learning. This type of learner is able to access mental activity in each of the four quadrants. This ability is not a measure of intelligence but rather is a result of preference based on learning experience. Whatever the demands of the learning situation, the "whole-brained" learner is able readily to adapt to the learning requirements. Because "whole-brained" learners are situational in their approach, the term "chameleon" (changing colors to blend into the environment) is often used, explaining well the ability to change learning preferences to suit the learning situation. Internal conflicts as to how to approach a situation are inevitable for the "whole-brained" learner because of the opposite or "pulls and tugs" between opposing preferences. This creates many challenges for the "whole-brain" learner.

Should you aim to become a "whole-brained" learner? As learners, all of us have strengths and weaknesses. Rather than striving to become a "whole-brained" learner, it is important for you to capitalize on your learning strengths as well as to recognize your limitations and improve on them. As you strengthen your limitations you will become more effective in learning and thinking. Learning will be more complete when avoided modes of knowing become preferred, or at least usable. The goal is to increase mental activity in areas that tend to have low preference, though not necessarily to become a "whole brained" learner. This improvement is possible if you learn to adapt to new situations and new learning experiences.

(A sample exercise to help determine your preferences is on the following page.)

Herrmann Thinking Styles Dichotomy Exercise

This is not the Herrmann Brain Dominance Instrument but an alternate non-validated exercise that will give you some insights about the direction of your preferences.

EXAMPLE

A		D
MOST		SOME
LEAST		SOME
B		C

A		D

This exercise contains four sets of dichotic word pairs. For each set, review the 13 dichotic pairs on the basis of your general preferences for one or the other. Indicate your degree of preference for each of the two by dividing 100 points between them as illustrated in this example. Example:

A–D DICHOTIC PAIRS
Analytic 30 / 70 Holistic

Force a choice between all 13 pairs in each set. In doing so, try to avoid a 50/50 split.

After completing all four sets, add up the totals in each column (A, B, C, D). Since all for columns are involved twice, you end up with two totals for each column. Enter these totals below, and determine a grand total for each column. Then write **most** in the box under the column (A, B, C, or D) with the highest total. (If there is a tie, write **most** in both boxes.) Write **least** in the box below the section(s) containing the lowest total(s), and **some** in the boxes under the remaining sections.

___ A	___ B	___ C	___ D
+	+	+	+
___ A	___ B	___ C	___ D
=	=	=	=
Total A	Total B	Total C	Total D

A–D Dichotic Pairs

	A		D	
Analytic	___	/	___	Holistic
Argument	___	/	___	Experience
Rational	___	/	___	Intuitive
Digital	___	/	___	Analogue
Explicit	___	/	___	Tacit
Analytic	___	/	___	Gestalt
Focal	___	/	___	Diffuse
Logical	___	/	___	Impetuous
Directive	___	/	___	Reflective
Words	___	/	___	Images
Realistic	___	/	___	Imaginative
Factual	___	/	___	Metaphoric
Literal	___	/	___	Approximate
Total A	___		___	Total D

B–D Dichotic Pairs

	B		D	
Detailed	___	/	___	Holistic
Sequential	___	/	___	Flexible
Safekeeping	___	/	___	Experimental
Rule Maker	___	/	___	Rule breaker
Avoids Ambiguity	___	/	___	Accepts Ambiguity
Evaluative	___	/	___	Non-judgmental
Disciplined	___	/	___	Playful
Execution	___	/	___	Conception
Planned	___	/	___	Impulsive
Structured	___	/	___	Free Flow
Controlled	___	/	___	Open
Operational	___	/	___	Strategic
Organized	___	/	___	Non-organized
Total B	___		___	Total D

B–C Dichotic Pairs

	B		C	
Verifies	___	/	___	Feels
Controlled	___	/	___	Emotional
Implements	___	/	___	Performs
Procedural	___	/	___	Free Form
Hard	___	/	___	Soft
Form	___	/	___	Feeling
Organization	___	/	___	Relationships
Dominate	___	/	___	Accommodate
Sequential	___	/	___	Harmonious
Dogmatic	___	/	___	Spiritual
Conservative	___	/	___	Charitable
Articulates	___	/	___	Talks
Detailed	___	/	___	Approximate
Total B	___		___	Total C

A–C Dichotic Pairs

	A		C	
Informational	___	/	___	Interpersonal
High-Tech	___	/	___	High-Touch
Intellectual	___	/	___	Sensuous
Here and Now	___	/	___	Eternity
Active	___	/	___	Receptive
Objective	___	/	___	Subjective
Analytic	___	/	___	Intuitive
Words	___	/	___	Music
Worldly	___	/	___	Spiritual
Facts	___	/	___	Feelings
Knows	___	/	___	Senses
Things	___	/	___	People
Rational	___	/	___	Emotional
Total A	___		___	Total C

Reading # 3   Excerpt from an Autobiography of Malcolm X

You may or may not agree with Malcolm X's politics, or with some periods of his life. Nevertheless, you should agree that he was a person of great determination who became a strong person through much dogged perseverance. Malcolm's story is a story about his dedication and commitment to learning. As you read about him, contemplate how you can develop a greater commitment toward your own learning.

The first man I met in prison who made any positive impression on me whatever was a fellow inmate, "Bimbi." I met him in 1947, at Charleston. He was a light, kind of red-complexioned Negro, as I was; about my height, and he had freckles. Bimbi, an old-time burglar, had been in many prisons. In the license plate shop where our gang worked, he operated the machine that stamped out the numbers. I was along the conveyor belt where the numbers were painted.

Bimbi was the first Negro convict I'd known who didn't respond to "What'cha know, Daddy?" Often, after we had done our day's license plate quota, we would sit around, perhaps fifteen of us, and listen to Bimbi. Normally, white prisoners wouldn't think of listening to Negro prisoners' opinions on anything, but guards, even, would wander over close to hear Bimbi on any subject.

He would have a cluster of people riveted, often on odd subjects you never would think of. He would prove to us, dipping into the science of human behavior, that the only difference between us and outside people was that we had been caught. He liked to talk about historical events and figures. When he talked about the history of Concord, where I was to be transferred later, you would have thought he was hired by the Chamber of Commerce, and I wasn't the first inmate who had never heard of Thoreau until Bimbi expounded upon him. Bimbi was known as the library's best customer. What fascinated me with him most of all was that he was the first man I had ever seen command total respect...with his words.

Bimbi seldom said much to me; he was gruff to individuals, but I sensed he liked me. What made me seek his friendship was when I heard him discuss religion. I considered myself beyond atheism--I was Satan. But Bimbi put the atheist philosophy in a framework, so to speak. That ended my vicious cursing attacks. My approach sounded so weak alongside his, and he never used a foul word.

Out of the blue one day, Bimbi told me flatly, as was his way, that I had some brains, if I'd use them. I had wanted his friendship, not that kind of advice. I might have cursed another convict, but nobody cursed Bimbi. He told me I should take advantage of the prison correspondence courses and the library.

When I had finished the eighth grade back in Mason, Michigan, that was the last time I'd thought of studying anything that didn't have some hustle purpose. And the streets had erased everything I'd ever learned in school; I didn't know a verb from a house....

Many who today hear me somewhere in person, or on television, or those who read something I've said, will think I went to school far beyond the eighth grade. This impression is due entirely to my prison studies.

It had really begun back in the Charleston Prison, when Bimbi first made me feel envy of his stock of knowledge. Bimbi had always taken charge of any conversation he was in, and I had tried to emulate him. But every book I picked up had few sentences which didn't contain anywhere from one to nearly all of the words that might as well have been in Chinese. When I just skipped those words, of course, I really ended up with little idea of what the book said. So I had come to the Norfolk Prison Colony still going through only book-reading motions. Pretty soon, I would have quit even these motions, unless I had received the motivation that I did.

I saw that the best thing I could do was get hold of a dictionary--to study, to learn some words. I was lucky enough to reason also that I should try to improve my penmanship. It was sad. I couldn't even write in a straight line. It was both ideas together that moved me to request a dictionary along with some tablets and pencils from the Norfolk Prison Colony school.

I spent two days just riffling uncertainly through the dictionary's pages. I'd never realized so many words existed! I didn't know which words I needed to learn. Finally, just to start some kind of action, I began copying. In my slow, painstaking, ragged handwriting, I copied into my tablet everything printed on that first page, down to the punctuation marks. I believe it took me a day. Then, aloud, I read back, to myself, everything

I'd written on the tablet. Over and over aloud, to myself, I read my own handwriting.

I woke up the next morning, thinking about those words--immensely proud to realize that not only had I written so much at one time, but I'd written words that I never knew were in the world. Moreover, with a little effort, I also could remember what many of these words meant. I reviewed the words whose meanings I didn't remember. Funny thing, from the dictionary first page right now, that "aardvark" springs to my mind. The dictionary had a picture of it, a long-tailed, long-eared, burrowing African mammal, which lives off termites caught by sticking out its tongue as an anteater does for ants.

I was so fascinated that I went on--I copied the dictionary's next page. And the same experience came when I studied that. With every succeeding page, I also learned of people and places and events from history. Actually the dictionary is like a miniature encyclopedia. Finally, the dictionary's A section had filled a whole tablet--and I went on into the B's. That was the way I started copying what eventually became the entire dictionary. I went a lost faster after so much practice helped me to pick up handwriting speed. Between what I wrote in my table, and writing letters, during the rest of my time in prison I would guess I wrote a million words.

I suppose it was inevitable that as my word-base broadened, I could for the first time pick up a book and read and now begin to understand what the book was saying. Anyone who has read a great deal can imagine the new world that opened. Let me tell you something: from then until I left that prison, in every free moment I had, if I was not reading in the library, I was reading on my bunk. You couldn't have gotten me out of books with a wedge. Between Mr. Muhammad's teachings, my correspondence, my visitors--usually Ella and Reginald--and my reading of books, months passed without my even thinking about being imprisoned. In fact, up to then, I never had been so truly free in my life....

As you can imagine, especially in a prison where there was heavy emphasis on rehabilitation, an inmate was smiled upon if he demonstrated an unusually intense interest in books. There was a sizable number of well-read inmates, especially the popular debaters. Some were said by many to be practically walking encyclopedias. They were almost celebrities. No university would ask any student to devour literature as I did when this new world opened to me, of being able to read and understand.

I read more in my room than in the library itself. An inmate who was known to read a lot could check out more than the permitted maximum number of books. I preferred reading in the total isolation of my own room. When I had progressed in really serious reading, every night at about ten P.M. I would be outraged with the "lights out." It always seemed to catch me right in the middle of something engrossing.

Fortunately, right outside my door was a corridor light that cast a glow into my room. The glow was enough to read by, once my eyes adjusted to it. So when "lights out" came, I would sit on the floor where I could continue reading in that glow.

At one-hour intervals the night guards paced past every room. Each time I heard the approaching footsteps, I jumped into bed and feigned sleep. And as soon as the guards passed, I got back out of bed onto the floor area of that light-glow, where I would read for another fifty-eight minutes--until the guard approached again. That went on until three or four every morning. Three or four hours of sleep a night was enough for me. Often in the years in the streets I had slept less than that.

I have often reflected upon the new vistas that reading opened to me. I knew right there in prison that reading had changed forever the course of my life. As I see it today, the ability to read awoke inside me some long dormant craving to be mentally alive. I certainly wasn't seeking my degree, the way a college confers a status symbol upon its students. My homemade education gave me, with every additional book that I read, a little bit more sensitivity to the deafness, dumbness, and blindness that was afflicting the black race in America. Not long ago, an English writer telephoned me from London, asking questions. One was, "What's your alma mater?" I told him, "Books." You will never catch me with a free fifteen minutes in which I am not studying something I feel might be able to help the black man....

Every time I catch a plane, I have with me a book that I want to read--and that's a lot of books these days. If I weren't out here every day battling the white man, I could spend the rest of my life reading, just satisfying my curiosity--because you can hardly mention anything I'm not curious about. I don't think anybody ever got more out of going to prison than I did. In fact, prison enabled me to study far more intensively than I would have if my life had gone differently and I had attended some college. I imagine that one of the biggest troubles with college is there are too many distractions, too much panty-raiding, fraternities, and boola-boola and all of that. Where else but in prison could I have attacked my ignorance by being able to study intensely sometimes as much as fifteen hours a day?

250

Reading # 4   We Need a Nation
of Scholar-leaders

Reprinted from J. B. Ritchie and Paul Thompson, Organization and People: Readings, Cases, and Exercises in Organizational Behavior, 3rd edition, 1984, pp. 13-18. St. Paul: West Publishing Co. Reprinted by permission of the author.

Bonner Ritchie is a Professor of Organizational Behavior in Brigham Young University's Marriott School of Management. Ritchie draws a parallel between the contrived dichotomy of student-scholar and the organizational and personal drives of institutions and those who work to survive within institutional society. As you read the article, verify for yourself to what extent there is a student-scholar dichotomy and, if there is one, to what extent Ritchie's arguments support his concerns for scholar-leaders in society and in its institutions. In Ritchie's terms, are you a student or a scholar, and does it matter?

Personal Responsibility and Organizations: We Need a Nation of Scholar-leaders

In the book, *The Once and Future King*, T. H. White retells the legend of King Arthur. In so doing, he captures an interesting dimension of growing up, learning, and accepting responsibility. When the young Arthur, affectionately referred to as "Wart" in the account, is despondent, a little confused, and sad, he goes to Ector and asks what he should do. Ector says he should go see the magician, Merlin, for some advice as to how to handle his frustrations. When he approaches the magician, Merlin responds as follows:

"The best thing for being sad," replied Merlin, beginning to puff and blow, "is to learn something. That is the only thing that never fails. You may grow old and trembling in your anatomies, you may lie awake at night listening to the disorder of your veins, you may miss your only love, you may see the world about you devastated by evil lunatics, or know your honor trampled in the sewers of baser minds. There is only one thing for it then--to learn. Learn why the world wags and what wags it. That is the only thing which the mind can never exhaust, never alienate, never be tortured by, never fear or distrust, and never dream of regretting. Learning

251

is the thing for you. Look at what a lot of things there are to learn--pure science, the only purity there is. You can learn astronomy in a lifetime, natural history in three, literature in six. And then after you have exhausted a milliard of lifetimes in biology and medicine and theocriticism and geography and history and economics why, you can then start to make a cartwheel out of the appropriate wood, or spend fifty years learning to begin to learn to beat your adversary at fencing. After that you can start again on mathematics, until it is time to learn to plough."

Learning: A Solution to Life's Frustrations

I subscribe to that advice. The solution to life's aggravations is to learn. And the solution to a frustrating life is to develop an attitude of learning. Each of us needs to develop an attitude toward life, toward organizations, toward the university, toward the Church, toward the state, toward the corporation, and toward each other of learning and of growing. We reduce the anxieties and confusion of life by developing a criterion for thinking that is based on analysis, interpretation, extrapolation, and extension of ideas rather than on judgment, classification, and rigid acceptance or rejection.

Student Versus Scholar Perspective

The term *student* is a revered term to me. Although I will suggest a metaphor that may not reflect my reverence toward students, I do so only to make a point. Students are like computers. The system sits there waiting for an input to be determined by something like a professor, a textbook, or an expert source that tells the student what is appropriate or what is desirable or what is true. The information is put into the computer, and by some previously designed operational system, is classified, perhaps processed a bit, and then stored in some way for easy retrieval. That retrieval is triggered by something like a question in a classroom, an assignment to write a paper, or a question or an examination.

I wonder if our student model has corrupted us in the ability to learn and to grow. I wonder if we have simply mastered the art of taking a class. That can be pretty empty. There is life after college!

We should develop an eternal perspective rather an a semester perspective. We have different people reviewing and evaluating rather than a single teacher, and sometimes the student model gets in the way.

252

Sometimes the student model undercuts our capacity to cope in a complex world. What is needed today is a scholar model.

A student asks what to do, a scholar searches and proposes what to do. A student blames the system for failure, a scholar has no need to blame anyone. He or she accepts responsibility for correcting a failed system. A student listens to judge, a scholar listens to learn. A student transfers to the university, to the professor, to the boss, or to God both credit and blame that the individual should accept. In the process of so doing, we default in the most important function we have to perform: to decide what the meaning of life is.

The Scholar and Personal Responsibility

From the scholar perspective, we do not search for the meaning of life, we define it, we develop it, we create it. We don't seek out who we are. Our identity is not found by searching across the land. Our identity is something we decide. Students expect someone else to define them; scholars accept the responsibility of defining themselves. Students expect the textbook to have the answer, and they want to know whether it is A or B.

I was intrigued recently in reading Norman Cousin's book, *Anatomy of an Illness*, where he describes how he accepted the joint responsibility with his doctor for his own health. He was told that his odds for getting better were 500-1 against, and he said when that announcement was made he decided he had to become a participant in this process in a way he had not considered previously. Norman Cousins, as the editor of the Saturday Review, had available to him a research staff. He sent his research staff out to do a survey of various medical findings, and he found that what his doctors were prescribing was not accurate. Norman Cousins did not blindly accept the diagnosis and prescriptions his doctor had arrived at working with incomplete data. Norman Cousins took the scholar-leader role and asked why. He found that the prescribed medication and the hospital environment were inappropriate. He determined that what he really needed was some Vitamin C, some laughter, and a pleasant environment. He moved himself out of a hospital into a nice hotel room. He started taking Vitamin C and watching Laurel and Hardy movies and he got better.

Cousins became part of the healing process. He applied the power of the participant, rather than to sit back and defer to the expert doctor.

Another example touches upon an uncomfortable and a difficult issue, but one that I find terribly compelling. Victor Frankl in *Man's Search for Meaning*, describes the fate of people in the concentration camps in Nazi captivity. He argues that what was needed was a fundamental change in attitude. Attitudes towards life, he said, had become too self-indulgent, too narcissistic, too self-serving, to really understand what was going on and to survive the brutality of the camp. In talking about the men in his camp, he said, "what was really needed was a fundamental change in our attitude towards life. We had to learn ourselves and furthermore we had to teach others that the issue was not what we expected from life but what life expected from us. We needed to stop asking what the meaning of life was and instead think of ourselves as those who were being questioned by life daily and hourly."

Beyond "Looking Out for Number One"

Our answers must consist not simply in talk and meditation, but in right action and conduct. Life ultimately means accepting responsibility to define appropriate answers to each problem as it comes up. The more you look for the meaning of life, I would argue, the less you would find it. We can only be trapped by the contemporary pop psychology of "looking out for No. 1," "winning through intimidation," "pulling your own strings," "being your own best friend," and the whole raft of pop psychology books that tell you how to beat the system, take care of yourself, indulge yourself at the expense of other people, be calloused and insensitive to the needs of the world around you in order to come out on top and win that game of competition with each other. The more we become victimized by such philosophies, the less capable we are of turning each of life's events into a learning experience rather than just a historical occurrence. We have got to become an involved part of the dynamic, rather than a simple part of a static system.

This issue of self-service is not new. It is not a product of our most recent five years. I refer to John Steinbeck's comments in *Grapes of Wrath*, where he described some of the landowners of the 1930s: "Some were kind because they hated what they had to do. Some of them were angry because they hated to be cruel. Some of them were cold because they long ago found that one could not be an owner unless one were cold. All of them were caught up in something larger than themselves. Some of them hated the mathematics that drove them and were afraid. Some worshipped the mathematics that drove them because it provided a refuge from thought and from feeling."

254

I think we have overdemanded our organizations to the point that we can only, ultimately, feel betrayed. Our economic, political, academic, social, and religious systems cannot answer all of the demands that we place on them. They cannot be aware enough. They cannot have an efficient enough information processing system to cope with the exponential explosion of information. They cannot acquire, digest, analyze, and resolve all of the complex and contradictory data received.

There is growing evidence of the failure of organizations just as there is growing evidence of shortcomings in the student perspective of life. Consider these examples: **Fifty percent of organizational decisions are ignored.** For the past 15 years, I have been collecting observations of managers, executives, people who seemingly are in positions where others expect them to run an organization. One of the things I found interesting was that about 50 percent of the decisions these people make are never carried out in organizations. Not 50 percent of the random comments in a hall "why don't you look into this, Sue," but 50 percent of the formal decision you can trace to board minutes, to memoranda that are distributed in an organization. Half of those decisions are not carried out! Why are they not carried out? Because no one person knows enough to account for all the variables in making those decisions. No one person nor one group--not the Soviet Politburo, not the Board of Directors of Exxon—can make all the decisions that will dictate the behavior of every member of that organization. "Democracy by default" may not sound elegant, but I think it comes from the inability to account for or control all the variables. The result of these decisions based on incomplete information: 50 percept of the decisions are not carried out.

When I was collecting my observations on this particular issue, I attempted to ask many people for their evaluations. When I would fly in an airplane, I would try to sit next to a person I felt was a business executive. (Sometimes I was badly mistaken, and that was an interesting experiment in itself.) I would sit next to someone that looked like an executive and I would say, "I am doing a research project, and I have been working in an organization where I find that half of the decisions made are not carried out. What do you think? It seems high to me. Can you believe that this is really true?" The responses I got were almost all confirming. In fact, one individual said, "Gee, I think that is right and maybe it is even a little low. If 50 percent of my decisions got carried out, I would be delighted."

The wrong decisions are carried out. This same respondent went on to make another point about failings in organizations. After confirming that many decisions are, in fact, ignored, he went on to say, "But I would argue that the survival and success of business depends on that 50 percent that are not carried out."

That is a telling argument, the fact that many decisions shouldn't be carried out. Now again, that is not comfortable to the administrator or the executive who sits back frustrated because orders are not followed. And, unfortunately, I have observed that ofttimes it is the wrong 50 percent that are not carried out. The good decisions are resented by the rebellious deviants, and the bad decisions are implemented by enthusiastic zealots. Somehow we need a nation of scholars, a nation of leaders, to discriminate as to which decisions ought to be carried out. But the more important point is not to sit back in judgment of which 50 percent, but to become part, in a responsible way, of that process.

There is a crisis in organizational leadership. I have been collecting other data about organizations which reveal an interesting trend. There is a crisis of leadership. There is, indeed, a crisis of confidence in our institutions: government, corporate, union, and military. I have been measuring the attitudes that people have toward those above and below them in organizations. I found it interesting that 15 years ago when I started studying this, I asked people to rate some of their character traits on seven-point scales. Consistently, these self-ratings came out about 5.7. Now there is nothing very significant about that particular point until we use it as a reference for comparison.

In the course of this research I also asked people to rate, using the same seven-point scales, their bosses and their subordinates. Fifteen years ago, they saw their bosses at about a 6.0 (three-tenths of a point above themselves) and they saw their subordinates at a 4.2 (about a point and a half below them). That was a consistent pattern regardless of organizational level. Vice-presidents saw the president at about a 6, themselves at 5.7, and the department heads at about a 4.2. First-line supervisors saw themselves at about a 5.7, their foreman at about 6.0 and their subordinates at about the same point of 4.2. These people saw themselves as a lot better than their subordinates, and almost as good as their boss. Therefore, when they communicate with the boss, they expected the boss to have full confidence in them and to think they were almost as good as the boss. Conversely, however, they expect subordinates to be inferior clods, and they talk down to them, disregard them, and belittle them. They have little confidence in subordinates' ability to function, and, therefore, they overcontrol them and harass them.

256

Those indicators held for several years. But as the 1970s began, I started getting different data. People still rated themselves at 5.7 on an average, still put their subordinates at about a 4.2, but now the bosses were coming in at a 5.7 also. So now my conclusions about their relationships changed. They now saw themselves as a lot better than subordinates, and as good as their boss. Many people now felt that they could do the boss's job as well as the boss. They were losing confidence in their superiors. By the middle of the seventies the data changed again. Starting in 1975 or 1976 the data started to look this way: Individuals still rated themselves at 5.7, subordinates about 4.2 and bosses were averaging 5.3. Now my interpretation changed one more time: they now see themselves as a lot better than their subordinates and quite a bit better than the boss. They concluded that there is nobody in the world as good as themselves!

Organizational lying. One further bit of evidence of the failing organization was reflected in a recent study of organizational lying--outright misstatements of the truth. The study discussed the external pressures on organizations to misrepresent their performance. The emphasis is on the facade rather than substance. Organizational rewards come from positive external reports, valid or not, instead of the internal criterion of genuine service.

There are pressures to lie and to misrepresent in all organizations. These need to be identified.

The Organization as a Haven from Self-responsibility

The organization has become a mechanism that many of us use to absolve ourselves of the burden of making decisions that only we can make and of accepting responsibility for thinking. Organizations will not and cannot replace the individual's need to become a scholar-leader who participates in the dynamic process of deciding. We cannot be spectators. We cannot shift the burden for self-development to others. Besides, organizations simply don't work that well.

As a "student" society, we have come to expect of organizations functions that only we as individuals can be responsible for. And when they fail to meet these expectations, our confidence in organizational leadership drops. We all need to be scholar-leaders. Our contemporary society is so complex, that is behooves each of us to become not only minimally informed, not passive members, but incredibly well-informed, active members. The burden is severe on all of us to be scholars and leaders, to develop the analytical tools to understand what organizations in our societies are doing, and to make fewer demands upon them. Not fewer demands in terms of morality or ethics, but fewer demands in terms of the universality of organizations serving needs we must ultimately be responsible for as individuals. We must demand of leaders of essential organizations, dignity and morality. We must expect less in terms of total output.

Our civilization depends on that informed citizenry in a way we have never depended on it before. The information available is too complex, the demands and opportunities for misrepresentation are too great, and the opportunity for organization encroachment in private lives is too great.

But the positive opportunities are also great for accepting responsibility for our own involvement in life as scholars, defining our own learning and performance objectives, evaluating ourselves, making proposals instead of simply asking questions, and listening to learn rather than to judge. I hope we can do that. I hope we can become enthused, committed, informed participants rather than ones who sit back condemning the system because it does not define things our way. And in the process, I hope that we clearly can gain an increased confidence in ourselves. I hope that we don't wait for the university or the nation, or the state, or the corporation to change our world—but instead, accept responsibilities for being part of it. When organizations fail, don't just blame the system, but accept the opportunity to become part of a changing process of the world in which we live.

Reading # 5 Feeding the Mind

Carroll, Lewis, *Feeding the Mind*. Chatto and Windus, 1907.

In the following section Lewis Carroll makes the point you are what you read. Do you find his case convincing? How do Carroll's suggestions for digesting material compare with the learning principles in Chapter 11?

Breakfast, dinner, tea; in extreme cases, breakfast, luncheon, dinner, tea, supper, and a glass of something hot at bedtime. What care we take about feeding the lucky body! Which of us does as much for his mind? And what causes the difference? Is the body so much the more important of the two?

By no means; but life depends on the body being fed, whereas we can continue to exist as animals (scarcely as men) though the mind be utterly starved and neglected. Therefore Nature provides that, in case of serious neglect of the body, such terrible consequences of discomfort and pain shall ensue as will soon bring us back to a sense of our duty; and some of the functions necessary to life she does for us altogether, leaving us no choice in the matter. I would fare but ill with any of us if we were left to superintend our own digestion and circulation. "Bless me!" one would cry, "I forgot to wind up my heart this morning! To think that it has been standing still for the last three hours!" "I can't walk with you this afternoon," a friend would say, "as I have no less than eleven dinners to digest. I had to let them stand over from last week, being so busy—and my doctor says he will not answer for the consequences if I wait any longer!"

Well it is, I say, for us, that the consequences of neglecting the body can be clearly seen and felt; and it might be well for some if the mind were equally visible and tangible—if we could take it, say, to the doctor and have its pulse felt.

"Well, doctor, it has not had much regular food lately, I gave it a lot of sugar-plums yesterday."

"Sugar-plums! What kind?"

"Well, they were a parcel of conundrums, sir."

"Ah! I thought so, now just mind this: if you go playing tricks like that, you'll spoil all its teeth, and get laid up with mental indigestion. You must have nothing but the plainest reading for the next few days. Take care now! No novels on any account!"

Considering the amount of painful experience many of us have had in feeding and dosing the body, it would, I think, be quite worth our while to try and translate some of the rules into corresponding ones for the mind.

First, then, we should set ourselves to provide for our mind its *proper kind* of food; we very soon learn what will, and what will not, agree with the body, and find little difficulty in refusing a piece of the tempting pudding or pie which is associated in our memory with that terrible attack of indigestion, and whose very name irresistibly recalls rhubarb and magnesia; but it takes a great many lessons to convince us how indigestible some of our favorite lines of reading are, and again and again we make a meal of the unwholesome novel, sure to be followed by its usual train of low spirits, unwillingness to work, weariness of existence—in fact by mental nightmare.

Then we should be careful to provide this wholesome food in *proper amount*. Mental gluttony, or overreading, is a dangerous propensity, tending to weakness of digestive power, and in some cases to loss of appetite; we know that bread is a good and wholesome food, but who would like to try the experiment of eating two or three loaves at a sitting?

I have heard of a physician telling his patient—whose complaint was mere gluttony and want of exercise—that "the earliest symptom of hypernutrition is a deposition of adipose tissue," and no doubt the fine long words greatly consoled the poor man under his increasing load of fat.

I wonder if there is such a thing in nature as a fat mind? I really think I have met with one or two minds which could not keep up with the slowest trot in conversation, could not jump over a logical fence to save their lives, always got stuck fast in a narrow argument, and, in short, were fit for nothing but to waddle helplessly through the world.

Then, again, though the food be wholesome and in proper amount, we know that we must be consuming too many kinds at once. Take the thirsty haymaker a quart of beer, or a quart of cider, or even a quart of cold tea, and he will probably thank you (though not so heartily in the last case!). But what think you his feelings would be if you offered him a tray containing a little mug of beer, a little mug of cider, another of cold tea, one of hot tea, one of coffee, one of cocoa, and corresponding vessels of milk, water, brandy-and-water, and buttermilk? The sum total might be a quart but would it be the same thing to the haymaker?

Having settled the proper kind, amount, and variety of our mental food, it remains that we should be careful to allow proper intervals between meal and meal, and not swallow the food hastily without mastication, so that it may be thoroughly digested; both which rules for the body are also applicable at once to the mind.

260

First as to the intervals: these are as really necessary as they are for the body, with this difference only, that while the body requires three or four hours' rest before it is ready for another meal, the mind will in many cases do with three or four minutes. I believe that the interval required is much shorter than is generally supposed, and from personal experience I would recommend any one who has to devote several hours together to one subject of thought to try the effect of such a break, say once an hour—leaving off for five minutes only, each time, but taking care to throw the mind absolutely "out of gear" for those five minutes, and to turn it entirely to other subjects. It is astonishing what an amount of impetus and elasticity the mind recovers during those short periods of rest.

And then as to the mastication of the food: the mental process answering to this is simply thinking over what we read. This is a very much greater exertion of mind than the mere passive taking in the contents of our author—so much greater an exertion is it, that, as Coleridge says, the mind often "angrily refuses" to put itself to such trouble—so much greater, that we are far too apt to neglect it altogether, and go on pouring in fresh food on the top of the undigested masses already lying there, till the unfortunate mind is fairly swamped under the food. But the greater the exertion, the more valuable, we may be sure, is the effect; one hour of steady thinking over a subject (a solitary walk is as good an opportunity for the process as any other) is worth two or three of readings only.

And just consider another effect of this thorough digestion of the books we read: I mean the arranging and "ticketing," so to speak, of the subjects in our minds, so that we can readily refer to them when we want them. Sam Slick tells us that he has learned several languages in his life, but somehow "couldn't keep the parcels sorted" in his mind; and many a mind that hurries through book after book, without waiting to digest or arrange anything, gets into that sort of condition, and the unfortunate owner finds himself far from fit really to support the character all his friends give him.

"A thoroughly well-read man. Just you try him in any subject, now. You can't puzzle him!"

You turn to the thoroughly well-read man: you ask him a question, say, in English history (he is understood to have just finished reading Macaulay); he smiles good-naturedly, tries to look as if he knew all about it, and proceeds to dive into his mind for the answer. Up comes a handful of very promising facts, but on examination they turn out to belong to the wrong century, and are pitched in again; a second haul brings up a fact much more like the real thing, but unfortunately along with it comes a tangle of other things—a fact in political economy, a rule in arithmetic, the ages of his brother's children, and a stanza of Gray's Elegy; and among all these the fact he wants has got hopelessly twisted and entangled. Meanwhile every one is waiting for his reply, and as the silence is getting more and more awkward, our well-read friend has to stammer out some half-answer at last, not nearly so clear or so satisfactory as an ordinary schoolboy would have given. And all this for want of making up his knowledge into proper bundles and ticketing them!

Do you know the unfortunate victim of ill-judged mental feeding when you see him? Can you doubt him? Look at him drearily wandering around a reading-room, tasting dish after dish-we beg his pardon, book after bookkeeping to one. First a mouthful of novel-but no, faugh! he has had nothing but that to eat for the last week, and is quite tired of the taste; then a slice of silence, but you know at once what the result of that will be-ah, of course, much too tough for his teeth. And so on through the old weary round, which he tried (and failed in) yesterday, and will probably try, and fail in, tomorrow.

Mr. Oliver Wendell Holmes, in his very amusing book <u>The Professor at the BreakfastTable</u>, gives the following rule for knowing whether a human being is young or old. "The crucial experiment is this. Offer a bulky bun to the suspected individual just ten minutes before dinner. If this is easily accepted and devoured, the fact of youth is established. " He tells us that a human being, "if young, will eat anything at any hour of the day or night."

To ascertain the happiness of the mental appetite of a human animal, place in its hand a short, well-written, but not exciting treatise on some popular subject—a mental bun, in fact. If it is read with eager interest and perfect attention, and if the reader can answer questions on the subject afterwards, the mind is in first-rate working order; if it be politely laid down again, or perhaps lounged over for a few minutes, and then, "I can't read this stupid book! Would you hand me the second volume of <u>The Mysterious Murder?</u>" you may be equally sure that there is something wrong in the mental digestion.

If this paper has given you any useful hints on the important subject of reading, and made you see that it is one's duty no less than one's interest to "read, mark, learn, and inwardly digest" the good books that fall in your way, its purpose will be fulfilled.

WEEKLY SCHEDULE

Name _____ Beginning Date _____ Ending Date _____

	MONDAY	TUESDAY	WEDNESDAY	THURSDAY	FRIDAY	SATURDAY	SUNDAY
Prioritized Tasks							
Schedule							
7 AM							
8							
9							
10							
11							
12 PM							
1							
2							
3							
4							
5							
6							
7							
8							
9							
10							
11							

SETTING SHORT-TERM GOALS

Identify your short-term goals and list the activities that will lead to accomplishing your goals. Indicate the time and place you will carry out each activity and then transfer it to your weekly schedule.

Goal #1: _____

Activities: _____
_____
_____

Goal #2: _____

Activities: _____
_____
_____

Goal #3: _____

Activities: _____
_____
_____

Goal #4: _____

Activities: _____
_____
_____

ORGANIZING YOUR TIME

❶ *Build your schedule around your fixed time commitments.* FIXED: organizations, classes, church, and employment. FLEXIBLE: eating, sleeping, study, personal grooming, and recreation.

❷ *Consider your short-term goals.* Budget the time needed for activities that will accomplish each goal, and then schedule the activity.

❸ *Budget enough time to study for each subject.* Most college classes require about two hours of outside work for every one hour spent in class. By multiplying your credit load by two, you can get a good idea of the time you should provide for studying each week.

❹ *Study just before or just after class.* Study of class notes should take place the same day as the class. Studying class notes more than 24 hours after the class usually means you must relearn rather than review the material. Previewing just before class facilitates class participation and permanent learning.

❺ *Borrow time--don't steal it.* A few hours each week should be set aside to trade for time borrowed to handle unexpected emergencies.

BUDGETING TIME

Sample Activities	Hours per week	Total
Class Time		
Class/Study	____	
Class/Study	____	
Class/Study	____	
Class/Study	____	
Class/Study	____	
Class/Study	____	
Class/Study	____	
Work		
Time	____	
Travel	____	
Church		
Service Projects	____	
Meetings	____	
Relationships		
Clubs and Projects	____	
Family Visits	____	
Diversion		
Recreation	____	
Exercise	____	
Miscellaneous		
Eating	____	
Traveling	____	
Sleeping	____	
Other	____	
Total Hours Per Week		168

USING THE WEEKLY SCHEDULE

Take 10-15 minutes before the week begins to review your goals, budget your available time and make a list of priorities. Spend 5 minutes each night to review your day and reschedule your priorities and plan the next day. Make any changes you need. Remember: The schedule is designed to serve you. Keep it flexible.

① *Schedule your fixed time commitments first.* This should be done at the beginning of each week.

② *Make a "To-Do" list of the tasks for the week.*
● List your tasks in order of importance on the day they take place. Include any exams, projects or assignments that are due.
● Review your tasks at the end of each day, cross off completed activities and reschedule incomplete items on a future day.

③ *Schedule your flexible time commitments.* These include: studying, eating, grooming, recreation and hobbies, sleeping, etc.
● Allow enough study time for each class. A good rule of thumb is to begin by planning two hours of study for every one hour of class; later adjust up and down according to your experience with each class.
● Set a regular time for study for each class. Your study hours should be as regular as possible and in the same place to avoid distraction.
● Find time for other essential activities.

WEEKLY SCHEDULE

Name _____   Beginning Date _____   Ending Date _____

	MONDAY	TUESDAY	WEDNESDAY	THURSDAY	FRIDAY	SATURDAY	SUNDAY
Prioritized Tasks							

Schedule	MONDAY	TUESDAY	WEDNESDAY	THURSDAY	FRIDAY	SATURDAY	SUNDAY
7 AM							
8							
9							
10							
11							
12 PM							
1							
2							
3							
4							
5							
6							
7							
8							
9							
10							
11							

SETTING SHORT-TERM GOALS

Identify your short-term goals and list the activities that will lead to accomplishing your goals. Indicate the time and place you will carry out each activity and then transfer it to your weekly schedule.

Goal #1: _____

Activities: _____

Goal #2: _____

Activities: _____

Goal #3: _____

Activities: _____

Goal #4: _____

Activities: _____

ORGANIZING YOUR TIME

❶ *Build your schedule around your fixed time commitments.* FIXED: organizations, classes, church, and employment. FLEXIBLE: eating, sleeping, study, personal grooming, and recreation.

❷ *Consider your short-term goals.* Budget the time needed for activities that will accomplish each goal, and then schedule the activity.

❸ *Budget enough time to study for each subject.* Most college classes require about two hours of outside work for every hour spent in class. By multiplying your credit load by two, you can get a good idea of the time you should provide for studying each week.

❹ *Study just before or just after class.* Study of class notes should take place the same day as the class. Studying class notes more than 24 hours after the class usually means you must relearn rather than review the material. Previewing just before class facilitates class participation and permanent learning.

❺ *Borrow time--don't steal it.* A few hours each week should be set aside to trade for time borrowed to handle unexpected emergencies.

BUDGETING TIME

Sample Activities	Hours per week	Total
Class Time		
Class/Study	|||	
Class/Study	|||	
Class/Study	|||	
Class/Study	|||	—
Class/Study	|||	
Class/Study	|||	—
Work		
Time	|||	
Travel	|||	—
Church		
Service Projects	|||	
Meetings	|||	—
Relationships		
Clubs and Projects	|||	
Family Visits	|||	—
Diversion		
Recreation	|||	
Exercise	|||	—
Miscellaneous		
Eating	|||	
Traveling	|||	
Sleeping	|||	
Other	|||	—
Total Hours Per Week		168

USING THE WEEKLY SCHEDULE

Take 10-15 minutes before the week begins to review your goals, budget your available time and make a list of priorities. Spend 5 minutes each night to review your day and reschedule your priorities and plan the next day. Make any changes you need. Remember: The schedule is designed to serve you. Keep it flexible.

① *Schedule your fixed time commitments first.* This should be done at the beginning of each week.

② *Make a "To-Do" list of the tasks for the week.*

● List your tasks in order of importance on the day they take place. Include any exams, projects or assignments that are due.

● Review your tasks at the end of each day, cross off completed activities and reschedule incomplete items on a future day.

③ *Schedule your flexible time commitments.* These include: studying, eating, grooming, recreation and hobbies, sleeping, etc.

● Allow enough study time for each class. A good rule of thumb is to begin by planning two hours of study for every one hour of class; later adjust up and down according to your experience with each class.

● Set a regular time for study for each class. Your study hours should be as regular as possible and in the same place to avoid distraction.

● Find time for other essential activities.

WEEKLY SCHEDULE

Name _____ Beginning Date _____ Ending Date _____

	MONDAY Prioritized Tasks	TUESDAY Prioritized Tasks	WEDNESDAY Prioritized Tasks	THURSDAY Prioritized Tasks	FRIDAY Prioritized Tasks	SATURDAY Prioritized Tasks	SUNDAY Prioritized Tasks

Schedule	Schedule	Schedule	Schedule	Schedule	Schedule	Schedule	Schedule
7 AM	7 AM	7 AM	7 AM	7 AM	7 AM	7 AM	7 AM
8	8	8	8	8	8	8	8
9	9	9	9	9	9	9	9
10	10	10	10	10	10	10	10
11	11	11	11	11	11	11	11
12 PM	12 PM	12 PM	12 PM	12 PM	12 PM	12 PM	12 PM
1	1	1	1	1	1	1	1
2	2	2	2	2	2	2	2
3	3	3	3	3	3	3	3
4	4	4	4	4	4	4	4
5	5	5	5	5	5	5	5
6	6	6	6	6	6	6	6
7	7	7	7	7	7	7	7
8	8	8	8	8	8	8	8
9	9	9	9	9	9	9	9
10	10	10	10	10	10	10	10
11	11	11	11	11	11	11	11

SETTING SHORT-TERM GOALS

Identify your short-term goals and list the activities that will lead to accomplishing your goals. Indicate the time and place you will carry out each activity and then transfer it to your weekly schedule.

Goal #1: _____

Activities: _____

Goal #2: _____

Activities: _____

Goal #3: _____

Activities: _____

Goal #4: _____

Activities: _____

ORGANIZING YOUR TIME

❶ *Build your schedule around your fixed time commitments.* FIXED: organizations, classes, church, and employment. FLEXIBLE: eating, sleeping, study, personal grooming, and recreation.

❷ *Consider your short-term goals.* Budget the time needed for activities that will accomplish each goal, and then schedule the activity.

❸ *Budget enough time to study for each subject.* Most college classes require about two hours of outside work for every hour spent in class. By multiplying your credit load by two, you can get a good idea of the time you should provide for studying each week.

❹ *Study just before or just after class.* Study of class notes should take place the same day as the class. Studying class notes more than 24 hours after the class usually means you must relearn rather than review the material. Previewing just before class facilitates class participation and permanent learning.

❺ *Borrow time--don't steal it.* A few hours each week should be set aside to trade for time borrowed to handle unexpected emergencies.

BUDGETING TIME

Sample Activities	Hours per week	Total
Class Time		
Class/Study	___	
Class/Study	___	
Class/Study	___	
Class/Study	___	___
Class/Study	___	
Class/Study	___	
Class/Study	___	
Work		
Time	___	
Travel	___	___
Church		
Service Projects	___	
Meetings	___	___
Relationships		
Clubs and Projects	___	
Family Visits	___	___
Diversion		
Recreation	___	
Exercise	___	___
Miscellaneous		
Eating	___	
Traveling	___	
Sleeping	___	
Other	___	___
Total Hours Per Week		168

USING THE WEEKLY SCHEDULE

Take 10-15 minutes before the week begins to review your goals, budget your available time and make a list of priorities. Spend 5 minutes each night to review your day and reschedule your priorities and plan the next day. Make any changes you need. Remember: The schedule is designed to serve you. Keep it flexible.

① *Schedule your fixed time commitments first.* This should be done at the beginning of each week.

② *Make a "To-Do" list of the tasks for the week.*
● List your tasks in order of importance on the day they take place. Include any exams, projects or assignments that are due.
● Review your tasks at the end of each day , cross off completed activities and reschedule incomplete items on a future day.

③ *Schedule your flexible time commitments.* These include: studying, eating, grooming, recreation and hobbies, sleeping, etc.
● Allow enough study time for each class. A good rule of thumb is to begin by planning two hours of study for every one hour of class; later adjust up and down according to your experience with each class.
● Set a regular time for study for each class. Your study hours should be as regular as possible and in the same place to avoid distraction.
● Find time for other essential activities.

WEEKLY SCHEDULE

Name _____ Beginning Date _____ Ending Date _____

	MONDAY	TUESDAY	WEDNESDAY	THURSDAY	FRIDAY	SATURDAY	SUNDAY
Prioritized Tasks							

Schedule	MONDAY	TUESDAY	WEDNESDAY	THURSDAY	FRIDAY	SATURDAY	SUNDAY
7 AM							
8							
9							
10							
11							
12 PM							
1							
2							
3							
4							
5							
6							
7							
8							
9							
10							
11							

SETTING SHORT-TERM GOALS

Identify your short-term goals and list the activities that will lead to accomplishing your goals. Indicate the time and place you will carry out each activity and then transfer it to your weekly schedule.

Goal #1: _____

Activities: _____

Goal #2: _____

Activities: _____

Goal #3: _____

Activities: _____

Goal #4: _____

Activities: _____

ORGANIZING YOUR TIME

❶ *Build your schedule around your fixed time commitments.* FIXED: organizations, classes, church, and employment. FLEXIBLE: eating, sleeping, study, personal grooming, and recreation.

❷ *Consider your short-term goals.* Budget the time needed for activities that will accomplish each goal, and then schedule the activity.

❸ *Budget enough time to study for each subject.* Most college classes require about two hours of outside work for every hour spent in class. By multiplying your credit load by two, you can get a good idea of the time you should provide for studying each week.

❹ *Study just before or just after class.* Study of class notes should take place the same day as the class. Studying class notes more than 24 hours after the class usually means you must relearn rather than review the material. Previewing just before class facilitates class participation and permanent learning.

❺ *Borrow time--don't steal it.* A few hours each week should be set aside to trade for time borrowed to handle unexpected emergencies.

BUDGETING TIME

Sample Activities	Hours per week	Total
Class Time		
Class/Study		
Class/Study		
Class/Study		
Class/Study		
Class/Study		
Class/Study		
Class/Study		
Work		
Time		
Travel		
Church		
Service Projects		
Meetings		
Relationships		
Clubs and Projects		
Family Visits		
Diversion		
Recreation		
Exercise		
Miscellaneous		
Eating		
Traveling		
Sleeping		
Other		
Total Hours Per Week		168

USING THE WEEKLY SCHEDULE

Take 10-15 minutes before the week begins to review your goals, budget your available time and make a list of priorities. Spend 5 minutes each night to review your day and reschedule your priorities and plan the next day. Make any changes you need. Remember: The schedule is designed to serve you. Keep it flexible.

① *Schedule your fixed time commitments first.* This should be done at the beginning of each week.

② *Make a "To-Do" list of the tasks for the week.*
- List your tasks in order of importance on the day they take place. Include any exams, projects or assignments that are due.
- Review your tasks at the end of each day , cross off completed activities and reschedule incomplete items on a future day.

③ *Schedule your flexible time commitments.* These include: studying, eating, grooming, recreation and hobbies, sleeping, etc. A good rule of thumb is to begin by planing two hours of study for every one hour of class; later adjust up and down according to your experience with each class.
- Set a regular time for study for each class. Your study hours should be as regular as possible and in the same place to avoid distraction.
- Find time for other essential activities.

WEEKLY SCHEDULE

Name _____   Beginning Date _____   Ending Date _____

	MONDAY	TUESDAY	WEDNESDAY	THURSDAY	FRIDAY	SATURDAY	SUNDAY
Prioritized Tasks							

Schedule	MONDAY	TUESDAY	WEDNESDAY	THURSDAY	FRIDAY	SATURDAY	SUNDAY
7 AM							
8							
9							
10							
11							
12 PM							
1							
2							
3							
4							
5							
6							
7							
8							
9							
10							
11							

ORGANIZING YOUR TIME

SETTING SHORT-TERM GOALS

Identify your short-term goals and list the activities that will lead to accomplishing your goals. Indicate the time and place you will carry out each activity and then transfer it to your weekly schedule.

Goal #1: _____

Activities: _____

Goal #2: _____

Activities: _____

Goal #3: _____

Activities: _____

Goal #4: _____

Activities: _____

ORGANIZING YOUR TIME

❶ *Build your schedule around your fixed time commitments.* FIXED: organizations, classes, church, and employment. FLEXIBLE: eating, sleeping, study, personal grooming, and recreation.

❷ *Consider your short-term goals.* Budget the time needed for activities that will accomplish each goal, and then schedule the activity.

❸ *Budget enough time to study for each subject.* Most college classes require about two hours of outside work for every hour spent in class. By multiplying your credit load by two, you can get a good idea of the time you should provide for studying each week.

❹ *Study just before or just after class.* Study of class notes should take place the same day as the class. Studying class notes more than 24 hours after the class usually means you must relearn rather than review the material. Previewing just before class facilitates class participation and permanent learning.

❺ *Borrow time–don't steal it.* A few hours each week should be set aside to trade for time borrowed to handle unexpected emergencies.

BUDGETING TIME

Sample Activities	Hours per week	Total
Class Time		
Class/Study		
Class/Study		
Class/Study		
Class/Study		
Class/Study		—
Work		
Time		
Travel		—
Church		
Service Projects		
Meetings		—
Relationships		
Clubs and Projects		
Family Visits		—
Diversion		
Recreation		
Exercise		—
Miscellaneous		
Eating		
Traveling		
Sleeping		
Other		—
Total Hours Per Week		168

USING THE WEEKLY SCHEDULE

Take 10-15 minutes before the week begins to review your goals, budget your available time and make a list of priorities. Spend 5 minutes each night to review your day and reschedule your priorities and plan the next day. Make any changes you need. Remember: The schedule is designed to serve you. Keep it flexible.

① *Schedule your fixed time commitments first.* This should be done at the beginning of each week.

② *Make a "To-Do" list of the tasks for the week.*
- List your tasks in order of importance on the day they take place. Include any exams, projects or assignments that are due.
- Review your tasks at the end of each day , cross off completed activities and reschedule incomplete items on a future day.

③ *Schedule your flexible time commitments.* These include: studying, eating, grooming, recreation and hobbies, sleeping, etc.
- Allow enough study time for each class. A good rule of thumb is to begin by planning two hours of study for every one hour of class; later adjust up and down according to your experience with each class.
- Set a regular time for study for each class. Your study hours should be as regular as possible and in the same place to avoid distraction.
- Find time for other essential activities.

WEEKLY SCHEDULE

Name _____ Beginning Date _____ Ending Date _____

	MONDAY Prioritized Tasks	TUESDAY Prioritized Tasks	WEDNESDAY Prioritized Tasks	THURSDAY Prioritized Tasks	FRIDAY Prioritized Tasks	SATURDAY Prioritized Tasks	SUNDAY Prioritized Tasks

Schedule	Schedule	Schedule	Schedule	Schedule	Schedule	Schedule	Schedule
7 AM	7 AM	7 AM	7 AM	7 AM	7 AM	7 AM	7 AM
8	8	8	8	8	8	8	8
9	9	9	9	9	9	9	9
10	10	10	10	10	10	10	10
11	11	11	11	11	11	11	11
12 PM	12 PM	12 PM	12 PM	12 PM	12 PM	12 PM	12 PM
1	1	1	1	1	1	1	1
2	2	2	2	2	2	2	2
3	3	3	3	3	3	3	3
4	4	4	4	4	4	4	4
5	5	5	5	5	5	5	5
6	6	6	6	6	6	6	6
7	7	7	7	7	7	7	7
8	8	8	8	8	8	8	8
9	9	9	9	9	9	9	9
10	10	10	10	10	10	10	10
11	11	11	11	11	11	11	11

SETTING SHORT-TERM GOALS

Identify your short-term goals and list the activities that will lead to accomplishing your goals. Indicate the time and place you will carry out each activity and then transfer it to your weekly schedule.

Goal #1: _____

Activities: _____

Goal #2: _____

Activities: _____

Goal #3: _____

Activities: _____

Goal #4: _____

Activities: _____

ORGANIZING YOUR TIME

❶ *Build your schedule around your fixed time commitments.* FIXED: organizations, classes, church, and employment. FLEXIBLE: eating, sleeping, study, personal grooming, and recreation.

❷ *Consider your short-term goals.* Budget the time needed for activities that will accomplish each goal, and then schedule the activity.

❸ *Budget enough time to study for each subject.* Most college classes require about two hours of outside work for every hour spent in class. By multiplying your credit load by two, you can get a good idea of the time you should provide for studying each week.

❹ *Study just before or just after class.* Study of class notes should take place the same day as the class. Studying class notes more than 24 hours after the class usually means you must relearn rather than review the material. Previewing just before class facilitates class participation and permanent learning.

❺ *Borrow time—don't steal it.* A few hours each week should be set aside to trade for time borrowed to handle unexpected emergencies.

BUDGETING TIME

Sample Activities	Hours per week	Total
Class Time		
Class/Study		
Class/Study		
Class/Study		
Class/Study		
Class/Study		
Class/Study		
Class/Study		
Work		
Time		
Travel		
Church		
Service Projects		
Meetings		
Relationships		
Clubs and Projects		
Family Visits		
Diversion		
Recreation		
Exercise		
Miscellaneous		
Eating		
Traveling		
Sleeping		
Other		
Total Hours Per Week		168

USING THE WEEKLY SCHEDULE

Take 10-15 minutes before the week begins to review your goals, budget your available time and make a list of priorities. Spend 5 minutes each night to review your day and reschedule your priorities and plan the next day. Make any changes you need. Remember: The schedule is designed to serve you. Keep it flexible.

① *Schedule your fixed time commitments first.* This should be done at the beginning of each week.

② *Make a "To-Do" list of the tasks for the week.*
● List your tasks in order of importance on the day they take place. Include any exams, projects or assignments that are due.
● Review your tasks at the end of each day, cross off completed activities and reschedule incomplete items on a future day.

③ *Schedule your flexible time commitments.* These include: studying, eating, grooming, recreation and hobbies, sleeping, etc.
● Allow enough study time for each class. A good rule of thumb is to begin by planning two hours of study for every one hour of class; later adjust up and down according to your experience with each class.
● Set a regular time for study for each class. Your study hours should be as regular as possible and in the same place to avoid distraction.
● Find time for other essential activities.

SIX UNIT STUDY PLAN

Name _____ Target Content Course _____ Grade Expected _____

FIRST TIME STUDY: Creation of lecture notes, reading notes, summaries, visual diagrams, and questions.

						Approx.
1 TOPIC	**2** TOPIC	**3** TOPIC	**4** TOPIC	**5** TOPIC	**6** TOPIC	
Reading Notes *	Reading Notes	Reading Notes	Reading Notes	Reading Notes	Reading Notes	1-3 Hrs
D____ T____	D____ T____	D____ T____	D____ T____	D____ T____	D____ T____	
Lecture Notes *	Lecture Notes	Lecture Notes	Lecture Notes	Lecture Notes	Lecture Notes	
D____ T____	D____ T____	D____ T____	D____ T____	D____ T____	D____ T____	

Review arrows (shaded region):

						Approx.
1 D____ T____	2 D____ T____	3 D____ T____	4 D____ T____	5 D____ T____		15 Min
	1	2	3	4	5	5 M
		1	2	3	4	3 M
			1	2	3	2 M
				1	—	1 M

Review Study:
To include a review of cues, summaries and sample test questions.

LAST REVIEW FOR FINAL EXAMS: To include a review of the text, notes, summaries and sample questions.

	Approx.
1 D____ T____	30 M
2 D____ T____	30 M
3 D____ T____	30 M
4 D____ T____	30 M
5 D____ T____	30 M
6 D____ T____	30 M

* Note: Work your study plan into your weekly time schedule. When complete, record on this sheet the date and the time the reading notes and lecture notes were finished.

SIX UNIT STUDY PLAN

Name _____

Target Content Course _____   Grade Expected _____

FIRST TIME STUDY: Creation of lecture notes, reading notes, summaries, visual diagrams, and questions.

		Approx.
1 TOPIC _____	**2** TOPIC _____	
Reading Notes *	Reading Notes	1-3 Hrs
D_____ T_____	D_____ T_____	
Lecture Notes *	Lecture Notes	
D_____ T_____	D_____ T_____	

3 TOPIC _____	**4** TOPIC _____	**5** TOPIC _____	**6** TOPIC _____
Reading Notes	Reading Notes	Reading Notes	Reading Notes
D_____ T_____	D_____ T_____	D_____ T_____	D_____ T_____
Lecture Notes	Lecture Notes	Lecture Notes	Lecture Notes
D_____ T_____	D_____ T_____	D_____ T_____	D_____ T_____

Review Study:
To include a review of cues, summaries and sample test questions.

	Approx.
1 → D_____ T_____	15 Min
2 → D_____ T_____	5 M
3 → D_____ T_____	3 M
4 → D_____ T_____	2 M
5 → D_____ T_____	1 M

LAST REVIEW FOR FINAL EXAMS: To include a review of the text, notes, summaries and sample questions.

	Approx.
1 D_____ T_____	30 M
2 D_____ T_____	30 M
3 D_____ T_____	30 M
4 D_____ T_____	30 M
5 D_____ T_____	30 M
6 D_____ T_____	30 M

* Note: Work your study plan into your weekly time schedule. When complete, record on this sheet the date and the time the reading notes and lecture notes were finished.

SIX UNIT STUDY PLAN

Name _____

Target Content Course _____

Grade Expected _____

FIRST TIME STUDY: Creation of lecture notes, reading notes, summaries, visual diagrams, and questions.

	Approx.

1 TOPIC

Reading Notes *
D _____ T _____
Lecture Notes *
D _____ T _____

2 TOPIC

Reading Notes
D _____ T _____
Lecture Notes
D _____ T _____

3 TOPIC

Reading Notes
D _____ T _____
Lecture Notes
D _____ T _____

4 TOPIC

Reading Notes
D _____ T _____
Lecture Notes
D _____ T _____

5 TOPIC

Reading Notes
D _____ T _____
Lecture Notes
D _____ T _____

6 TOPIC

Reading Notes
D _____ T _____
Lecture Notes
D _____ T _____

1-3 Hrs

Review Study:
To include a review of cues, summaries and sample test questions.

1 D _____ T _____   15 Min
2 D _____ T _____   5 M
3 D _____ T _____   3 M
4 D _____ T _____   2 M
5 D _____ T _____   1 M

LAST REVIEW FOR FINAL EXAMS: To include a review of the text, notes, summaries and sample questions.

1 D _____ T _____	30 M
2 D _____ T _____	30 M
3 D _____ T _____	30 M
4 D _____ T _____	30 M
5 D _____ T _____	30 M
6 D _____ T _____	30 M

* Note: Work your study plan into your weekly time schedule. When complete, record on this sheet the date and the time the reading notes and lecture notes were finished.

SIX UNIT STUDY PLAN

Name _____ Target Content Course _____ Grade Expected _____

FIRST TIME STUDY: Creation of lecture notes, reading notes, summaries, visual diagrams, and questions.

	Approx.
1 TOPIC	1-3 Hrs
Reading Notes * D ___ T ___	
Lecture Notes * D ___ T ___	

	Approx.
2 TOPIC	
Reading Notes D ___ T ___	
Lecture Notes D ___ T ___	

	Approx.
3 TOPIC	
Reading Notes D ___ T ___	
Lecture Notes D ___ T ___	

	Approx.
4 TOPIC	
Reading Notes D ___ T ___	
Lecture Notes D ___ T ___	

	Approx.
5 TOPIC	
Reading Notes D ___ T ___	
Lecture Notes D ___ T ___	

	Approx.
6 TOPIC	
Reading Notes D ___ T ___	
Lecture Notes D ___ T ___	

Review	Approx.
1 D ___ T ___	15 Min
2 D ___ T ___	5 M
3 D ___ T ___	3 M
4 D ___ T ___	2 M
5 D ___ T ___	1 M

Review Study:
To include a review of cues, summaries and sample test questions.

	Approx.
1 D ___ T ___	30 M
2 D ___ T ___	30 M
3 D ___ T ___	30 M
4 D ___ T ___	30 M
5 D ___ T ___	30 M
6 D ___ T ___	30 M

LAST REVIEW FOR FINAL EXAMS: To include a review of the text, notes, summaries and sample questions.

* Note: Work your study plan into your weekly time schedule. When complete, record on this sheet the date and the time the reading notes and lecture notes were finished.

The Elements of Reasoning Worksheet

The objective for which reasoning has taken place.

The reasoning started somewhere and took something for granted.

The theories, axioms, principles, or rules used while reasoning.

The place or end to which the reasoning leads.

The issue or problem to be solved by reasoning.

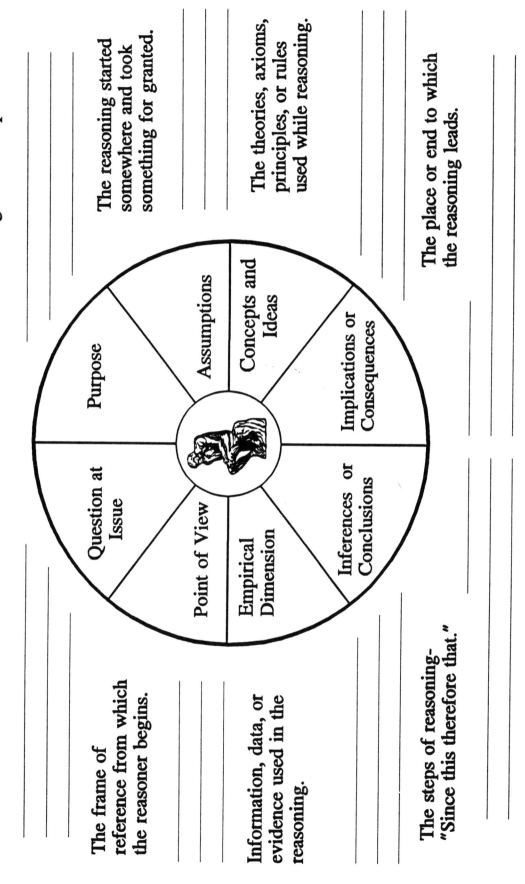

The frame of reference from which the reasoner begins.

Information, data, or evidence used in the reasoning.

The steps of reasoning-
"Since this therefore that."

The Elements of Reasoning Worksheet

The objective for which
reasoning has taken place.

The reasoning started
somewhere and took
something for granted.

The theories, axioms,
principles, or rules
used while reasoning.

The place or end to which
the reasoning leads.

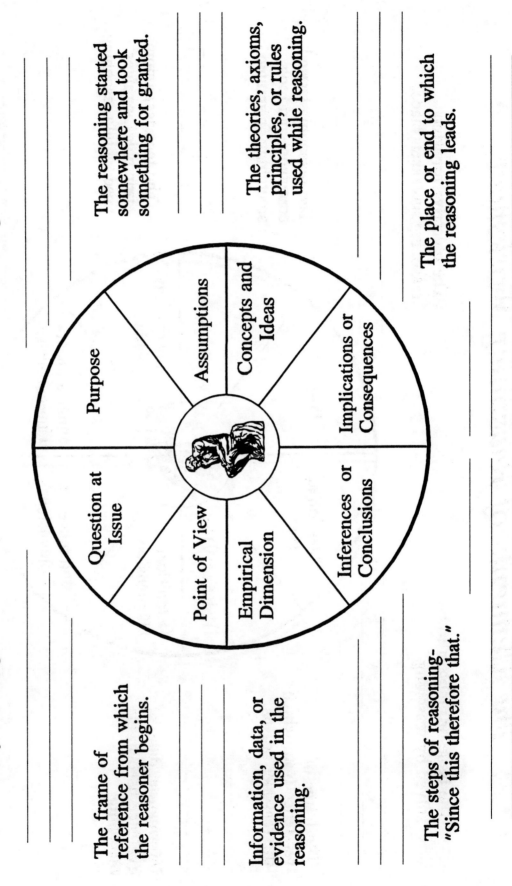

The issue or problem to be
solved by reasoning.

The frame of
reference from which
the reasoner begins.

Information, data, or
evidence used in the
reasoning.

The steps of reasoning-
"Since this therefore that."

The Elements of Reasoning Worksheet

The objective for which reasoning has taken place.

The reasoning started somewhere and took something for granted.

The theories, axioms, principles, or rules used while reasoning.

The place or end to which the reasoning leads.

The issue or problem to be solved by reasoning.

The frame of reference from which the reasoner begins.

Information, data, or evidence used in the reasoning.

The steps of reasoning—"Since this therefore that."

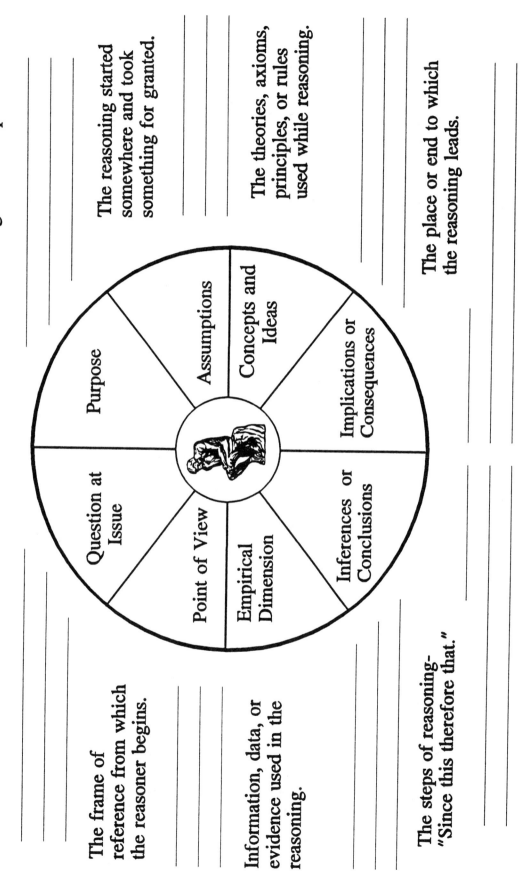

Purpose

Assumptions

Concepts and Ideas

Implications or Consequences

Question at Issue

Point of View

Empirical Dimension

Inferences or Conclusions

The Elements of Reasoning Worksheet

The issue or problem to be solved by reasoning.

The frame of reference from which the reasoner begins.

Information, data, or evidence used in the reasoning.

The steps of reasoning- "Since this therefore that."

The objective for which reasoning has taken place.

The reasoning started somewhere and took something for granted.

The theories, axioms, principles, or rules used while reasoning.

The place or end to which the reasoning leads.

Purpose

Assumptions

Concepts and Ideas

Implications or Consequences

Question at Issue

Point of View

Empirical Dimension

Inferences or Conclusions

Index

284